Mary A Humphrey

The squatter sovereign

Kansas in the 1850s

Mary A Humphrey

The squatter sovereign
Kansas in the 1850s

ISBN/EAN: 9783743382152

Manufactured in Europe, USA, Canada, Australia, Japa

Cover: Foto ©ninafisch / pixelio.de

Manufactured and distributed by brebook publishing software (www.brebook.com)

Mary A Humphrey

The squatter sovereign

THE
SQUATTER SOVEREIGN,

OR

KANSAS IN THE '50'S.

A

LIFE PICTURE

OF THE

EARLY SETTLEMENT

OF THE

DEBATABLE GROUND.

A STORY, FOUNDED UPON MEMORABLE, AND HISTORICAL EVENTS, WHOSE CHARACTERS HAVE BEEN CAREFULLY CHOSEN TO REPRESENT THE VARIOUS TYPES OF MEN, AND WOMEN WHO MET UPON THE KANSAS PLAINS INTENT ON SETTLING THE VEXED QUESTION AS TO WHETHER THE TERRITORY SHOULD COME INTO THE UNION AS A FREE, OR SLAVE STATE.

By *MARY A. HUMPHREY.*

ELEGANTLY ILLUSTRATED.

CHICAGO, ILL.:
COBURN & NEWMAN PUBLISHING CO.,
1883.

DEDICATION.

TO THE PIONEERS OF KANSAS.
THE NOBLE MARTYRS

WHO GAVE UP THEIR LIVES IN DEFENCE OF
THE PRINCIPLES OF LIBERTY AND JUSTICE,
THE SURVIVORS OF THAT OLDEN TIME
WHO SUCCEEDED IN REARING UPON HER PLAINS,
THE RAMPART WHICH TURNED BACK THE ADVANCING
TIDE OF SLAVERY,
AND
THE GALLANT ARMY OF WORKERS,
WHOSE TOILS AND PRIVATIONS MADE
POSSIBLE THE GLORIOUS PROSPERITY NOW
ENJOYED BY HER PEOPLE, THIS VOLUME IS
REVERENTLY DEDICATED.

THE AUTHOR.

AUTHOR'S PREFACE.

Having long been deeply impressed with the national significance of the preliminary strife engendered upon the plains of Kansas on the promulgation of the doctrine of Squatter Sovereignty, by the determination of each section of the Union to obtain supremacy, and filled with admiration for the patriotic and noble souls who led the vanguard of freedom in the irrepressible conflict, through hardship and toil, through privation and danger, through misunderstanding, contumely, and misrepresentation, I have been impelled to disinter some of the leading events from beneath the weight of later memories of the civil war and its great achievements, and to embody them, while sources of information are still accessible, in a more enduring form.

And, believing that the highest form of history is that which makes apparent to the reader the effect of great movements upon individuals and communities, I have carefully collected and strung together the threads of fact, weaving them into a story with the golden woof of fiction, hoping that the web might prove acceptable for the intrinsic value of the material though wrought by a prentice hand.

MARY A. HUMPHREY.

List of Illustrations.

"The Way to that Man is over my Dead Body." *Frontispiece.*	
Kansas Farm Scene.	25
Jacob Schmidt. "I sends for my Katrina."	37
Agnes Langtry.	55
Sile Hardiker's Store.	65
Bachelors' Sunday.	82
New Year's Callers. "Much Good."	94
Grace Alden.	111
The Polls, "Hurray for Missoury."	144
Sile Hardiker.	182
Mabel Delaney.	211
Shawnee Water Works.	229
Sile's er' Poppin. "Yer Mighty Purty Miss Grace."	267
"She Kissed the Cold Lips."	285
"My Blood be upon the Cause They Represent. Agnes, Oh! Agnes."	320
Zeke and Bets Having a Flirtation.	336

Table of Contents.

CHAPTER I.
THE VENTURE.

CHAPTER II.
THE RETURN.

CHAPTER III.
ON THE TOWN SITE—VISITORS.

CHAPTER IV.
NEW FRIENDS.

CHAPTER V.
THE FIRST INVASION.

CHAPTER VI.
THE "RAISING"—DUTCH JAKE.

CHAPTER VII.
NEW COMERS—LANGTRY'S WIFE—ARTHUR FAIRCHILD—NEWS FROM AMY.

CHAPTER VIII.
OUR LADY—SOUTHERN COLONIES—ELECTION OF WHITFIELD.

CHAPTER IX.
ARTHUR'S LOVE—AGNES' ACQUISITION—THE FREE NEGRO.

CHAPTER X.
ARTHUR'S MISSION—WARSAW GROWING—AIR-CASTLES.

CONTENTS.

CHAPTER XI.
CHRISTMAS—PIONEER CHURCH—THE ESCAPED SLAVE.

CHAPTER XII.
NEW YEAR'S CALLERS.

CHAPTER XIII.
LETTERS—ARTHUR'S CLAIM JUMPED.

CHAPTER XIV.
A JOYFUL REUNION—A NEW LOVER—COL. DELANEY.

CHAPTER XV.
THE NEW HOME—TEA AT LANGTRY'S—VISIT TO WARSAW—BEAUTY'S COURT.

CHAPTER XVI.
AN AMUSING VISITOR—BLUE LODGE SECRETS—GRACE ENTERTAINS THE SQUIRE.

CHAPTER XVII.
ELECTION DAY—LANGTRY IN DANGER.

CHAPTER XVIII.
RODERICK AT THE CABIN—POLITICAL GATHERING—AGNES AND AMY.

CHAPTER XIX.
THE GOVERNOR'S MANSION—THE PROPOSAL.

CHAPTER XX.
THE WIDOW—HER VISIT TO LAUDERDALE—A PRESENT FOR GRACE—A FATHER'S ADVICE.

CHAPTER XXI.
THE FIRST LEGISLATURE.

CHAPTER XXII.
THE FOURTH OF JULY—RODERICK AND MABEL DELANEY—ARTHUR'S RETURN—OF HER OWN FREE WILL.

CHAPTER XXIII.
PREPARATIONS FOR THE WEDDING—THE BOGUS LEGISLATURE—THE JEWELLED HAND THAT MOVES THE PUPPETS—RODERICK IN OPPOSITION—CAPITAL OFFENCES—TESTS FOR JURORS—LEGISLATURE INDORSED BY SUPREME COURT—LANGTRY'S CIRCULAR.

CHAPTER XXIV.
RODERICK'S DISAPPOINTMENT—CONVENTION AT WARSAW—AGNES' APPEAL.

CHAPTER XXV.
WHITE SPRINGS—A WARNING TO LANGTRY.

CHAPTER XXVI.
THE NEW HOUSE — "SILE'S-ER-POPPIN" — RAGE AND JEALOUSY.

CHAPTER XXVII.
DEPREDATIONS ON ARTHUR'S CLAIM—BURNING OF HIS HOUSE.

CHAPTER XXVIII.
A DEMAND FOR JUSTICE — THE ASSASSIN'S AIM—THE LONE TREE ON THE PRAIRIE.

CHAPTER XXIX.
BENEATH THE SOD—ARREST OF ALDEN—A MIDNIGHT TRAMP—"WE WILL PROTECT YOU."

CHAPTER XXX.
LAW AND ORDER CONVENTION—SECRET PLANS.

CHAPTER XXXI.
FORCED TO FLEE—ON A WAR BASIS.

CHAPTER XXXII.
LANGTRY SHAKES THE DUST OF WARSAW FROM HIS FEET—WARD AND ALDEN—IN THE BORDER RUFFIAN CAMP.

CHAPTER XXXIII.

"One more look at that dead face,
Of his murderer's ghastly trace!
One more kiss, oh widowed one!
Lay your left hand on his brow,
Lift your right hand up and vow,
That his work shall yet be done."

CHAPTER XXXIV.

"Bear him comrades to his grave,
Never over one more brave,
Shall the prairie grasses weep,
In the ages yet to come,
When the millions in our room,
What we sow in tears shall reap."

CHAPTER XXXV.

ALDEN A WANDERER—GRACE GOES TO OHIO—ELECTION OF OFFICERS UNDER TOPEKA CONSTITUTION—PRISONERS AT LECOMPTON.

CHAPTER XXXVI.

A CHAPTER OF HISTORY.

CHAPTER XXXVII.

"What, we have many goodly days to see,
The liquid drops of tears that we have shed,
Shall come again, transformed to orient pearls,
Advantaging their loan with interest."
                                SHAKESPEARE.

CHAPTER I.

THE VENTURE.

"Be sure to bring back a fortune, John," were Amy Alden's last words as she bade her husband "good bye," in that long ago when the California gold fever was at its height.

"That I will, Amy;" was the answer. "You shall keep your carriage and wear diamonds yet, my little wife, only be brave, and very patient."

For thirteen years these two had walked life's path together. At first, joyously, like happy children, gathering the flowers, chasing the birds and butterflies, in every festive throng the gayest of the gay.

Then, more sedately, as the swift years went gliding by, bringing now a care, anon a disappointment, and then, Alas! a grief.

"Having a good time," was at first their only object in life, and like many a young couple in our own day, they lived in a style beyond their means. Not that they exceeded their income—they had a very little prudence, but they should have left a margin, and that never seemed possible.

"I have too much pride," John said, "to go more poorly dressed or less comfortably housed than my associates."

"I must have *this* and *that*, as all my friends have. One can't be old-fashioned and look like a fright," said Amy.

But after a while, when the little daughter, whose coming had given a deeper current to their thoughts, had grown to be a fair-haired, lovely little lass, they suddenly awoke to a consciousness of the fact that many humble plodders who had begun life at the same time they did, and whose frugal manner of living they had laughed to scorn, were taking possession of homes of their own, and otherwise giving evidence of progressive fortunes while they remained pecuniarily at the starting point.

To John and Amy Alden this was a very unpalatable truth, one which they were unwilling to admit. But the proofs were plainly before them and would not be gainsaid. They realized fully the harsh fact that the fruits of economy and industry can only be enjoyed after the practice of the frugal virtues necessary to their growth.

And now they began to plan each year how much should be spent for this, and that, and how much should be deposited in the savings bank; but somehow the savings bank deposit invariably came out a minus quantity. There were always a hundred little expenses cropping up like vile weeds to absorb the surplus. Many of them, no doubt, might have been lopped off with a hoe of moral courage sufficiently incisive; but our friends were yet not toned up to the point of declaring decisively, "I cannot afford it." Old habits asserted themselves, false pride was still strong within them; they could not deny themselves the little indulgences of which all around them partook, and, of course, they failed to accumulate property.

Amy became discontented and envious. Ugly little lines made their appearance on her hitherto lovely face—the happy childlike expression was gone from her eyes, and a harsh note intruded itself in the tones of her voice.

John grew moody and misanthropic. The daily routine of business, standing as he did for hours at a desk in a dull counting room, entering credits, and bills of merchandise, and bills of lading, and summing up long rows of figures, grew very distasteful to him. It seemed such a treadmill, and to do this year after year—for a fixed salary—a weary round of existence.

Just at this time came the discovery of gold in California. Ah! here was a rift in the cloud. Here was deliverance from this dull monotony. Who would tread the painful jagged paths of economy when he might gain the smooth heights of competence by one daring effort?

What were a few years of absence from home and family compared to the long years of comfort and affluence that absence might bring.

John Alden pondered long. Over and over again, in imagination, he traveled by land to the Atlantic coast—sailed to, and over the Gulf of Mexico—safely crossed the isthmus of Panama, took ship again on the Pacific—reached San Francisco, and joined the hurrying throngs who were making their way to the gold mines.

How hope and expectation reveled high within his soul. What stores of yellow ore he made his own, and with what exultation returned to receive the welcome reception which ever awaits the successful fortune-hunter.

These dreams, ever recurring, haunted him by day, and by night. Sometimes the journey was made by the Cape, and home across the continent; sometimes with one series of adventures, and sometimes with another, but the end was always success and a return to spend his days and fortune in the old home, and mid the old friends.

At last he gathered courage to broach the scheme to Amy, from whom he expected strong opposition; but to his great surprise she was not only willing for him to go, but he found her a most valuable member of his ways and means committee. Fertile in resources, she had soon matured a plan which she urged upon him, and never for a moment did she permit herself, or him to falter, or to hesitate.

To obtain the means for John's long journey they sold

their costliest furniture, and like Isabella, of Spain, she brought all of her jewels and laid them at the feet of an adventurer. Then, with her daughter, when she had seen her hero fairly launched on his voyage of discovery, she sought the paternal home, from which she had gone forth thirteen years before, a happy bride.

Poor Amy! she turned from John on that eventful morning, sad at the separation, it is true—and yet, so distasteful of late had become the petty economies of housekeeping, the constant struggle to keep up the appearance of lavish expenditure, and yet make ends meet and lap over a little, so much had John's moodiness and anxiety for the future worn upon her, that she felt as if a great burden were rolled away, and she turned to her childhood's home, set in memory amid green fields and blue and smiling skies, as to a haven of rest where she might await in peace a successful lord's return.

And as for John, foot-loose at last, and free to pursue the glorious visions which had so long danced before his eager eyes, his spirits rose within him. His soul took no cognizance of the present pain of parting, but his hope-winged thoughts went bounding forward through the brightly looming future in fond anticipation of the hour of meeting.

CHAPTER II.

THE RETURN.

CLEVELAND, OHIO, June 1, 1854.

MY DEAR, DEAR HUSBAND:

This is the anniversary of your departure. Six years—six weary years have dragged their slow length along, since you set forth in quest of that fortune which was to bring us happiness. They have been to me years of loneliness, toil, and grief.—And to you, I dare not think what they have been to you. Long, long since have I learned that happiness is within ourselves, and not in our surroundings, in our aims and purposes and not in our possessions, and long since would my love have annihilated the barriers of space between us but for the chains of duty which have held me fast.   *   *   *   *

So long you have been an exile from the sweet delights of home. Come back to me! oh! come back to me, and never again shall an envious murmuring word pass my lips. A crust of bread, a cup of water, a roof to shelter us, and your love and presence, are all the fortune I ask you to bring, to your loving and lonely wife,

AMY ....

Across the continent sped this loving missive sent by no self-indulgent, pleasure-loving wife. It was no miracle, this change so radical! t'was growth, development. The purest gold must with hard rubbing burnished be. The diamond polished by rough hands before it sparkles in the light. When real troubles rack the soul all fancied ills soon vanish. Amy Alden had gone back to her father's house with anticipations of the old childlike feeling of security and repose. She would have been disappointed had even the outward conditions remained the same. States of feeling never repeat themselves, there are too many fleeting factors entering into each adjustment.

She was very welcome there and her presence soon became a necessity. Her father had long been an invalid, dependent on her mother's care and solicitude, and during the second year of her stay at home, this loving mother suddenly sickened and died. Her mantle of devotion fell upon our Amy. Each day brought urgent duties which could neither be evaded nor postponed. Thus tried as in a crucible, the little imperfections which marred her character were worn away. How foolish and petty seemed all her former aims. How vain her desire for show and extravagance, and Alas! how more than doubly dear, the love and care of her husband, which in her folly she had put far from her.

How often she reproached herself, unjustly too, for she was not alone to blame, for his absence. Every disappointment, every misfortune that came to him, and they were many, she stored up against herself as so many sins for which she was accountable. But now her father's death had relieved her. Her duty to him was ended. She had also received as a share of his estate, a small sum of money sufficient to enable them to begin house-keeping again in a modest way. She would have an opportunity to try again, another chance to do right by John, and by herself. Thank heaven always for another chance to do right. So she sent the white-winged, love-laden messenger to that far away land, with many hopes and prayers that it might not be too late.

Weary and despondent, John Alden lay supinely upon his blankets within a well worn tent. All up and down the river bed from which the waters had been turned by a wooden flume, roughly dressed men were bending over pans of golden sand. He could hear an occasional shout of exultation as some fortunate washer secured an unusual find, and he could hear also the curses of contention and the groans of dis-

appointment, but each, and all fell alike unheeded upon his
ear. His whole being was inert. Repeated disappointments
had dried up the well-spring of hope which had once bubbled
high within him.

Ah! he had thought himself at the last point of discouragement six years before, when weary of his book-keeping—but this—this was exhaustion, physical and mental.

At first he had been successful and had even been able to make remittances to his wife and child, but unfortunately he imbibed the spirit of eagerness, which pervaded the time and place, and worked incessantly, scarcely allowing himself the hours for necessary sleep. Recreation there was none in which he cared to indulge. This unceasing toil, combined with exposure and change of climate, brought on an illness during which all that he had accumulated wasted away. Money does not last long when one is sick, among strangers who require pay for every slight service.

After a time he recovered and resumed his labors, but without marked success. His next pile, the result of a years work, was stolen. Then "the diggings" of that vicinity seemed to be exhausted and he was obliged to seek another place.

Cursing his luck, and yet unwilling to give up and return home penniless, John Alden worked on doggedly and persistently haunted by desperate thoughts of what his fate might ultimately be, should he thus continue his exertions deprived of every comfort, and subject to an increasing depression of spirits which he was unable to throw off.

"Hallo! Buckeye," he heard a rough voice say in kindly tones. "Hallo pard, old fellow! wake up, here's a letter for you."

"A letter? give it to me," and the thin hand clutched the missive eagerly.

Gently John Alden's fellow exile raised his weary head

placing beneath it his own bundle of blankets, saying as he did so :

"There, read it old fellow, it will do you good."

It was Amy's letter, and as John Alden read the loving words he seemed to hear her voice, to feel her presence. Slowly the tears trickled down his wan cheeks, and as their fountain was unsealed, the vital forces rallied, and life and hope once more came back to him.

He slept that night as he had not done in weeks previous, and in his dreams he was again at home, his arm was round his wife, and his little daughter sat upon his knee. The world was bright without, for his heart was glad within. The voices of the miners singing in the distance a favorite song with this refrain:

"Can't stay in the wilderness,
A few days, a few days."

sounded like the chanting of angel hosts.

The clear cool air of morning woke him and he rose with new energy. Yesterday he had felt like an old man, his knees were bent together, and his hands trembled with weakness; to-day he was a young man again and there was courage in his heart, and strength in every limb.

Yes, he would go back. The dread of being compassionated by friends and relatives as a "failure", which had hitherto acted as a spur to his resolve to remain until he had achieved a fortune, was for the time forgotten, what cared he for wealth if Mary and Grace were but with him, contented and happy.

And now, strange to say, fickle fortune turned about and began to smile upon him, like a wayward flirt, who sees with vexation a victim escaping from her toils. His washings this morning proved richer than they had done for many a long day.

He accepted her proffered favors, dallying but long enough however, to amass a sufficient sum to carry him home respectably.

The overland route had been opened by Col. Fremont. Trains were continually coming and going across the country, and John found no difficulty in securing a passage homeward.

Ah, what a journey, through defile and seemingly inaccessible pass, over the Rocky Mountains whose towering peaks reach the region of eternal snows, their sides covered with pines and cedars, the beginning of whose growth dates back to by-gone ages, their branches festooned with vines, and the sward beneath them gay with flowers of every hue.

There were sparkling cascades crowned with rainbows dashing from romantic and inaccessible cliffs. There were bubbling rivulets, and placid lakes, gentle slopes and dark canons, all combining to give such a variety to the route that days of travel with a slow moving freight train did not produce weariness. But how different the country beyond; a sterile and vast level expanse covered with waving lines of sand in which the rivulets are lost as they descend from the bare ridges around.

John Alden was introspectively and retrospectively inclined, and the long, weary days required to cross this desert gave him time to muse on every act of his past life, to analyze the motives which had actuated him and to reflect upon the consequences which had followed, and there were still left hours and days which he gave to the construction of a vast air castle for future habitation.

But the great American desert has a limit, and leaving it, the train entered the region of "Buffalo Grass", where the monotony was occasionally varied by the starting of a herd of elk or buffalo. Beyond this they came upon fertile rolling prairies, watered by large streams skirted by heavy timber, with here and there a range of bluffs whose gray tops were capped with stone, arranged in regular layers as if disposed by the hand of man, and for a purpose.

"What a glorious scene," exclaimed John Alden, as the train halted one evening on the top of a high hill, two days after leaving Fort Riley, then upon the uttermost bounds of civilization; "how still, how peaceful! It seems as if the rude passions and conflicting interests of mankind might never break its calm or mar its harmony."

To the east he looked through the clear atmosphere, over ten miles of rolling prairie, the zig-zag lines of timber marking the courses of the streams with waving lines of green, to a range of hills in the distance, upon whose brown tops rested the deep blue and gold horizon.

To the north, after the first abrupt descent of the hill, there was a gradual slope, then almost a level, beyond which the land declined to meet a river whose sparkling waters shadowed on their surface the large trees which fringed the opposite bank.

Beyond and spreading out, far as the eye could reach, lay a fertile and broad expanse, the small patches of timber visible here and there resembling the orchards of an old settled country.

A large mound reared its shapely form to the south-west, whose carpet of grass was marked by many lines of brown, the effect of the intense heat of the summer sun.

Westward lay a beautiful valley, beyond that a high hill, and to the northwest a varied scene, hill and dale, prairie and woodland, ravine and gently flowing river, all intensified and glorified by the brilliant rays of the setting sun.

And as John stood there on the hill top, entranced with the beauty of the land on every side, a vague idea which had taken possession of him since having learned at Fort Riley that the territory was thrown open for settlement, shaped itself definitely and became resolve.

As he neared the bounds of civilization all the old dread of meeting those polite assurances of sympathy which partake so largely of pity, and which to him savored of contempt, had returned, accompanied with a horror of returning from the free air and sunshine to the old treadmill in the counting room.

He walked down to the river. He strolled along its banks, went southward to the little creek, then westward to the mound, and the moon was high in the heavens ere he again made his way to the encampment, but his resolution was fixed.

"Jake," said he the next morning to the boss of the train, a good natured Dutchman, to whom our traveler had become indebted for many kindly offices by the way,

"Jake, I want you to do a favor for me."

"So, goot! Meester Alten, speak out already, and it vas done."

"Well, Jake, I want you to carry a letter for me to the nearest post office."

"Vat for you not yourself go?"

"Because I have decided to remain here and invite my wife and daughter to join me;" then noting the Dutchman's look of amazement,

"I shall make my fortune in this quiet valley, Jake."

"Mein Got in Himmel! How you makes him? Nottings to sell unt nopody to puy. Vare you get your money, hey, Meester Alten?" and Jake planted himself squarely upon this, to him, unanswerable argument.

"I shall dig it from the earth, perhaps," was the reply. And in spite of Jake's protestations that he wouldn't find a pan of "pay dirt" in the whole valley, and a very emphatic assertion, "Meester Alten you is von tam fool!" John remained firm.

He ordered his baggage to be taken from the train and carried to the valley below; and soon after, with great bustle and noise, and the usual amount of swearing, the train was got underway, moving its slow length along to the eastward, and he was left alone on the prairie, monarch of all he surveyed.

CHAPTER III.

ON THE TOWN SITE—VISITORS.

No sooner had the last wagon of the long train disappeared in the distance, than a revulsion of feeling came over him.

"John Alden, you are a fool!" he said to himself. "What do you expect to accomplish on this wide prairie, alone. It was a rash impulse that bade you stop, and a wise man would have disregarded it."

Then he seated himself upon his box, took out an old and cherished pipe, filled it with tobacco, lit it, assumed an easy position and judicial frame of mind, and as the clouds of smoke went curling upward, called for arguments on the other side of the question.

"Your head is level," said the attorney for the opposite side. "By this act you have constituted yourself a Squatter Sovereign, possessed in fee simple of one hundred and sixty acres of the finest land the sun ever shone upon, in the most beautiful valley in the world—a very respectable amount of moss to attach to a rolling stone. You have learned from others, and you have seen for yourself that people are coming into the territory from every direction. This valley is near the great highway and others will soon join you. At any rate, the weather is warm, your tent is the only shelter you need, your supply of provisions is sufficient for a month, that piece of timber-land in sight certainly contains game, and the river, fish. You have the prospect of sport and a savory addition to your bill of fare, wherewith I rest my case."

The decision rendered completely restored John Alden's confidence in his own good judgment, and he began to look about him. Seeing several large stones in juxtaposition, he placed his tent near them. Within, he put blankets in one corner, the large box containing provisions, clothing, etc., etc., in another. His working utensils he deposited outside on one of the large stones. Then he undertook to search for water, and found a small spring issuing from one side of the ravine to the north, the sides of which were covered with a thick growth of underbrush. After enjoying a cool draught he filled his coffee pot with water, and carrying with him a few sticks for fuel, returned to his camp.

Having thus disposed of his household affairs with a wise forethought, he placed a package of crackers and dried beef in his pocket, and taking his gun, departed on a tour of exploration.

It was a long tramp in the hot sun, and by the time he reached the creek, he had also arrived at the determination that all future expeditions, while the warm weather continued, should be made in the early morning.

After resting awhile, however, he proceeded slowly through the underbrush, with which the low ground was covered, and after a trudge of several miles, was rewarded by the sight of a flock of wild ducks which started up just in front of him, and luckily succeeded in bringing down three at a single shot.

Picking up the game, he retraced his steps to a small spring of water, where he enjoyed a lunch and cool drink, and then proceeded to return slowly to the tent, wherein he sought shelter, incapable of further exertion until the decline of the summer sun moderated the intense heat. Then, issuing forth, he dressed the game, a process in which he had long since become an expert, built a fire, placed thereon a frying pan and coffee pot. Into the latter he put some coffee, and to

KANSAS FARM SCENE.

the former consigned his ducks, with a little bacon to prevent their burning, and salt and pepper to flavor, and presently served up with great satisfaction, upon a large flat stone an appetizing meal, to which he brought that wholesome sauce, a good appetite.

Then removing the remains of his repast, our Squatter Sovereign stretched himself out on the grass with his blankets rolled up for a pillow, and his pipe as an aid to digestion, the blue sky lighted by the silvery moon for a canopy, and his own thoughts for company. His first reflection was: "How very simple the process of house-keeping becomes when under the sole management of the sterner sex. Left to man alone, all the complicated mysteries, all the differentiations of divers courses, and devious methods of preparation, the pomp and circumstance, the expensive paraphernalia of serving disappears, and the creature returns to the simple style of the aborigines, which style possesses double advantages, for all elaborate processes of dining having been dispensed with, the labors entailed by the clearing up process are likewise avoided. I take mine ease on my blanket, and the kitchen work awaits my pleasure."

Presently the shining river visible in the distance invited to a bath and a swim, from which he returned to enjoy a night's refreshing slumber within his tent.

Several days passed away thus with little variation, save in his bill of fare, quails, prairie chickens, and wild pigeons, each in turn gracing the stony board.

But this isolation was not destined to continue long. E're it became positively painful, John was agreeably startled by the sound of human voices and the clatter of horses hoofs. It was in the early morning, and he was inside the tent engaged in performing the duties of his toilet, which consisted chiefly in putting on his boots. The voices were not pleasant, on the contrary, they were harsh, discordant and uncultivated, but the sound thrilled him with pleasure as it broke upon the solitude.

"Halloa there! Halloa, halloa!"

"Halloa yourself!" he replied.

"Come out here and show your colors," said a rough voice.

"They are true blue," was John's reply as he stepped to the door of the tent and confronted three rough looking customers on three very fine-looking horses. They were well armed, having pistols and knives strapped in their belts, and an additional bowie peeping from their boots. They all wore slouch hats, but here the resemblance ceased. The first, who seemed to be the leader, was a medium-sized, tolerably well made man. He had long brown hair, weather beaten features and gray restless eyes, His mouth, though quite large might not have been disagreeable but for an inveterate habit of chewing tobacco, that had drawn down the left corner, from which a little brooklet of the juice of the weed trickled constantly down his chin. He wore butternut pants of Kentucky jeans, and a bright blue flannel shirt embroidered on the front and back with red wool. The expression of his face indicated the predominance of the selfish propensities. His movements and voice displayed energetic aggressiveness and combativeness. He would not hesitate to posess himself of that which he desired, forcibly if necessary, and would enjoy it the more for the effort.

The second was decidedly different in physique and in character as well, if facial expression can give indication of what lies beneath. He was long, lean, lank and loose-jointed, slow of movement and of speech, was too indolent for much exertion, and yet when roused might perhaps exceed the other in strength. There was a more frank look in his face, though even less of symmetry, his chin protruding and his cheek bones rising high, while his nose was short and broad. He too wore the jeans pants, but they were blue, matching his shirt, and upon his neck he wore a massive gold chain, while several very striking rings were upon his fingers.

The third was a little weazen-faced dried-up Irishman, whose red shirt matched his hair in color, and whose blue eyes snapped and sparkled inquisitively as he sat uneasily on his horse, and that the evident disappointment and surprise which John's appearance created, may be understood, it must be stated that he was himself the roughest looking customer in the group. His hair and beard, slightly tinged with gray, were long, his boots old, his buckskin pants considerably worse for wear, and he too wore the blue shirt, but t'was faded in color, and the embroidered figures on the front and back were but faintly visible. Judged by externals he was "one of them," and a most dilapidated one, and the answer he had given " true blue" happened to be one of the pass-words of their order, consequently when he emerged from the tent and drew himself up to his full height before them, they looked at him and then at each other and burst into a loud laugh.

"Gentlemen," said John indignantly, "have you come here to insult me?"

The leader now managed to control his risibles sufficiently to ejaculate: "Euchred by hokey! and a moment afterward continued: " Stranger the larf comes in on us, we haint got nothin agin you. You're all right on the goose, any fool can see that with half an eye. But here was us three fellars, ha, ha, ha, ha, border-ruffians we are, stranger, ridin like mad down to this here tent, darnation sure as we'd treed a dog-gauned biled-shirted abolitionist, and to see you walk out, so kinder cool like, in that ar uniform, gin us a set back, well it did!" and he laughed again.

"Whar did you come from any way old hoss?" "And be jabers!" cried Pat, "ye must have dhropped down from the sky I'm thinkin'. It's on the rampage we've bin now for a wake, guardin of the country forninst," pointing to the east, "and niver a b'y have we seen with a pack on his back comin into the territory."

"Well gentlemen," said John, "dismount and smoke the pipe of peace with me, and I will give you all the information about myself you desire."

They accepted his invitation by dismounting immediately, turning their horses loose to graze upon the prairie. Pat first unwinding a strap which was fastened about the neck of each animal, and which hanging loosely served to seize them by, when they were again wanted. John in the meantime, brought forth his tobacco box, each man furnished his own pipe, the stones before mentioned served as seats, and they were soon puffing away, a picturesque group—the Irishman with his red shirt and hair of the same hue, giving color to the scene.

Our Squatter opened the conversation by stating: "My name is John Alden, and I came here on a return trip from the west. I've been to the mines—"

"An' g-g-got b-b-busted," stammered the long, lean visitor, which caused another laugh in which Alden himself joined, as he replied—

"Well, yes, I am pretty well used up, it is true; but I've got a nice piece of land here, which I propose to make something out of."

"Bully for you!" shouted the other Missourian, slapping John familiarly on the back. "You're a hoss! You're a gol darned snorter! an' you've struck it rich this time. You've squatted right squar' on the town site."

"What town site?" Alden inquired in surprise; "Why, the dog-gon Abolitionist town site, of course. There's a whole company on em, drat 'em! comin' up here, an' we heered they wor a kalkilatin' to lay out a town on the Kaw, beyond the mouth of the Areposa. In course, this must be the place. An' now you've got it, you hold on to it. We'll stand by yer. I'm Zeke Fagin, otherwise known as Pineknot Zeke, 'cos I'm hard to lick, ye see; and this hyer's Sile Hardiker, he aint much on the talk, but git him roused, mad him, stranger, an' he can fight like thunder. That ar's Pat Malone; he's little, but he's tough, an' he hates niggers like sin."

"An nagur worshippers like the divil!" put in Pat.

"We'll stand by yer," continued Zeke; "Jist plant yerself hyer, and we'll back yer."

"Ya-as, we'll b-b-b-b-back yer," said Sile approvingly.

"And faith, its good backin' there is forninst us," said Pat; "Swhorn to clane out the nagur worshippers intirely, begorra! A shwate time they'll have of it sure, makin' a free shtate of this territory."

"They've no right here," said Zeke; "Let 'em go to Nebrasky, where they belong. Yanks and Sons of the South wont do to mix. Stranger, we've took a solemn oath, by the Eternal! to make this a slave state, an' we mean to do it. The fellers are all drillin' over thar an' gittin' ready for the fun. The big-bugs furnish the ammunition and whisky, an' us fellers furnish the grit."

"Och, whishky!" cried Pat; "Shmoke is a good thing, Misther Alden, but whishky is a better; an' by me troth, I like a little of both."

"Gentlemen," said John, "I am very sorry that I have no liquor of any kind to offer you."

"Murther!" screamed Pat; "Did you ever hear the likes of it? Shquattin' on the lone prairie, and niver a dhrop of the crather to cheer him the whiles. It's a case of pauperism I see before me.

"T-t-t-take up a c-c-collection!" stuttered Sile.

Pat immediately sprang up, seized Alden's cup, poured some liquor from his own bottle into it, and passed it to each of his companions who did the same, then handing it to John, he said:

"We'll drink now, 'Success to the sons of the South.'" Remembering the old adage, "When in Rome, do as Romans do," John discreetly raised the cup to his lips, but managed to spill some of the liquid unperceived to the ground. The smell of it was enough for him, but his visitors seemed to relish it, for each took a long pull at his respective bottle.

"The b'yes will shtick to the Colonel, while the whishky howlds out," said Pat.

Long Sile's eyes flashed as he stammered:

"The S-s-sons of the South w-w-will stick to the bitter end, d-d-darn yer, l-l-licker or no licker."

Little Pat might have been annihilated then and there, but Zeke came to the rescue.

"Here, Pat," said he, "You git them horses up; we've got to stake out our claims in this hyer valley, an' git back to Bean's cabin to meet the boys to-night." Turning to Alden, he said, "We've got no call to interfere with you; but our instructions from the Colonel are to hold this valley and prevent the Yanks from gittin' in."

"Are you going to settle on the land?" Alden inquired.

"Wa-al, no. At least, not now; but we're goin' to put our mark on it, and hold it too.

The horses being brought up by this time they were soon galloping off, and in the south John saw them pause; and on examination afterward, he found that each man had set up a stake, tacked to it a card with his name on, and also a threat of death to any one who should disregard this notice and presume to take up the land as a claim.

CHAPTER IV.

NEW FRIENDS.

Two days longer John Alden held undisputed sway, and then a number of men on horseback, followed by a long line of wagons and carriages, bringing freight and passengers, came bearing down upon him from the east.

The iron wheels crushed pitilessly the tender grass and bright flowers on the bosom of the virgin prairie, and there was no outcry; but the echoing hills resounded cheerily, in a new key, to the sound of many human voices,—those hills whose tones till late had but replied to the wild bird's call, the baying of the wolf, and the gutteral accents of the savage. The placid river flowing idly to the sea, now gently and now swiftly, to suit the mood of wind and current, shadowed back in the sunshine the new faces which bent over her, as if in welcome, and cooled the heated hands which rippled her bright surface, unknowing or unheeding the harsh fact that those same hands had come to chain her waters to the wheel.

So gently, Nature bends herself to do the will of man, the conqueror.

From the height on which John Alden stood when first looking down on the quiet valley, he saw them come, witnessed all the pleasant commotion of alighting, the stretching of limbs which is so grateful after long confinement in an uncomfortable position—saw little groups of two or three, or more, scattering off in various directions, others attending to the horses, and still others unloading and opening various boxes as if to make preparations for the evening meal.

One party set up a tent on the side of the hill on which Alden stood, and ever and anon the sound of cultivated voices came floating up to him with memories of home in every accent. Suddenly in the presence of this busy scene in which he had no lot or part, a sense of unutterable loneliness came over him, and stealing down by a side-path he made his way to his tent, hoping to hide his buckskin pants and blue shirt, of whose hideousness he had all at once become conscious, within its sheltering folds, when a voice called out in friendly tones the accustomed salutation:

"Halloa there stranger!"

And he was constrained to reply:

"Halloa yourself!"

The interlocutor was a tall, hatched-faced individual with an inquiring expression of countenance, an unmistakable son of Vermont, and he continued:

"Is this your tent?"

Alden replied in the affirmative:

"How long have you been here?"

"A week yesterday."

"A native of Missouri, I guess?"

"You guess wrong, try again."

"Arkansas then, or Alabama?"

He shook his head. Quite a group had by this time gathered around them and another voice suggested:

"Illinois sure!"

"No."

"Kentucky?" Still another asked.

"Wrong still."

"Indiana?"

"Wrong again."

"Well where in thunder did you come from then?" said the Vermonter, "I'll give it up."

"Well," said John, "I came from Northern Ohio, and can

boast of as good Yankee blood as any of you." There was a laugh and an expression of incredulity on every face, but when he explained that he had come to the territory by way of the Isthmus and California, and had been six years on the way, incredulity gave way to kindly interest, and he was soon quite at home among them.

Alden evinced friendly feelings by guiding them to the spring in the ravine, and also taught them how to build a fire on scientific principles, by digging a hole in the ground and then arranging the sticks in such a manner that the draught should be from beneath, carrying the smoke off with the wind. This settled his status with that mess, and he received an invitation to take supper with them, which was gladly accepted.

During the meal, which, though served in the open air from the top of several large boxes and cooked under many disadvantages, yet was the nearest approach to the civilized manner of doing things which John Alden had enjoyed for many a long day, he learned many things of interest. His messmates informed him that they came under the auspices of the "New England Emigrant Aid Society" an association formed for the purpose of encouraging emigration on a large scale, thus securing reduced rates for passengers and freight, the use of capital for building store-rooms, hotels, mills, etc., and besides avoiding that isolation from society which under the old method rendered the life of the pioneer so dreary. He also learned much of the political condition of the country which in his exile had come to him, if at all, in such a manner as to make little impression on his mind.

The triumph of the slave-power in the passage of the fugitive slave-law, the enforcement of which roused the latent sense of justice in many Northern hearts, the repeal of the Missouri Compromise—that breaking of the plighted faith, which proved the last straw on the back of that patient camel, northern forbearance.

Then came the passage of the Kansas-Nebraska act, which with its different interpretations North and South, transferred the scene of conflict from legislative halls to distant prairies.

All this came to him with force, as related in eloquent and stirring language by his new friend Langtry, the Vermonter. " And," he continued, " we accept this issue thus forced upon us and propose to fight this battle to the bitter end." His words so prophetic of his own fate called to Alden's mind what Sile Hardiker had asserted of the sons of the South, and he related the incident of his Missouri visitors.

" We shall not be dismayed by these threats," said Langtry, " we have received numerous warnings on our route, that it would be dangerous for us to attempt to make a settlement, but we have not come so many hundreds of miles to be turned back by threatening words."

The next morning John Alden received a message to present himself in the tent of the leader of the colony, Dr. Francis Rulison. Desiring to appear as presentable as possible, he went to his box, dived into its depths profound, and drew from thence a time-honored shirt whose yellow folds suggested faintly the opprobrious epithet " biled," at the same time however, fixing the era of that process far back in the dim and shadowy past. A pair of pants which had made the round trip in undisturbed security, his boots fresh blackened, a straw hat he had purchased from one of the new comers, and his hair and beard cut into comeliness by another, completed the costume in which to receive his introduction to the free-state chief.

He found Dr. Rulison seated on a camp chair, by the side of a small table, within a large tent used as an office for the transaction of business. Books and papers upon, and inside a large box, which served as table and writing-desk, and several additional camp chairs, completed the list of furnishings.

He was a man of grave and dignified demeanor, calmness and equability were engraved upon his countenance, coolness and caution expressed in every movement. In person he was tall, well made and commanding, with brown hair and a keen grayish blue eye, which seemed to look one through and through. In a pleasant voice he bade John be seated, and then said kindly:

"I understand you have been in possession of a part of this valley for some days."

"A week to-day," was the reply.

"And did you intend to pre-empt the land with a view to making a settlement?"

"I did, sir; and have written my wife to come and join me."

"In that case we must endeavor to compromise the matter with you. Have you any reason for preferring this particular spot as the site of your future home?"

"None sir, except its rare beauty. It was that which first suggested to me the thought of remaining, and induced me to leave the homeward bound train, and take possession of it."

"Ah! you did not know then that we intended bringing a colony to this point?"

"I did not hear of it until afterward. Several Missourians, who came a few days ago, and who have also set up stakes in the valley, informed me of your coming; but I was uncertain as to the reliability of the information."

"As to their claims, we shall disregard them. They are not *bona fide* settlers and never intend to become such; but finding you in actual possession, we are obliged to make terms with you."

This did not prove a difficult matter, however. Alden was anxious to retain the favor and companionship of his new found friends, and felt more than satisfied with his investment of a week's time, when in return for vacating his Squatter

"I SENDS FOR MY KATRINA."

right to one hundred and sixty acres of the town site, he received a membership in the town company entitling him to twenty lots and a vote in all the affairs of the "association," besides a good team of horses and a wagon, while his right of pre-emption still remained intact, and he could look about and select a place somewhere in the neighborhood of the city, that was to be.

An arrangement had been made by the town company for mail connection with the outside world, so he immediately dispatched a letter to his wife, giving her a detailed account of all that had taken place during the past week, the advantageous arrangement he had made with the town company, and his strong desire to begin life again, surrounded by the earnest hopeful spirits of his new associates. In the evening at a regular meeting of the town association, it was decided to call the new place Warsaw, a name which suggested the idea of what its founders intended it should become—a stronghold of freedom. The conical hill to the southwest was named Greenmound, and the high mount to the west called Mount Olympus.

The next day the members of the town company, John Alden included, set off in various directions to look up desirable claims. As he was now the proprietor of a vehicle of transportation, quite a number of persons, among them his first acquaintance and interlocutor, Mr. Langtry, wished to accompany him; and the latter suggested that timberland would be most likely to yield immediate returns, as the saw mill furnished by the "Aid Society," would soon arrive and lumber become a cash article.

Acting upon this suggestion, Alden turned his horses' heads toward the south, striking the Areposa creek and following its course as it flows north-east to join the Kaw. As they drove over the beautiful prairie country, one by one, those who accompanied them, attracted by the beauty of some particular spot, alighted from the wagon to take possession, until Langtry and Alden were left alone, and these two continued onward until they reached a good fording place, and then crossed the creek to an extensive tract of timber which lay on the opposite side. So large were the trees and the wood of such excellent quality, that they decided the distance from Warsaw of small importance; besides there stretched out beyond the woods a beautiful prairie tract where they hoped to be able to purchase land for farming purposes, if a sufficient quantity to meet their needs did not, on survey being made, come within the limits of the one hundred and sixty acres which they had the right to pre-empt.

Here they halted and remained during the day, examining and selecting lands and hewing a few logs to be used in improvements, agreeing to work together and to build their cabins as near each other as possible.

Langtry was quite communicative and related during the day, many things concerning his former life, none of which tendered to lessen the great respect Alden had conceived for him. He was thirty-six years old, and had been a farmer all his life, having inherited from his father, one of those rocky little places in Vermont, where the stones stubbornly dispute proprietorship with man, for almost every rod of ground. He had inherited also the family mortgage, which he had early resolved to liquidate ere he married; and this resolution he adhered to steadily, until the age of thirty, when having vanquished that arch enemy, debt, he became enamored of, and married a lady some ten years his junior. She was the orphan daughter of a Unitarian clergyman, was the teacher of the village school, and it was her unfriended lot, as well as her beauty of character and sympathetic, impulsive nature, which had attracted him towards her. The marriage, though childless, had proved a happy one, and he already looked forward with eager anticipation to the end of this their first separation. He was quite liberal in his religious views, having become an ardent disciple of Theodore Parker, whose noble sentiments and eloquent words had at this time stirred the fountains of New England thought to their depths. In politics he was a radical abolitionist, the question of slavery having swallowed up all others in his mind.

Of course, John Alden gave him confidences in return, and from that day they became warm friends.

Towards evening they returned to Warsaw, picking up their passengers of the morning by the way. And this they continued to do for some time. The town was their base of supplies, and besides there was a charm in the meetings held for conference and discussion. Seated on the ground, on camp-chairs, boxes, or whatever else could be pressed into service, in front of the business tent, members related to each other the various incidents of the day, giving descriptions of the claims they had taken, stating their plans and prospects of making them profitable. There were many crude ideas and wild projects indulged in by some of the members of the company; but the majority were sober-minded men with reasonable hopes, and all seemed inspired by the consciousness that their acts were not self regarding alone, but they were each a factor in the great combination which was to mold the institutions of this vast and fertile territory into conformity with the enduring principles of justice.

Many of them were unaccustomed to hard labor, and weary limbs and blistered hands were the result of their attempts to hew out homes from the raw material which nature had provided. Those who had taken prairie claims were awaiting the advent of the saw-mill, as it was really cheaper for them in building, to use boards rather than logs, and the labor of fashioning them much less.

CHAPTER V.

THE FIRST INVASION.

For three weeks the two friends worked on in the best of spirits. Pleasant companionship sweetens toil and each task willingly performed accelerates the motions of the wheels of time.

Langtry had hewn out logs for his house, and with John's assistance and the use of his team, had drawn them to a piece of rising ground beyond the timber.

Another day and they were to have a "raising," that is a number of their friends were coming from Warsaw to help them rear the ponderous walls of the new structure. They had made great preparations for the event, laying in quite a stock of provisions including game from the surrounding woods.

As soon as the "raising" was over and the cabin roofed and chinked, it would be in some measure fitted for woman's habitation, and then Langtry's wife, Agnes he called her, would come to him. She was now in Iowa with friends, anxiously awaiting a summons.

Alden had contented himself with hewing out a pile of logs ready for transportation to the mill, knowing that they would bring ready cash in case Amy decided adversely to joining him. He had not yet heard from her, but felt sure the next week's mail would bring him a letter.

August had declined into September, and here and there the trees were taking on a tinge of yellow and red. Gentle breezes from the north occasionally prevailed over the warm winds from the south. The wild grapes and plums with which the woods abounded, were thoroughly ripe, and as a last preparation, our friends had gathered some of the finest to serve for the morrow's dinner, and as they lifted on the wagon bed that had been removed to permit the hauling of logs, and harnessed the horses that they might return to Warsaw, they were in a boyishly exultant mood.

"To-morrow night" said Langtry striking an attitude and pointing his emphasis with a significant gesture,

> "My castle-walls shall proudly rear,
> O'er looking all this wide domain."

"I say Alden," he continued, "don't you think we had better sleep here at least a part of the time hereafter."

"It might be well," John replied, "as actual possession is necessary to pre-emption you know."

"I hardly think any one will dispute our ownership when they see how well we have carved out our rights on this timber, but if we sleep here we shall feel more as if it were really our home, and we shall get on faster with our work."

"Very well, I will bring up my tent and place it on my side of the road, and then we can take turns staying all night with each other, as we did with our young friends in boyhood's days."

"By jove, that's a good idea, and we will begin to-morrow night, but hark! what's that?"

"I don't know I'm sure, its a queer noise to be heard on these prairies. It sounds like a jollification in a miner's camp. Take the team, Langtry please, behind the thicket yonder, while I go to the road and reconnoitre."

He did so, and securing a place where he could observe without being seen, John Alden witnessed the approach of the advance guard of the "Sons of the South". In wagons and on horseback, pistols in their belts, and bowie knives in their boots, red-shirted, coatless and with battered hats, weather-beaten, loud-voiced, swearing, halloing and singing to the music of two violins, accompanied by an occasional blast on an ear-piercing dinner horn, they came, while now and then a shot from a musket gave warning that their expedition was a war-like one. Each wagon bore " A Banner with a strange device," a lone star or a lion rampant on a blood-red ground, above some soul-inspiring motto, such as " war to the death", " knife to the hilt ", "no quarter to abolitionists". The banner-poles were decorated on the tops with an inverted whiskey bottle, beneath which bowie knives were crossed and secured by long streamers of hemp, and each man wore a suggestive badge of the latter, tied in his button-hole.

And, ever and anon, as they continued on their way, the festive jug went round, and louder still the clamor grew, as each potation swelled each empty head, till out of all proportion grew each man's conception of his own exploits, and each essayed in turn, and all at once, to wake that admiration in his fellows which he felt his wondrous feats, so thrillingly related, should excite.

Zeke Fagin was there, his burly form sat proudly on his handsome horse. The red head of Pat was plainly visible and the lank visage of Sile Hardiker.

The three rode in the van and under their guidance the procession wound its way down through the timber to the ford and onward towards the free-state settlement.

As they entered upon the town site, the invading hosts did not as might have been expected, precipitate an attack, but turned aside, crossed to the north of the ravine and there intrenched themselves.

They were perhaps one hundred in number, and when with the shades of night the free state men had all gathered in, they were of equal strength though but sixty of them were armed.

The first instruction given by Dr. Rulison, who with the

consent of all assumed command, was: "Look to your arms!" and all obeyed. Then he dispatched a committee to the opposite camp, inquiring "why this warlike demonstration and wherefore have you come out with music and banners and bearing arms?"

The answer came, quick, sharp and imperative: "We have come to clear this territory of abolitionists, and will give you until ten o'clock to-morrow morning to take down your tents and depart in peace. After that hour, any man who remains takes his life in his own hands. We are armed and we are determined. Your blood be upon your own heads if you heed not this warning."

"No reply to that message is needed until to-morrow morning at ten o'clock," said the Doctor coolly, "yet I warn you all to sleep lightly, they are not to be trusted." Sentinels were appointed for the different watches of the night, and then they retired to await the events of the coming morning.

There was no need of the injunction to sleep lightly, fatigue was forgotten, by some in fear and by others in eagerness for the conflict. The latter were anxious to go over and attack the enemy in the midst of their revelry, which continued long into the night, prophesying a complete route. But wiser counsels prevailed.

"We may defend ourselves, if attacked, but we are not here to commit aggression," said Dr. Rulison; and to this doctrine he adhered firmly through all the events which followed.

At length the weary night was over. The morning sun shone down upon the white tents of the free state men still resting in the valley. But their inmates were astir—a hurried breakfast and they gathered in front of the large office tent, and all who were armed began to go through the evolutions of a military drill. Silent, yet firm; undemonstrative, yet resolute; they moved as calmly as though the occasion was but a New England training-day.

An hour later, and across the ravine all was commotion and excitement, tumult and disorder, amazement and surprise at the appearance of resistance where they had anticipated a terrified slinking away. Accustomed to associate silence with fear, and calmness with despair, they were bewildered with the new psychic problem which presented itself.

All at once a tremendous shriek rent the air, again and again. Then an answering yell from the east, and looking in that direction, the free state men saw approaching, another body of men similarly armed and caparisoned with the first. "Were they to be attacked from two sides at once?" was the question in every mind. Perhaps we had better go back and wait until the thing is settled," piped some fainting soul, which suggestion was received with a most contemptuous "Bah!" But no; they pass on to the north and join their friends, who receive them with many demonstrations of joy.

The new-comers brought a fresh supply of bottled inspiration, and this imbibed, the sinking courage of the party rose, and they too, marched and countermarched, exultant in the consciousness of superior numbers, and at ten o'clock were drawn up in line to witness the inglorious departure of freedom from the territory. But the tents still stood defiantly, and the drill went calmly on.

A half hour passed, and then a consultation was held and a messenger dispatched.

It was Zeke Fagin, and swelling with gratified conceit at the honor thus conferred upon him, his already exaggerated estimate of himself, elevated beyond the balancing power of his uncultivated judgment, he galloped across the intervening distance in advance of the four associates deputed to attend him, and halted in front of the large tent, directing them as they came up, with a lordly gesture, to form a line in his rear.

No attention was paid to the imposing array. The armed men went on with their drill, not even so much as turning a head to look at them. A lounger near the door of the tent deliberately took out his pocket-knife and began to whittle. This reception somewhat disconcerted Zeke, who, big with his message, had expected to meet with obsequious attention. At length he called out.

"I say, Whittler, wher's your Cap'n?"

The man addressed looked up with an indifferent air and asked in an assumed nasal tone, "Be you desirin' to speak to him?"

"Yes, dog-gon ye! I've a message for him from Gen. Watkins, commander in chief of the 'Missouri Rangers,'" and Zeke drew himself up pompously, and sat his horse as firmly as though the concentrated dignity of the whole slave power was represented in his burly person.

No visible effect was produced on the whittler, however, by this assumption of consequence. The easy motion of his pocket-knife was undisturbed, his eye blankly unconscious of any unusual significance in the name of Watkins, even with the prefix, General, and his voice was without a tremor as he replied;

"Wal, I guess he's in this 'ere tent, least wise that's where he generally keeps himself, when he aint somewhere else."

"Tell him to come out here, dog-gon ye! an' keep yer guessin' for them as likes it. Be quick now! Say a messenger from Gen. Dave Watkins, wishes to see him *immediately!*" this with emphasis and renewed pomposity.

The whittler disappeared within the tent for a moment, and then returned with the reply; "The Dr. will be happy to receive a messenger from Gen. Watkins. Will he please dismount and enter."

Zeke's indignation, which had been gradually rising, now reached the boiling point, and bubbled over.

"What! git off and wait on a dog-goned abolitionist! No! I'll be d— ef I do! I'll see him in h—l, first! Tell him that I am a messenger from BRIGADIER-GENERAL, David Watkins, and I want to see the Cap'n of this hyer dog-goned, biled-shirted, abolition crowd, *out hyer!*" with cumulative emphasis, reaching a climax on the last two words.

The message was carried, and the reply delivered with exasperating indifference, by Whittler, as follows:

"The Dr. is very much engaged at present, and if you do not wish to dismount you may send the message through myself."

Zeke was unable to contain himself at this. He reared his horse upright, advanced toward the tent as if he would like to trample in the dust the unoffending canvas with all that it contained, then halted suddenly, and ejaculated sardonically;

"By the great horned, flat-footed d—l! I 'low he thinks he's the 'Pope o' Rome!' but I'll be dog-goned if I'm goin' to kiss his big toe!" and with this he wheeled about and carried his insulted dignity back to the more congenial atmosphere of his own camp, leaving his retainers to follow at their leisure.

Zeke's account of his mission was received with a yell, whether consoling or excruciating to his feelings, could not be determined. They only knew that three embassadors, of less pretentious appearance, and less *exactions* temper, approached, one of whom dismounted and was conducted by Whittler to the Dr.'s presence, where he delivered himself of the following message:

"Gen. Watkins wishes the free state men to strike their tents and take up a line of march for Nebraska. An earnest desire to prevent the effusion of blood, induces him to extend the time until 1 o'clock, P. M. At that hour his men are coming over in force, and all who remain will be put to the bowie knife, or shot."

The Dr. listened to the message, then fixing his calm blue eye upon the messenger, replied in a mild, though resolute tone:

"Tell Gen. Watkins that we have come here to stay," and then resumed his writing as serenely as though he had received an invitation to dinner and accepted with pleasure.

The discomfited envoys retired, waiting until some distance off before giving vent to their anger in oaths.

One o'clock came and went, and yet the September sun blazed down upon those obnoxious tents in undisturbed possession of the town site, and still the squatter soldiers, who for the sake of greater comfort having removed their coats, might have been styled the "biled shirt brigade", went on with their drill.

The enemy were now drawn up in line, as if to advance at the word of command, and a single messenger, Pat Nelson, came galloping forward and without dismounting called out: "Halloa there yez! Yez kin have jist twenty minutes to move your tints and save yer scalps, be jabers!"

He was greeted with a shout of laughter, so loud and long that it must have reached across the ravine.

Consternation was now clearly perceptible among the invading hosts. One party led by Zeke Fagin was for advancing immediately to put their threats into execution, while others, seeing in the composure which pervaded the free state camp, indications of some concealed force or power on which the squatters relied to offset the difference in numbers—a cannon perhaps, or Sharp's rifles, of whose destructive capacity they had heard marvelous stories, were in favor of giving "a little more time." The leaders themselves, having failed to succeed in their game of "bluff", suddenly awoke to a sense of the responsibility to be incurred by a deliberate, unprovoked attack on unoffending settlers, and agreed with the conservatives, whereat Zeke and his followers swore, "they didn't propose to make fools of themselves by running with such a dog-goned skeery crowd," and to the number of sixty departed toward the east. The remainder lingered until twilight and then followed in his wake.

Thus bloodlessly ended the first invasion, and there was joy and peace and rest that night in Warsaw. But when morning came and a happy party joyously proceeded to Langtry's claim, to do the work and enjoy the feast postponed from yesterday, alas! alas! upon his head and that of Alden had fallen the ruthless vegeance of the retiring and crestfallen foe. A smoking pile of coals and ashes was all that remained of Langtry's castle walls, or of John Alden's pile of logs, and each claim bore an upright pole decorated with streamers of hemp, to which a card was attached announcing, that Zeke Fagin, or Carr Withers, respectively, would dispute possession with any man who attempted to take up that claim.

Disappointed and disheartened they returned to town, nor did the inevitable, "I told you so," from those who had warned them against settling so far away from Warsaw, tend to enliven their dejected spirits.

CHAPTER VI.

THE "RAISING."—DUTCH JAKE.

Langtry and Alden were not the only workers in the colony. The sounds which greeted them on reaching the town site, "Steady there now!" "A little to the left!" "Heave away!" "Up with her!" "All right!" as each integral part of a gradually rising structure, in the shape of a huge log hewn at the ends, was lifted from the ground, carefully hoisted and deposited in its allotted position, by a jolly company of men in their shirt sleeves, indicated as much, while the laughter which followed some awkward movement or some sally of wit, as clearly proclaimed their genuine enjoyment of their first experience in log cabin raising.

"There Alden," said Langtry, "that's the place for us, nothing like hard work to cure the sting of disappointment."

"All right," John responded, and consequently, after thanking their friends, as they alighted from the wagon, not only for intended assistance but for sympathy in their misfortunes, and listening once more to the well meant but irritating injunction;

"Begin nearer home next time, and when you are ready again we will gladly come and help you," they joined the merry party.

The building thus undergoing the process of architectural development, and at the same time rising into historic eminence as the first house on the town site, was the property of Jacob Schmidt, a rotund jolly little Dutchman, who had hitherto served as chief in the culinary department, driving a thriving business in bread and pies, the latter a luxury which a true Yankee can ne'er forego when attainable, baking the same in a stone oven of his own construction, and disposing of them at a good price, being patronized by the whole community.

And now, inspired by that wholesome discontent which reaches forth after higher and better things, Jake coveted the distinction of Hotel-proprietor. What human heart hath not its pet ambition? and what heights of eminence may not be attained if steadily pursued in the line of the least resistance? Conscious of the true bent of his genius, Jake had confined his exertions strictly to catering for the appetites of his patrons, thus securing for himself their good will and verifying the old proverb "the way to a man's heart is through his stomach," and what was of more value to Jake, coining at the same time the wherewithal to pay more stalwart workers to prepare the material for his twin cabins, for such the hotel as it assumed form and shape proved to be; twin cabins with a connecting link, one roof extending over the ten feet of open space between them.

They were each sixteen feet square, eight feet high and covered with a thatched roof made of poles slightly elevated at their joining place in the centre, forming a slope on either side and covered heavily with prairie grass.

Though rough and unsightly in appearance, this formed a water-proof roof—floor there was none, that luxury Jake proposed to add when the coming saw-mill should make it more readily procurable,

One of the rooms was to be devoted exclusively to sleeping, and consequently was furnished with two bedsteads, made of hickory poles, extending entirely a cross two sides of the room. They were designed to accommodate, each, some six or seven sleepers, but proved a sort of omnibus bed, capable of indefinite extension.

The other cabin, being intended for the dining room, was furnished with two immovable tables, each twelve feet in length, with benches on either side. A small building near the oven was erected as a protection for Jake while pursuing the arduous duties of his profession, and no prouder man walked the town site than he, when the whole was finished and a large sign, with the words "Pioneer House, Jacob Schmidt, Proprietor," swung above the door. His round rubicund phiz was radiant with complacency, and a broad, contagious grin was continuously disseminated from his good natured, wide-spread mouth, as he waddled hither and thither, puffing and blowing with his efforts to wait on his guests, the workers, whom, at the conclusion of their labors, he invited to be seated around the new tables and partake of a bountiful dinner of various kinds of game and bread, with potatoes procured from Missouri.

Hard work in the open air induces good appetites, and the consciousness of having performed a friendly act, however humble the recipient, arouses agreeable sensations conducive to enjoyment. This dinner party thus possessed two elements of success lacking to many a grander spread—and the climax was reached, when with the dessert of pies and pudding made from the wild fruits found in the woods, Jake brought forth from some mysterious recess, a keg of root beer of his own brewing, prepared expressly for the occasion, and filling the cups of his guests, desired that they should drink, "Success to the Pioneer house."

"And its proprietor," sung out a voice from the company. The amendment was received with cheers and the toast drank standing. Then there was a unanimous call for a speech from Jake; but conscious that it was his mission to fill mouths, rather than ears; to tickle the palate, rather than to enlighten the understanding, Jake had disappeared, nor did he return until the company were dispersing when he came to say, "I tank you, shentlemens ferry mouch!"

" You must get you a wife, now, Jake," suggested Langtry.

" I vas dink of dot myself already," was the reply. " Sometime I send for my Katrina."

"Ah, so it is! "Love rules the camp, the court, the grove," said Langtry, as himself and Alden turned away towards the tent, their sleeping place, for rest. The atmosphere of good cheer which had surrounded them during the day had restored their equanimity, and they were able to discuss plans for the future with renewed hopefulness, and ere they slept to devise a feasible scheme for retaining the claims of their choice, and yet providing for the possible contingency of an attempt to dispossess them.

A large addition to the colony was expected daily, and the idea was to induce a sufficient number from among them to unite for mutual protection, and take up the whole wooded tract beyond the Areposa. With the adoption of this plan, Alden and Langtry became the progenitors of a long line of far-famed Kansas land agents; and the morrow brought a large number of land seekers, mostly from Iowa and Ohio.

CHAPTER VII.

NEW-COMERS—LANGTRY'S WIFE—ARTHUR FAIRCHILD—NEWS FROM AMY.

"Saw-mill's come!" "Saw-mill's come!" was the cry as a long train of white-covered wagons halted on the town site.

"It is in the rear," was replied to anxious inquiries, and Langtry and Alden started with the crowd who were making their way, eager to inspect the anxiously awaited piece of machinery.

They had gone but a short distance when a woman's voice called out "Edward!" "Edward!" Langtry paused. "Edward!" the voice called again, nearer, and he turned to find a woman's arms about his neck, and to clasp warmly to his bosom, oblivious to everything but the joy of her presence, his wife, Agnes.

She had come on the train with some of her Iowa friends —had been well taken care of—and enjoyed the novel incidents of an otherwise tedious journey. "It was all so new and strange to me," she said; "And then every day was bearing me nearer you. I could not remain longer away from you, Edward. An uncontrollable impulse bade me come, but—" noting the shade that passed over his face as he thought of that cabin, to which he should, by rights, have taken her, "Are you not glad to see me?"

"Indeed I am, dear," and the fond pressure of the arm which still lingered around her waist, and a look of unutterable tenderness from his eyes made assurance doubly sure. "But then, being glad to see you is one thing, and knowing

AGNES LANGTRY.

what to do with you is another. I fear I cannot make you comfortable."

"But I did not come to be comfortable, Edward. I came to be a pioneer and to endure the hardships and privations of frontier life. To make me comfortable would destroy all the romance," said she, archly smiling into his face.

"A very convenient frame of mind under present circumstances," said he, with a shrug of his shoulders, then reassuringly, "I am glad you have come, at any rate, and shall, I have no doubt, soon find some place for you."

Turning to Alden, he said, "Agnes, this is my friend, Mr. Alden, and a very good friend, too." She turned to John one of the most winning faces he had ever beheld. It was not strictly beautiful, the nose was rather long and slightly Roman, the forehead low and broad, the chin a little pointed, but the eyes were large and blue and clear as the summer sky. They were eyes through which one might look into the depths of the earnest soul beneath, and yet they could sparkle with mischief, for the tell-tale lines about the expressive mouth, suggested a wealth of concealed smiles. There was tenderness, and steadfastness, and sympathy in every lineament of her countenance. Her hair was blonde with a golden tint, and though drawn back in waving lines and twisted in a coil on her neck, little stray fringes had crept out and rippled and sparkled like sunshine on the white forehead. Her form was tall and willowy, and her voice exceptionally sweet and musical, as she acknowledged her pleasure at meeting any friend of her husband.

"My tent is at your service, Langtry," said John.

"Oh, no, Alden! We cannot thus dispossess you," said he, deprecatingly.

"But you must. You have no alternative, and as for me, I shall patronize Jake's establishment and sleep in the 'field-bed,' to-night. I want to make the acquaintance of some of these new-comers, you know, and proclaim the merits of the 'Walnut Grove Colony.'"

Necessity compelled Edward Langtry to accept this kind offer, and he soon after carried to the tent one of Agnes' trunks. The others, with several boxes of freight were left in the wagon, in which they had been transported, for the present.

When Alden had seen them safely settled he left them, saying:

"I will order supper for three at Jake's, come down in an hour."

He had gone but a few steps when he was confronted by a young man who came straight towards him smiling, and holding out his hand, saying as he did so:

"You are John Alden of Cleveland, Ohio, are you not?"

"The same sir."

"And do you not recognize me?"

"Indeed I do not."

"Well, I do not wonder at it, for when you last saw me I was a schoolboy. I did not wear this then," indicating his mustache, and after a moments pause: "I sometimes escorted a little lady, Miss Grace Alden, to and from school on my sled. Do you know me now?"

A smile passed over John Alden's face.

"You must be Arthur Fairchild, though the resemblance is very slight indeed to the little Arthur whom I remember."

"Time changes us all, I should never have recognized you, had you not been pointed out to me. I bring a letter from your wife," and he handed John a bulky envelope which the latter took eagerly. "And I also bear many messages from your old time friends which I will repeat to you at your leisure," and then with a thoughtfulness indicative of good breeding, "I will leave you now and join you again when you have read your letter," he was turning away but Alden detained him with:

"No, I must walk down to the hotel and order supper for some friends who are occupying my tent. Come with me."

"The hotel, where is it?"

"Just before you."

"What! that mass of hay and logs? I thought it a poor apology for a stable; ha, ha, ha, this is pioneering truly."

"I hope you are not dismayed at the prospect already."

"Not a bit of it! everything must have a beginning I suppose. I think I prefer the tents however, or the white covered wagons, they are more picturesque."

"To be sure, but then you know, beauty is not what we are going in for just at present, we worship the necessary."

By this time they had reached Jake's establishment, and found him in his element, so many were the orders for supper he had received from the young men among the new comers. Most of the families came prepared to do their own cooking and were now encamped, gipsy-like, on the town site.

"If business continues thus brisk," said Alden to Jake, "you will have to send for Katrina immediately."

"I vos shust dinks of dot myself already," was Jake's reply.

Bidding Arthur meet him in an hour, John sought a place where he could read his letter undisturbed. He walked some distance before he found himself alone, and then trembling with emotion broke the seal, and read:

CLEVELAND, August, 1854.

"MY DEAR HUSBAND:

"It would ill become me who urged you so strongly to leave home in search of wealth to gratify my foolish longings and desires, to decline now to share your fortunes, whatever they may be, and whatever you may wish. I would not do so, even were the sundering of old home ties likely to be a painful sacrifice; but the truth is, there have been so many changes in the old place, among the old friends, and within myself during the past six years that I can even hail with joy a removal, particularly one which unites again our divided lives. As for privations, there are none so great as those we have already suffered in being separated."

"Dear, brave, loving Amy," John ejaculated, "may Heaven spare us many years in which I can prove my devotion." Then he read on:

"It will be unnecessary for you to send money to defray the expenses of our journey, as I have a sufficient sum at my disposal, and Grace and I will come as soon as you are ready for us. * * * * * * *

"And now a few words concerning the bearer of this letter. A well-mannered, honorable and studious boy, Arthur Fairchild has naturally developed into a high-minded, intelligent, and agreeable young man, the pride of his parents and friends, and the center of high hopes and expectations, which I sincerely believe may yet be realized, although he has chosen for himself a path widely deviating from the one parental ambition had marked out for him.

Anxiously desiring him to continue the study of law, upon which he had just entered, they received with dismay the announcement of his determination to 'do what one man could, to make Kansas a free State.' They might have anticipated as much however, for you know the Fairchild family have long been the main stay and support of the 'Anti-Slavery Society,' in this section of the country, and from a child, Arthur has listened to most eloquent appeals in behalf of the slave, and bitter denunciations of negro slavery, and furthermore, for four years he has breathed the atmosphere of Berlin College, where the spirit of human equality, without regard to sex or color, sits incarnate, and from whose teachings he is still fresh. What wonder then, that the stirring appeals now made to every lover of liberty, in the name of justice and humanity, to form in line at the point of aggression and hurl back the advancing tide of liberty's foes, should arouse all the ardor and enthusiasm of an earnest impulsive youth, and that he should desire, like a brave knight of olden times, to buckle on the armor and go forth to battle with the giant wrong of his day and generation. And if the roguish brown eyes and smiling face of a little maiden called 'Grace Alden,' soon to be in Kansas Territory, have somewhat influenced his decision, what matters it! Did not each knight of old have his '*fair ladye*' whose colors he wore and at whose feet he laid the trophies nobly won."

A shadow fell upon the page. John glanced up, and the young crusader stood before him, in a traveling suit of grey, with polished boots, and tall, silk hat, a flush on his handsome face, and a slight tremor in the tones of his voice betraying a suspicion that something of the relation to which he aspired had been disclosed. Yet in reality Alden had scarcely been conscious of the intimation concerning the young man, which his wife intended to convey. To him Grace was still a laughter loving little girl, and Amy's allusion to Arthur's admiration of her, made less impression upon him than his wife's expressions concerning the state of feeling and the wide-spread determination on the part of the North to prevent the establishment of slavery in Kansas. Amy knew all then—comprehended the situation more fully than did himself when first he invited her to join him, and yet she did not hesitate, nor shrink from, in fact, rather courted the change.

Arthur had come to announce that supper was in readiness, and friends waiting in the dining-room of the Pioneer House, and the two walked thither quickly and rather quietly, Alden being absorbed in thought and the young man too respectful to force conversation upon him. At table however, the conversation grew free and easy and soon Langtry related the story of the first invasion, and the destruction of his property. The youth's eye fired with indignation, and an expression of deep anxiety settled upon the fair brow of Agnes.

When Langtry concluded, John stated their intention of forming a colony, to settle on the timber land on the opposite side of the Areposa, and Arthur begged to be enlisted as the first recruit, offering also to introduce them to others from Ohio, in the morning.

"Why not to-night?" said John. "Never put off until to-morrow what can be done to-day." So Arthur and he sallied forth to find them, leaving the Langtrys to their "own sweet company."

CHAPTER VIII.

OUR LADY—SOUTHERN COLONIES—ELECTION OF WHITFIELD.

The hum of busy industry wakened in the pleasant valley during those autumn days of '54, has never ceased, but wafted on and on to the hillsides, to the river and beyond, an ever widening, ever deepening circle still resounds, stimulated by the constant stream of immigrants flowing in from every side, with needs to be provided for, and aspirations and expectations to be fulfilled.

And there was so much to be done, only strong arms and willing hands, guided by earnest, patient souls, could have so changed the face of nature in so short a time. There was hewing of timber and quarrying and hauling of stone, there was building of limekilns and burning of lime, for the winter was near, and the rude cabins must have chimneys. And after the human beings were provided for, there must be shelter for the horses and cattle, and grass cut from the far-reaching unclaimed meadows, for their subsistence.

Then, with an eye to the future, the breaking plow drawn by patient oxen must upturn the sod, that it may be in readiness for spring plowing and planting.

Meanwhile food must be obtained, and many were the teams and teamsters kept busy hauling supplies in their large wagons, from the Missouri River. Groceries, dry goods, and all manufactured articles shipped thither from the East, and vegetables, flour and fruits obtained in Missouri; for much as the inhabitants of the latter State collectively desired to oust the Free State men from the Territory, it had not yet occurred to them to place an embargo on the food supplies, the profits of which came to them individually.

Likewise, while things material, food, shelter, and raiment required immediate and untiring effort, things political were also pressing, and while the pioneers built up a home, they must also develop a fitting political environment. And here they were required to manipulate, not the easy, submissive forces of nature alone, in her most genial mood, but the widely differing temperaments and clashing interests of human beings.

Through the representations of Arthur Fairchild, about twenty of the newly arrived colonists went to Walnut Grove, and these were sufficient to form a nucleus round which others gathered, as the Free State men increased in numbers.

Claims were laid out in such a manner as to give each settler a fair share of timber and prairie lands. A written compact was made to maintain and defend each other's rights against all intruders, and then each set to work with a will.

For Mrs. Langtry's sake, Alden and Arthur offered to help Langtry hew out logs for his cabin before beginning work on their own claims, and their offer he accepted, providing they would allow him to work for them in return. And this he did with his keen sense of justice, persistently, day for day, though they would never have required it of him. To serve "our lady" would have been sufficient recompense, and so indeed thought all who came to the "raising," and by whose united efforts a cabin was reared so much resembling one of Jake Schmidt's rooms, with its thatched roof and ground floor, that it is unnecessary to describe it.

And thither Agnes Langtry came in her gentleness and refinement, a gem not fitly set within its rude, rough walls; but without, the trees, the shrubs, the clustering vines vied with each other, in rich and varied coloring to do her homage, and the whole forest, many hued and gorgeous, rejoiced in her sweet presence. Each beech, each ash, each cottonwood put on a tint of scarlet, or cherry, or orange. Walnuts were flecked with white, and poplars glowed with vermillion. Graceful willows bending o'er the creek bedecked themselves in yellow, and wild grapes in purple hung from many a clinging vine, while the box elders still retained their rich dark green, a fitting background for all this wealth of coloring, from which the wind whirled the superabundant leaves and lightly placed them on the ground, making a variegated carpet for her feet.

For three months, Agnes was the only woman in Walnut Grove Colony, yet she did not seem lonely nor conscious of fear, but so absorbed herself in the little world around her, that she became a part of it. No incident was too trivial to awaken her interest; the selection of a site by a settler, for his cabin; the discovery of a new kind of timber, or some unusually large, fine tree of a well known order; a different species of bird; a good day's hunt; or even the dispatching of a rattlesnake, when related by any of the colonists, all of whom came frequently in the evening, to Langtry's house, was listened to with attention. The failure of letters from home, or the reception of letters containing unfavorable news, always excited her sympathy. In fact, she had a word and a smile for each, to cheer him if lonely or dispirited, or to rejoice in his gladness; a salve wherewith to bind up some slight hurt, a cup of tea, or some little delicacy for the sick; thus endearing herself to all by manifestations of that sweet unconscious cordiality which ever evinces the close kinship of human kind.

The first boards obtained by any one in Walnut Grove, from the saw-mill, in Warsaw, which, although running night and day, was unable to meet the demands, were carried to Langtry by the roughest man in the association, who begged him to take them for a floor in his cabin. "I could not use them myself," said he, while 'our lady' lived on the ground."

Langtry himself, soon became quite a favorite. Superior to most of the men in education, as in judgment and knowledge of farming, they soon learned to consult him about every movement, every plan, and he always gave his opinion freely when asked, yet never obtruded his advice unsought, a species of self-restraint which few guiding spirits are able to exercise.

It was impossible for any one to come within the influence of such ardent friends of freedom as Mr. and Mrs. Langtry, without imbibing somewhat of their hatred of oppression in every form, and somewhat of zeal to combat it in that phase which presented itself. And they found in Arthur Fairchild an able and enthusiastic ally, untiring in his efforts to strengthen the wavering and confirm the weak in their determination to make Kansas a free State—and so it happened that the colony of Walnut Grove became no less a stronghold of freedom than Warsaw herself, notwithstanding the fact that it was soon hedged in on either side by pro-slavery settlements. The one to the west, beyond the Areposa, and between Walnut Grove and Warsaw, was composed principally of Missourians, and led by Sile Hardiker.

They laid out a town and called it Calhoun, brought lumber from Missouri and erected a few frame cabins, the largest of which, serving for a grocery store, was owned and occupied by Sile Hardiker, who, dealing in liquor supplies as well as groceries, became the presiding genius of the place. Alden and he frequently met on the way to and from Warsaw, and the former invariably saluted Sile in a friendly manner, but a gruff "H-H-how," the Indian salutation, was the only reply received. Evidently, Sile thought himself and his companions had been egregiously duped by a Yankee masquerading in Western costume, on that morning when they had smoked with him the pipe of peace.

SILE HARDIKER'S STORE.

Pat Malone too, his source of life and light Sile's grocery, had taken up a claim on the west side of the creek; while Zeke Fagin, comet-like in his eccentric motions, and irregular in his orbit, came and went at unexpected times and seasons, with a constantly increasing tendency to overshadow lesser orbs.

The colony to the east, called Charleston, was made up of families from South Carolina, who were evidently drawn from the class known there as "poor white trash." They were a scrawny-looking set, and seemed to have little energy and capacity, either for work or enjoyment, unless it might be called such for men to sit hours in uncomfortable places and ungainly positions, leisurely ruminating a wad of tobacco, or slowly puffing the smoke from a corn cob pipe—for sharp-featured, unkempt women, by a fire in the open air to prepare the meal of bacon and corn-dodgers, improving meanwhile each leisure moment to solace themselves with the kindred indulgence of a "dip," while sandy-haired, half-clad children, whose young limbs had not yet exhausted their slight inherited tendency to active motion, frisked about in the sunshine. They had been sent thither by a South Carolina Aid Society, whose leading spirit was Col. Delaney, afterward a territorial officer of high position, and were led by his son Roderick, who having seen them safely to their destination and well provided with lumber and other necessaries for building cabins, and provisions to supply them during the winter, had returned to the South to organize another colony and bring them out in the early spring.

They did not seem anxious to make Northern acquaintances, though now and then a long, lanky fellow sauntered up to inquire:

"Air all them lumber lots taken?" and on receiving a reply in the affirmative, lazily sauntered off again. To one who seemed disposed to linger, Alden ventured the information,

SILE HARDIKER'S STORE.

Pat Malone too, his source of life and light Sile's grocery, had taken up a claim on the west side of the creek; while Zeke Fagin, comet-like in his eccentric motions, and irregular in his orbit, came and went at unexpected times and seasons, with a constantly increasing tendency to overshadow lesser orbs.

The colony to the east, called Charleston, was made up of families from South Carolina, who were evidently drawn from the class known there as "poor white trash." They were a scrawny-looking set, and seemed to have little energy and capacity, either for work or enjoyment, unless it might be called such for men to sit hours in uncomfortable places and ungainly positions, leisurely ruminating a wad of tobacco, or slowly puffing the smoke from a corn cob pipe—for sharp-featured, unkempt women, by a fire in the open air to prepare the meal of bacon and corn-dodgers, improving meanwhile each leisure moment to solace themselves with the kindred indulgence of a "dip," while sandy-haired, half-clad children, whose young limbs had not yet exhausted their slight inherited tendency to active motion, frisked about in the sunshine. They had been sent thither by a South Carolina Aid Society, whose leading spirit was Col. Delaney, afterward a territorial officer of high position, and were led by his son Roderick, who having seen them safely to their destination and well provided with lumber and other necessaries for building cabins, and provisions to supply them during the winter, had returned to the South to organize another colony and bring them out in the early spring.

They did not seem anxious to make Northern acquaintances, though now and then a long, lanky fellow sauntered up to inquire:

"Air all them lumber lots taken?" and on receiving a reply in the affirmative, lazily sauntered off again. To one who seemed disposed to linger, Alden ventured the information, that if he wanted wood to use for fuel, he would give him an opportunity of earning it, as there was plenty of work to be done, to which the Calhounite replied: "No you don't! work and me don't git on well. Never did."

"How then do you earn a living?" said John.

"Wal, pick it up mostly, when I'm to hum, and I reckon them big-bugs as brung us out hyer to this God-forsaken country, won't let us starve."

"But why should they support you when you won't work?"

'Look here now stranger," said he, squaring himself up as well as his loose joints would permit, and looking John for a moment full in the face, "I reckon you're a durned inquisitive Yank, an I'll be dog-goned ef it's any o' your business who feeds me, so long as I don't browse 'round in your pertater patch."

"Well no, I guess not, unless you swing your ax in my wood-pile."

He laughed. "You needn't be skeered on my account, stranger. I don't kalkilate gittin a leetle to north is goin fur to change the color of my hide, an ef them fellars want my vote when this ere question o' theirn comes up, they'll have fer to keep me an' my family in perwisions and licker, fire-wood thrown in, dern em! What right hev they to all the land and all the niggers any way?" and this born socialist took himself off. All the same, the loose wood disappeared, and with it any other small articles carelessly left about or unwatched.

At the November election for delegate to Congress, the men of this colony came up manfully and paid for their "keep," by voting for Whitfield, the pro-slavery candidate, and aided by seventeen hundred Missourians, who encamped for the day on Kansas soil, carried the election in his favor. This was the real opening of the Southern programme—the first demonstration that other than fair means were to be used at the polls, in settling the great question relegated by Congress to the Territory.

This duty done, the Charleston colonists turned their attention toward the construction of winter quarters, digging cellars and roofing them with boards, or else excavating a space in the side of a ravine or hill, and closing up the front, with the exception of a small space which served for ingress and egress. These dwellings, called "dug-outs," in which families of six or seven persons contrived to exist, were very common among pioneers from the South and Southwest.

CHAPTER IX.

ARTHUR'S LOVE—AGNES' ACQUISITION—THE FREE NEGRO.

At the time of the foundation of the Walnut Grove Colony, John Alden had hoped to be able to announce to his wife that her new home was in readiness for her by the expiration of six weeks at farthest, but that time had lengthened day by day into two months, and still he was not prepared to bid her come. When they first began to work in the woods, John had observed that Arthur made little headway in chopping, and that his hands, unaccustomed to rough usage, were swollen and bleeding, so he suggested that Langtry and himself do the cutting, and Arthur drive the team, hauling the logs to the mill. This proved a satisfactory arrangement, and a large amount was delivered at the mill, much of which was contracted for by other parties, and for which they received a good price. But they were obliged to wait their turn to have some sawed for the floors, and sheathing for the roof of the cabin, and it did not come until after the walls had been raised and the clumsy chimney built of stone, which they had quarried and hauled from a neighboring bluff. Not wishing to wait for lime, they had used a mortar made of clay and mud; and John proposed to use the same for chinking, while Arthur drove to Lauderdale for shingles and window-sash.

During two months' daily association with the lad, John Alden had conceived somewhat of his wife's partiality for him, and had learned for himself that a certain magnet, still in Ohio, had acted powerfully in deflecting Arthur's life-course from the one previously marked out for him.

Consciously, or unconsciously, he had been influenced in his determination to emigrate to Kansas, by the fact that there hereafter would be found Grace Alden. Perhaps the thought too had its weight, that, so far away from other competitors, his own claims might be more readily recognized, and this long delay chafed him not a little. There was some consolation however in extolling the charms of his idol, and John encouraged him to tell of her ways, her occupations, her companions, her studies, her musical acquirements, her beauty and her goodness. It was a theme of which the lover never tired, and what more sympathetic listener could a devoted admirer ask than a fond father who had long been separated from his child? They worshiped at the same shrine, and mutual homage forged a link to bind them together. But what of Grace, John wondered; did she reciprocate all this tender adoration? He had received a number of affectionate little notes from her, in which she mentioned Arthur with sisterly concern. "A bad omen," John thought, "a maiden's love is shy." Occasionally, too, Arthur received letters in the same handwriting, but John observed that they never seemed to give him that perfect happiness, that freedom from anxiety which a written expression or acknowledgement of the reciprocation of affection should bring to a lover.

Not until December were the boards obtained for floor and roof, and then adjusted. Soon after, Arthur departed for Lauderdale. John Alden worked away industriously during his absence, at chinking or filling the crevices between the logs with a plaster made of mud, his heart keeping time with his hands, for while the latter diligently essayed the impossible task of smoothing the rough surface, the first was full of pleasing memories and bright anticipations.

One evening when he went as usual to visit the Langtrys, Agnes came forward to meet him, her face radiant with happiness, as she exclaimed eagerly:

"I am so glad to see you Mr. Alden. I could scarcely wait till evening for your coming, but tried to induce Edward to go over and bring you—"

"Ah indeed! has anything unusual happened?"

"Oh yes! we have eight new members of the colony, just think of it, eight at once! and likely to be valuable acquisitions, though they are of Southern birth."

"Is that so, and when did they arrive?"

"Only this morning. Edward purchased them of an Arkansas man, whose wife was homesick and wanted to go back to her friends."

"Purchased them! purchased additions to our colony! Of course he means to set them free."

"Indeed he will not; we mean to keep them and profit largely by their possession," said she laughingly; "but before I conduct you to their quarters allow me to treat you to a pleasant beverage." She poured from a pitcher as she spoke, a glass of fresh milk, a sweet, delicious draught such as had not passed her visitor's lips in years. And then it dawned upon him what manner of colonists, at least one of the eight purchased ones, must be, and he was somewhat prepared, when, calling out gaily: "Come on," she led him to a haystack, behind which, calmly ruminating, stood a black and white spotted cow with crumpled horns, that received their admiration with unconcealed indifference, and helped herself to a fresh cud of hay in mild-eyed unconcern.

"Isn't she a beauty?" cried Agnes, with almost childish delight, "and her name is Dinah! Now who but a Southerner would have called a cow Dinah? It suggests to me a large darkey woman with a red bandana handkerchief around her head."

"Your cow is only parti-colored, but you might decorate her horns with red ribbons, or why not change her name if you don't like it?"

"No, I won't. It's unlucky to change names, besides I like it. Dinah she was named, and Dinah she shall be to the end of the chapter," stroking and patting the cow's face gently. "And now Mr. Alden we shall have all the cream and milk and butter we want. You must provide yourself with a little tin pail or pitcher and come over every day for milk, and once a week you must bring a plate for butter also."

"Thank you, I will certainly accept your generous offer."

"But this is not all; I have other treasures to display," and she conducted him to a chicken-coop, wherein rested half a dozen hens and a crested chanticleer.

"You are indeed rich, but I must warn Langtry to make that coop more secure or the prairie wolves will be after those chickens, with keen appetites."

"We are more afraid of two-footed wolves. If they let them alone we can provide against the others."

Returning to the house they found Langtry reading newspapers which he had received through a neighbor who had been down to Warsaw to bring up the mail for the settlement.

"I congratulate you on your acquisitions," remarked John, "we shall be able to live here in civilized style after awhile." To which Langtry replied:

"I hope so. We are making some progress, but I shall be better satisfied when we can have our mails more regularly. This thing of having to wait two weeks or more for a newspaper after it is published, and perhaps a month for a magazine, is tiresome."

"You must practice what you preach, my dear," said Agnes, "and submit with a good grace to what is an inevitable necessity."

Arthur returned in three days from Lauderdale with his wagon-load of shingles and sash, and a supply of provisions for the winter, bringing a quantity of apples and potatoes from Missouri, which were a welcome addition to their bill of fare. He brought also a passenger, a colored man with free papers in his pocket, whom he had picked up on the roadside intending merely to give him a lift by the way, but thus encouraged, the poor fellow ventured to ask for work and protection, telling a sad story of persecution on account of his color.

He had been continually suspected and arraigned as a runaway slave, and in Lauderdale came near having his free papers stolen, and himself remanded to slavery. Thinking perhaps he would be safer in the interior, and having heard of the Free State colony on the Kaw, he had started thither on foot. Arthur's sympathies were fully roused, and the poor man, overjoyed with kind treatment, begged so hard to remain in his employ, that he had consented to give him a trial.

The negro professed to be a proficient at rail-splitting, and also said he understood how to construct a lime-kiln, which Arthur thought might be a profitable investment; but on consideration concluded to let the colored man first try his hand on the rails.

Alden and Arthur not being adepts in the art of carpentry, encountered considerable difficulty in fitting the window-frames in the ponderous logs, yet by patient though not ingenious endeavor, they achieved a rather unsatisfactory result.

In the meantime Arthur's protege went daily to his work, and finding that he accomplished a fair amount, was quiet, and did not intrude himself upon his white protectors, John expressed approval of him; and then Arthur broached a little scheme which had no doubt been running in his mind for some time.

The holidays were at hand, and one accustomed to the merry-makings, the social gatherings, the gifts and pleasant surprises incident to the season in a large and well to do family, could not but turn with longing toward his home and friends.

"Mr. Alden," said he, "do you think it would be quite safe for Mrs. Alden and Grace to travel alone?"

"Oh no, I must find company for them, but there are so many families coming out now from Ohio, that I think there will be no difficulty in securing them an escort, between this time and spring."

"I was thinking that I should like to go home for the holidays. My mother has written me to come, and if you will hold my claim for me, and keep my man at work, I can do so, and then return with the ladies."

"With all my heart, Arthur. I'll do the best I can for you, and really there is very little that can be done until toward spring."

"But it is too bad to leave you out here alone and you have not seen them for so long. You ought to go and let me stay to guard our claims. I'll do it if you say so; come now, you get ready and go."

"No, don't tempt me. I've thought it all over and made up my mind that it would not be best. Besides the necessity of guarding my own claim, I feel responsible for those of the men who have settled in this neighborhood on my solicitation, not that I apprehend any trouble at present, but should anything go wrong I ought to be here. They depend upon me."

"Yes, I know Langtry and yourself are the pillars of this edifice and it would go to pieces, should you step out. It was rather presumptuous in me to think for a moment that I could supply your place."

"Not at all Arthur, but it will be best for you to go. Your plan suits me exactly."

Danger was indeed nearer than they apprehended, and the event proved Arthur not lacking in courage or coolness.

It had been noised about the settlements of Calhoun and Charleston, and borne on the wings of rumor to the few pro-slavery men hanging about in Warsaw, that a "nigger was at work in Walnut Grove," and very naturally they jumped to the conclusion that he was a runaway slave, and according to their tenets it was the duty and likewise the privilege of every law-abiding citizen to see that the fugitive was forthwith returned to his master.

Accordingly they mounted in hot haste. When duty leads in the path of desire, it is easy to obey her mandates, and to the number of at least thirty, they galloped across the prairie, their excitement gathering force at every bound, until, wrought up to the highest pitch, they presented themselves in front of Alden's cabin, where Arthur and he sat enjoying pleasant reminiscences of the old home, called up by the prospect of the young man's approaching visit. The negro, a short distance to the right, and seated on a new made stool, was enjoying a huge slice of corn-bread, and bowl of milk, the latter an offering from Dinah.

One glance at the heated faces, alive with the expression of malignant passion, and furious with hatred as they gazed on the innocent black man, was sufficient to show that something was wrong, nevertheless Arthur tipped his hat to them as the two men arose to their feet, and before Alden had found voice, said politely:

"Good morning, gentlemen. What can we do for you?"

"We have come down here to ketch that derned nigger, and send him back to Missouri ridin' on a rail," called out one, and a chorus of voices chimed in:

"We want that derned nigger."

Arthur's blue eyes flashed, but he controlled himself, and his voice was without a tremor as he replied:

"I have hired that man to work for me, and I acknowledge no man's right to interfere with my actions."

"Hear the dog-goned nigger-worshiper," sung out the chorus.

"Wouldn't you like to marry a nigger?" shouted a voice from the outside rank.

"Bring 'em both out here!" cried another, "and we'll tar and feather 'em and ride 'em on a rail together." There was a move forward at this, as if they were about to put the threat into execution, and the poor negro, trembling with fear, crouched down close to the cabin.

"The man is free," said Alden, "he has his free papers in his pocket," attracting the attention of the party to himself for a moment. That moment was sufficient for Arthur; like a flash he was into the cabin and out again, a revolver in his hand, and another in his belt. Placing himself directly in front of the negro, his slight form drawn up proudly, his pistol firmly held, and his eye meeting their scowls fearlessly, he said in a clear, defiant tone:

"The way to that man is over my dead body! Touch him if you dare!"

They drew back; they were like lions kept at bay by the moral courage of a clear, determined human eye. Yet it was only for a moment, infuriated as they were, and with such overpowering numbers, Arthur must soon have been disarmed and the negro taken; but for the forty Sharpe's rifles, which now came upon the scene, borne by as many Free State men, who had heard of this proposed attack just in time to come to the rescue, and before whom the raiders slunk away, muttering:

"Wal, if the man war free, they reckoned as how they had no call to interfere with him."

CHAPTER X.

ARTHUR'S MISSION.—WARSAW GROWING.—AIR-CASTLES.

Arthur hesitated somewhat about going East after this occurrence, especially as the negro was in such a nervous condition from extreme fright, that his services were likely to be of small value, and avowed his determination to leave as soon as he could do so with safety, but his hesitancy was soon ended by the action of the "Walnut Grove Association," at a meeting held on the day after the attack on the negro.

It was unanimously resolved in this meeting, to send Arthur Fairchild to Northern Ohio as a regularly accredited agent for the colony, and he was specially instructed to use all honorable means to secure a large immigration previous to the 30th of March, 1855, that being the day fixed upon by the first Governor of the Territory, who had arrived in October, for the election of the first territorial legislature. The selection of this legislature was a matter of grave importance to the settlers, as the laws and institutions of the future State depended in a great measure on their course of action. There were many indications of a large influx of pro-slavery men, as urgent appeals were being made all through the South for men and money, and organizations, secret and otherwise instituted, to aid and induce emigration.

It was well known that a great many were coming from the North in the spring, but very unlikely, unless specially urged that they would reach the scene of action in time to be at the polls.

Arthur was also instructed to represent clearly and distinctly all the difficulties and dangers of the situation, and the necessity of immigrants coming forearmed as well as forewarned. The association in return, was pledged to have a certain amount of work done on his claim, and to resist any and all attempts to jump the same. This agreement being formally entered into, Arthur was at liberty to depart, and he must needs hasten, as there still remained but a week in which to make the homeward journey before Christmas, and this was barely sufficient, four days' staging being necessary at that time to reach a railroad.

Alden carried him down to Warsaw in his wagon from which place he intended to take the stage for Lauderdale, and they could but remark the development which had taken place in the young city since Arthur's coming.

The white-winged tents were folded, and in their stead rose many a cabin of logs or frame. One or two stone buildings were in process of erection, and a large frame structure had replaced the office tent, serving as well for political and social gatherings during the week, and a place for holding divine service on Sunday.

There were quite a number of stores in which a great variety of goods were displayed, and several shops, where skillful-handed artisans plied useful trades. The village smithy stood upon the open plain. The smith was there, the forge, and merry children watched the flying sparks with glee, the only feature lacking to give the picture grace and beauty, and the smith and children shade, was the "spread-spreading chestnut tree."

The "Pioneer House, Jacob Schmidt, proprietor," had expanded by frame additions on every side, and the original twin cabins developing an upward tendency, now boasted a second story, and it was here Arthur intended to spend the night in order to be ready for the morning's stage.

John Alden bade him "good-bye," and God speed on his

journey, with many hopes for a speedy and safe return, and as they stood hand in hand, a thought seemed struggling in the younger mind for utterance; but although John had more than a faint suspicion of its purport, he did not propose to assist in its delivery. At length, however, Arthur said with evident effort, as one braces himself for a leap, " Mr. Alden, have I your permission, that is—if I can muster sufficient courage—and circumstances seem propitious, to ask Miss Grace to be my wife?"

How delightful it is when we have made the dreaded leap to find we come down easily and gently, and that it was not much of an undertaking after all. John smiled into the boyish, earnest face, happy in the thought that if his bird must leave the parent nest, it might be to find so secure a resting place as the inmost soul of this pure-minded, brave young man, for such their three months' daily intercourse had proven him to be.

" You have, my boy! and I wish you success. If my little girl rejects so precious a jewel as your heart, it is because she does not know its value."

" Thank you, my friend, for your good opinion. I will try always to deserve it. I wish you were going, too."

Alden shook his head. " That is impossible, in person; but my thoughts and my best wishes go with you."

" Good-bye!" and with another shake of the hand they parted. Arthur walked down the irregular, unpaved street, and John drove slowly homeward. His horses knew the way full well, and scarcely required guiding. The reins lay idly in his hands, and his thoughts, freed for the time from the leading strings of the present, took on their old-time habit and went bounding into the future, radiant as ever with beauty, and built therein a castle for the young folks, Arthur and Grace. A beautiful home near the placid waters of the Kaw, rising from amid tall trees, and surrounded by wide-spread, well cultivated fields--an abiding home whose foundations were laid deep in love and truth. He saw himself and Amy feeble and snowy-haired, yet made glad in the decline of life by the respect and love of their children's children, whose gladsome voices resounded in the spacious rooms, and whose tripping feet pressed the luxuriant grassy lawn. The picture pleased his fancy, and then his imagination followed the youth, and he strove to realize what manner of woman was the baby girl whose wee fat hands had fondled his face, whose glad footsteps had later hastened to his side, and the sweet tones of whose childish voice still lingered in his ear. And in search of her image his swift-winged thoughts went gliding backward through the ever-changing seasons of twenty years, until they gave to him once more the Amy he had in his own youth worshiped so ardently, so devotedly loved, and so proudly won.

And now he reflected with satisfaction on a letter penned the night before, and which Arthur bore with his own hand to his wife. A letter full of love and longing for her presence, and ending with a detailed account of the manly conduct of Arthur in defence of the poor negro. "Grace is already attached in a friendly way to her old schoolmate, and this account of his bravery and resolution will awaken an admiration which his presence must surely enkindle into love," thought John.

But the team halted at his cabin door. The dream was over. The castle vanished. The past sought with swift feet its dim and silent chamber. The future was dissipated and hung above and beyond, a vague, uncertain mist.

The stern, uncompromising present, with its call for action, alone confronted him.

CHAPTER XI.

CHRISTMAS—PIONEER CHURCH—THE ESCAPED SLAVE.

Christmas came to the pioneers, as to the world they had left behind, a clear, beautiful morning, the air crisp and bracing, but growing warmer as the sun mounted higher. With a sigh for those whose presence he would have so much enjoyed, John Alden sought the new friends whose society had already become dear, founded as their friendship was, in a congeniality of tastes, and forced into rapid growth by the atmosphere of mutual toils and privations which encompassed them.

Regularly church services were held on Sunday morning, in Free State Hall, as the large frame building in Warsaw devoted to public uses, was called, but Alden and the Langtrys were not regular attendants. It was a long drive, the sermons not particularly attractive to them, and besides, they were generally pretty much worn out with the week's work, and only too glad to make Sunday literally a day of rest, sleeping a little longer than usual, and then reading, writing, lounging about, or visiting each other. They had planned, however, to be present at the Christmas services in commemoration of the birth of the Great Teacher whose words and works, good seed sown in the hearts of men, have brought forth their harvest of rich fruit for more than eighteen centuries.

Accordingly Alden harnessed his horses and drove over for the Langtrys, and found in waiting besides themselves, Messrs. Harley and Bentz, two members of the colony who

BACHELORS' SUNDAY.

were to spend the day with them. Pleasant greetings were exchanged with all, and the usual remarks about the weather, with more than the usual emphasis on the adjective *fine*.

"How very delightful it is!" said Agnes, as her husband assisted her into the wagon. "Here am I, comfortable in this light spring shawl,"—a blue one with an oriental border—"and," glancing around, "not an overcoat in the party! and this on Christmas. Why, at home, I have no doubt they are shivering in furs, and riding over three feet of snow."

All agreed with her that it was exceedingly pleasant, except Langtry, who, shrugging his shoulders, said, "I don't know, I'm sure, whether I like this perpetual spring or not. I sometimes long for a good stiff north-easter, to brace me up."

"What wretched taste, my dear! For my part I shall never sigh for cold weather to come and shut us up in our cabins. I could live on forever in this balmy atmosphere," said Agnes.

"But it is so debilitating. Life moves on in such an easy channel that we shall grow degenerate. We New Englanders will lose all our vigor and energy if not continually aroused by physical necessities to combat with the sterner phases of nature."

"My most congenial habitat!" then said Alden. "I would like to glide down the stream of time smoothly and calmly, and do not care to combat with nature or with man."

"Nor I," said Agnes.

"And only think," said Harley, "in this genial climate, where human vitality is so largely economized, what a vast store of surplus energy you New Englanders will have wherewith to combat sin in various forms; slavery, for instance, or intemperance."

Langtry had read much and thought deeply on many subjects, and it was only necessary to suggest a starting point,—

give him the key note, as it were, to receive the benefit of his accumulation of facts and inferences. This time he discoursed on the influence of climate on character, the rest of the party putting in a word or two occasionally, to ask a question, or to express dissent, only ceasing when the vehicle drew up at the church door.

It was a rude sanctuary, the windows small, the walls unplastered, the rough board seats, the bare and echoing floor, all so in harmony with the surroundings of their daily lives, could wake no depths of feeling in the soul, nor tune its best emotions to the grandeur of the theme.

The motley congregation, too, made up from all the settlements around, both Free and Slave State, and comprising representatives of nearly every State in the Union, was provocative rather of curious study of the creature than worship of the Creator.

But a Bible, richly gilt, a gift from an Eastern church, lay on the rude box, which turned up endwise, served for a desk; and when the preacher rose, and from its pages read with well trained voice, how wise men came, a new star guiding them to the manger to bring their offerings to the regal child, while Earth and Heaven hailed with joy the Prince of Peace; and the choir sang with sweet voices, accompanied by the notes of a seraphine, the old hymn, " Coronation," they felt their spirits rising to the higher plane of devotion. The sermon following brought the hearers back to earth. It seems to be the peculiar office of common-place sermons, to chill the raptures which entrance the soul when absorbed by the contemplation of majestic themes. However, the pleasant greetings at the close of the meeting, were sufficient to repay all for their presence.

The programme of the party for the remainder of the day was to dine together at Langtry's house—a sort of picnic dinner to which each had contributed a share. Mr. Bentz,

Langtry's nearest neighbor to the south, an unmarried man, contributed the oysters, procured at an exorbitant price from an enterprising dealer in Warsaw, who had laid in a supply of extras for the holiday season. Harley—whose claim was next beyond that of Bentz, was an Illinoisan, and, like Alden, expecting his family to join him in the spring—had been lucky enough to shoot a wild turkey. The apples for pies and sauce, and the potatoes, were John's contribution; while the host and hostess made up the melange with bread, butter, and other necessary articles. Nor did the guests allow Mrs. Langtry to perform all the drudgery incident to the occasion. Gallantry forbid! Harley had dressed the turkey before bringing it, and of course only the fair hands of Agnes were considered eligible to the privilege of stuffing, but each contended for the honor of turning the spit before the kitchen fire, obsequiously playing at "fetch and carry," as faithfully though more awkwardly, than good-natured, well-trained Newfoundland dogs.

There were plenty of newspapers and books to fill up the intervals of attendance, and there was not lacking many a jest and many a witty repartee, to while away the time, until, at last, when Agnes had spread the snowy cloth and placed thereon the napkins, the china, and a few pieces of silver, with the shining knives whose unstained surface denoted a woman's care, their Christmas dinner was announced in readiness.

The soup-tureen with appetizing contents was brought on, and a merry company with good appetites sat down to the first course, which was soon disposed of. Then came the second—a juicy, tender, and delicious wild turkey, literally done to a turn, fragrant with its dressing of sage and summer savory, which condiments, with the accompanying jelly, must have been brought forth from Mrs. Langtry's secret store, and these, flanked by mealy potatoes, and tart apple sauce, so demoralized the attacking party that they were obliged to call a halt before laying siege to the third, which consisted of apple pie and a regular old-fashioned New England Christmas pudding. With the dessert came coffee—and such coffee—clear, strong and aromatic, rich with thick, delicious cream, fit complement for such a feast, and an aid to digestion with which they could not very well have dispensed.

It was growing dark, yet the company had not risen from the table, nor lighted a lamp, when there came an unexpected, uninvited guest. An interval of silence permitted his approaching footsteps to be heard, and then there framed itself in the doorway the form of a forlorn looking negro, in a battered old hat, a tattered shirt whose remnants scarcely concealed the scars on his broad back, and a pair of old thin pants covering his shivering limbs, while his feet were bare. A tawny face with beseeching, wide-open eyes, and a voracious, hungry look, conveyed without a word the story of his needs, and Agnes involuntarily arose and carried him a plate heaped full of food, and having seated himself in the doorway, he began to eat. Mrs. Langtry filled and re-filled his plate, until at last, when he had drank the third cup of coffee he seemed satisfied, his eyes lost the glare of a hungry animal, and something like a smile crept over his face, as he exclaimed: "May de good Lawd bress you, Missus, for your kindness to ole Mose!"

Agnes had not returned to the table when she had once moved away, but had placed her stool near the foot of the bed on the right-hand side of the door, where she now sat watching him with a look of interest and pity, and the others had all in the meantime changed their positions. Langtry, who was walking up and down the short, open space in the room, now paused in front of the negro, to ask from whence he came, and whither he was going.

"Am you from de Norf, Massa?" was the cautious reply.

"Yes, we are all from the North, all Free State people."

"Den bress de Lawd, Massa, I done tole you all 'bout it," but, glancing suspiciously into the darkening night, "Ole Massa might done come afore I get frew!"

"Ah! you are an escaped slave, then?"

"Jess so! Jess so, Massa!"

Taking a turn or two of the room a little more rapidly than before, and again pausing near him, Langtry said:

"You are shivering with cold in your bare feet and thin clothes. Come in; come to the fire. Here, take this seat;" placing him a stool in a warm corner. "Thaw out a little, and then begin your story."

The negro obeyed, and our host seated himself in the vacated place in the doorway, a certain watchfulness apparent in his demeanor, while poor Mose, thus encouraged, proceeded to relate his simple tale:

"I hain't no 'count now, Massa, but I done hoe my row wif de bes' ob dem in ole Varginny."

"You came from Virginia then?"

"Dat's jess whar I war raised, Massa, me an' my wife Cinthy an' de chillun, wot I nebber see no more in dis worl' I reckon. Nebber! nebber!" and he leaned his head upon his hands, swaying his body to and fro, and moaning piteously.

"You care for them so much, and yet leave them?" said Agnes.

The man's hands dropped from his face.

"Car for 'em? Car for 'em! Fore God, Missus, ole Mose 'ud go fru fire an brimstone fur dem little chillun. Ah, you dunno nuffin 'bout slavery, nuffin! You tink I leab dar ob my own cord? leab Cinthy an' dem young uns, an' de cabin, an' de chickens, an' de pig, an ole Massa an' Missus? No! no! I'd stayed dar till my dyin' day, but they sol' me, Missus, sol' me! de bes' han' in de fiel' and de fus at de backy pickin," shaking his head sorrowfully. "I nebber tought ole Massa Long would 'a dun it."

"And why did he do such a wicked thing?" said Agnes, her face all aglow with sympathy.

"I reckon, Missus, dey couldn't done help derselves," said he in a resigned, plaintive tone. "You see de niggas will increase so fas', so berry fas'. Ebery year, rain or shine, dat crop o' niggas am always shuah. In course de plantation can't hold 'em all. So ebery year, dere comes from de Souf, whar dey raise de cotton, a man wid de money in his fis', to buy up de spar hands. I seen 'm go many times, an' I hear dem cryin' an' moanin', an' I see de dead look in dere faces, but I didn' mind it much, 'cos as I tole yer, I was de bes' han' in de fiel' an' I tought Massa couldn' spar me, an', bress your soul! niggas is like chillun, when de sun shines to-day, dey don't tink ob de rain what may come to-morrow, an' dey nebber feel de sting ob de lash, until it strikes on dere own backs. An' it done come to me at las', jess like lightnin' from a clear sky, an it struck jess here, Missus," putting his great black hand over his heart. "When I war tole dat ole Massa done sold me, an' dat I must pack up my traps an' move along widout so much as goin up to de house to see Cinthy, 'cause Missus didn't want no flar-up, an' when de chillun cum runnin' to me wid de tears in dere eyes to say good-bye, an' I stoop ober to kiss dem, de new Massa's oberseer struck me with his whip an' tole me to 'Git along dar, an' hab done wid dat dam nonsense,' and Mose broke down completely, weeping and sobbing, while Agnes sobbed in sympathy, and tears stood in the eyes of the strong men who listened, two of whom, at least, could appreciate the strength of the ties thus rudely sundered.

"And how came you here?" inquired Alden.

"Wal I war taken to Louisianny an' put to work in de cotton fiel', but somehow I wor no 'count; I wor all broke down an' couldn't work no more, an' dey beat me, an' beat me, but it didn't do no good, nuffin hurts de back when de heart am clar done broke, Massa."

"But how came you here?" John inquired again.

"Wal, it's jess dis way: Massa Wilson he done got tired o' whackin, an gib me up, said I wor no 'count nohow, an' sole me to Massa Jenkins for free hundred dollars, me, de bes' han' in ole Massa Long's fiel' sol' for free hundred dollars!" and his eyes and tone of voice spoke volumes of wounded pride at the low value set upon him. "Massa Jenkins he wor comin' to Kansas an' he tought mebbe de wedder being colder might put some life inter me. Mebbe it has! Mebbe it has," brightening up, "for I learnt up dar," pointing west, "from a white man what done tuk a claim near Massa Jenkins, dat if I could git away to de Norf, I should be a free man, an' I might take de money what I could arn an' buy Cinthy an' de chillun from ole Massa Long, an' 'pears like I could work all day an' all night too, for *dat*, massa."

"How long since you left Mr. Jenkins?" inquired Harley.

"Free nights and two days, Massa. Dis hyer prairie country am mighty hard to hide in, an I' done had to trabbel mos'ly in de night, an' den I got lost sometimes, an' don' know which way to go." But looking earnestly and inquiringly at the listeners: "De good man wid de broad brimmed hat, wot tole me 'bout de Norf, said I would fin' somewhar 'bout hyer de road undergroun' dat leads straight to freedom. You don't none ob youun's know whar de startin' pint am? Couldn't you done put a po' feller on de right track!"

Langtry looked at Alden significantly. He knew well what was meant by the underground railroad, though he had never yet acted as a conductor, nor established a station at his own house. He did not reply immediately, but the womanly nature of Agnes was fully roused, and rising and coming toward her husband, who still sat in the doorway, the moon which had now risen, shining full into her earnest face:

"Edward," she said, "do you hesitate? If this man were

in danger of his life from savages, you would protect him at the hazard of your own. How much more then should you save him from those who would deprive him of his liberty, which is dearer than life. You might not offer it to him, but when he has put forth his own hand to grasp it, shall you thrust him back, or will you bring the precious boon within his reach?"

Before Langtry had time to reply, Harley broke in with: "But there is a law against harboring, or in any manner assisting fugitive slaves, and the penalty for its violation is fine or imprisonment."

She turned and looked him full in the face, with those clear blue eyes which never failed to see the right.

"Mr. Harley, there is a higher law, the law of God, the penalty for the violation of which is moral degradation. Edward," pleadingly, "you will not be misled by this seeming conflict of duties; you will help him?"

"Of course, Agnes, I had not for a moment thought of doing otherwise," said Edward, calmly.

"Forgive me dear," said she humbly, "but you seemed to hesitate."

"Did I? I was unconscious of it. My thoughts were busy, even before the story was finished, with the difficult problem of concealment, for of course he must remain hidden about here for some time until the search is over."

"I will never doubt you again, even for a moment. You always do right," said she joyfully, and then going over to the fire, where the negro sat with anxious face, looking from one to another, she exclaimed:

"He will take care of you. My husband will; you need not fear," and the poor runaway, his emotional nature strung up to the highest pitch, fell upon his knees, his hands upraised, crying:

"Bress de Lawd! Bress de Lawd, oh my soul!"

"I think," said Alden, taking Mrs. Langtry's place near the door and addressing his friend, who seemed lost in thought, "that I can furnish him a safe hiding place."

"Ah! Where?"

"Over on Arthur Fairchild's claim. You know where the creek turns so abruptly to the west? The bank is quite high and rocky there, and covered with a thick undergrowth of cedars."

"I know the place."

"There is a deep cave or 'dug-out' there, with its entrance completely hidden. It was constructed by Arthur's hired negro man, after the fright the ruffians gave him, and he slept there until he could get out of the Territory."

"But will he be warm there?" asked Agnes.

"Certainly, it is warm anywhere under ground; besides, there is a bed of hay, and I can let him take some blankets which the other one scented."

They all laughed at this, and then Langtry turned to Bentz and to Harley, who had sunk into a chair after the rebuff given by Agnes:

"You gentlemen, need not feel responsible for this affair. If in your opinion the law of the land is supreme, whether founded in justice or not, I shall not question your decision; but to me, no law comes with a supreme obligation which stifles the feelings of humanity, and robs us of the right to alleviate human suffering."

"I think," said Harley, "that after all, I will share the risk with you."

"And I, too," said Bentz. "My sympathies are with the poor man."

"Very well, then," said Langtry. "You stay here and keep my wife company, while Alden and I put Mose in a safe place."

"That's taking risks with a vengeance. You had better let me go with you," said Bentz.

"No, I think it better for you not to know exactly where the man is, in case you are asked. Alden shall show me where the place is, and I alone will see him safely housed. A little prudence combined with your zeal makes it a safe and healthy mixture," said he jocosely. "Put him up food for to-morrow, Agnes. It may not be safe to go near him until the day after; and give him the whistle with which you call me from the field. I will show him how to use it to bring us to his aid in case he is discovered in Alden's absolutely safe retreat."

She complied with both requests, and then the three started for the cave, halting at Alden's cabin for blankets. Near its entrance John turned away, and Langtry alone saw him enter.

The poor negro remained there in safety for four days, and then Edward Langtry borrowed Alden's team for a visit to a good Quaker, who lived twenty miles nearer the Nebraska line.

The day after Christmas, Major Jenkins, with a half dozen mounted men galloping at his heels, called at every house in the settlement to inquire for a runaway negro. Several had seen him, but no one knew of his present whereabouts, save one man, and him they did not encounter. The gallant Major who had traced him thus far, and then lost sight of him, was loth to give him up, but finally retired, vowing vengeance on the Free State party in general, and the Walnut Grove Colony in particular.

CHAPTER XII.

NEW YEAR'S CALLERS.

Mrs. Langtry had not announced a reception at her house on New Year's Day. She had not decorated her drawing room and prepared a feast. She did not, when the morning came, array herself in jewels and rich robes, and don her sweetest smiles and most engaging manners, to greet the friends who came to pay her the compliments of the season. She had some guests, however, who claimed her hospitality with somewhat of presumption in their manners.

The morning's work was done. Her kitchen, dining-room, bed-room, parlor, and sitting-room, combined in one, was neatly swept, the fire in the huge stone fire-place was smoldering low, the table cleared—its snowy cloth removed to give place to one whose crimson hue harmonized with the ribbons which looped the white Swiss curtains back from the one window opening to the south. The breakfast dishes nicely washed, were ranged upon the shelves with curtains drawn to shield them from the dust. The bed was neatly made and dressed in counterpane of white, the pillows covered with slips adorned with ruffles,—no shams. The milk was strained into shining pans, and then the rich cream skimmed and poured into the churn, whose painted sides of undimmed blue proclaimed its newness.

And now that order reigned, the blue-eyed mistress of the cabin seated herself on a low stool beside the churn, and swiftly moved the dasher to and fro, singing the while a

"MUCH GOOD."

cheerful song which bubbled forth as if unconsciously from a happy heart.

Her back was toward the door. She heard it open slowly, and turned, expecting to meet her husband's familiar face. Instead, her astonished gaze fell upon an unwonted sight, one which she had many times desired to see, declaring her pioneer experience incomplete without it, and yet a sight which startled and confused her, coming thus unexpectedly, and when she was alone.

It was three Indians, gaudy with feathers and war-paint, wrapped in gay blankets, who waited not for an invitation, but gravely uttering their salutations, " How!" " How!" entered, and proceeded to make themselves at home. Gazing around the room, and taking in at a glance all the little ornaments which served to soften its rough outline, they grunted out an approving, " Much good!" and then *nonchalantly* seated themselves near the fire, two of them letting their blankets fall as they did so. Agnes was somewhat reassured by perceiving that the dress of one, as well as her smaller size and more delicate form, showed her to be a squaw. They stretched forth their hands to the fire and seemed to luxuriate in the genial warmth, expressing their satisfaction in grunts, and the one phrase, " Much good!"

Then the larger one turning from the fire to the hostess, said: " Me Kantakee. Me much hunger," and opening wide his mouth and pointing therein, indicated that there was a vacuum beyond, and the second following the example of his chief, also introduced himself, " Me Wasumka," and the squaw, " Me Sandbar," and they too declared themselves by most expressive gestures and wide-open mouths, to be in the same unsatisfactory condition.

Hospitably inclined, Mrs. Langtry sought her stores and brought forth bread and meat, and cutting three large slices of each, she smilingly gave them to her visitors, who again grunted, "Much good!" though with never a smile on their stolid faces, and they gravely munched in unison, while the mistress resumed her churning, yet watching their motions with interest, and taking, woman-like, an inventory of their wardrobes.

Kantakee wore a girdle of red sustained by a leather strap; his hair was parted in the center, and the front portions brought down over each shoulder in plaits whose length was increased by the introduction of horse-hair and other substances, while the back hair was fastened in a brass ring, and the whole surmounted by a head-dress of feathers of gaudy colors. He wore ear-rings, a necklace of beads, and a heavy brass chain, besides, he had armlets of brass wire coiled to the elbows, and each finger had its ring. In his hand was a bow and a few arrows, the latter sharp at the point and fledged with goose quill. His moccasins were beaded in bright colors. Other adornment had he none save streaks of bright paint across his brow, and spots and patches of red and yellow in various places on his naked body.

Wasumka retained his blanket so closely drawn that his ornaments were not open to observation, and whether he had lost his scalp or not, Agnes could not say, but he wore a yellow handkerchief closely drawn about his head and tied underneath his chin, which gave him quite a grandmotherly appearance.

Sandbar was a gay-looking squaw, with beaded moccasins and a bright blue robe reaching to her bare knees, and held about her person by a stout leather belt, probably intended by the maker for a part of the harness of some Western team, but it was now ornamented with a triple row of brass buttons, and converted to fairer use. She had ear-rings, armlets big and little, and finger rings. Her hair was parted and plaited not wholly unlike that of some of her more civilized sisters, and adorned with feathers and beads.

Her forehead was daintily streaked with lines of beauty and grace in bright blue, flamingo, and yellow.

These three uniquely-costumed New Year's callers did full justice to the refreshments furnished them, and when the last mouthful of the first installment was disposed of, with the primitive manners of untutored nature, they greedily called for " more," asserting most positively in pantomime to Agnes, who at first shook her head, that there was still an aching void in each capacious form.

So persistent were they that she finally divided the remaining bread and meat between them, and they again munched contentedly; but this relay vanquished, and the sharp edge of hunger blunted, they sighed for something more dainty wherewith to appease their appetites, and with the remembrance of some former feast from hospitable Yankee hands still fresh in memory, Kantakee rose, took one of his long arrows and drew an imaginary circle on the floor, then tracing many a radius from center to circumference, as the sharp knife divides the luscious pie in pieces easy to handle, indicated thus that the dainty would please his taste.

The hostess heeded not. Then Wasumka gravely rose, his blanket clutched with one hand tightly, and with the other he seized the poker which stood near the fire-place, and he, too, marked off the magic circle, and traced the lines from center to circumference. Agnes shook her head decidedly. It was nearly noon. Mr. Langtry had a man at work with breaking plow, and these uninvited guests had already devoured the main part of the dinner that was to have been set before him, and she was loth to give them the dessert also.

But they were not thus to be balked. Sandbar arose, leaving her blanket on the stool, and began a search in which the others joined, the squaw taking in boxes and trunks which happened to be unlocked, while the two males attacked shelves and jars. From one of the latter they soon brought to light two pies which they divided between them, Sandbar, by this time, being too busily engaged before the looking-glass, whose use she had divined, in adjusting bows and ribbons, collars and jewelry, which she had discovered in her search, to heed them.

In her despair Mrs. Langtry thought best to summon her husband, and opening the door, blew a shrill blast on a whistle kept for the purpose, and whose sound could be heard on any part of the claim. Fortunately, Langtry was near at hand and came quickly, and at his coming, Sandbar quietly yielded up her treasures; the pie, alas! was irrecoverable. The whole party soon obeyed a polite but positive invitation, emphasized by the display of a Sharp's rifle, to "Be off!" saying as they went, "How! How! Much good!" with the same *sang froid* as that with which the polite guest repeats the stereotyped expression of thanks for a pleasant visit.

CHAPTER XIII.

LETTERS—ARTHUR'S CLAIM JUMPED.

On the tenth day of the New Year, John Alden received three letters from Ohio.

Mrs. Alden wrote:

* * * * * "I am glad Arthur has come for us, as I presume we ought not to travel alone through the border country in its unsettled and excited state; but he will not be ready to return before the last of February, and we have been in readiness for starting now over a month. We must have patience, I suppose, and some day or other, the meeting time so long delayed will surely come. * * * *

"We were all delighted to see Arthur, and his friends and acquaintances marked the improvement in his physique and his more manly carriage. His parents are very proud of him, and I am sure they glory not a little in the self-reliant spirit which leads him to take his own course, and bear himself with courage and dignity amid the hardships and dangers incident thereto. I read to an admiring circle of friends and relatives your account of his defence of that poor, persecuted free negro, and I assure you he became the hero of the hour.

"As for Grace, the story did not seem to make much impression on her. The fact is, she takes everything good and noble in Arthur as a matter of course and his unconcealed devotion to herself as merely her due. * * * * *

"Your loving wife,   AMY."

Arthur Fairchild wrote to John Alden:

"DEAR FRIEND:

'So far, I have not had the opportunity which I desired, so much of my time seems to be taken up by my friends. There are gay parties given in my honor by the young folks, which are well enough, providing I could always escort Miss Grace, and herself alone; but both young ladies and gentlemen seem to cluster around her like a swarm of bees, and if I find the field clear of the former, the latter are sure to be out *en masse*.

"I console myself, however, with anticipations of the long journey which lies before us, during which I may be able to secure her undivided attention. She does not care a penny for any one else, I'm sure of that. * * * * * * * ARTHUR."

Arthur wrote to the Walnut Grove Association:

"There is manifested here great interest in the coming struggle in the Territory. It is felt to be the battle between Slavery and Freedom. Nightly there are meetings held, and the subject is discussed in all its bearings. I shall be able to secure a large number of emigrants for our Colony, and I am urging upon them the necessity of an early start. The name Abolitionist is beginning to be accounted honorable. * * *

"I shall return by March 1st. ARTHUR."

The Association received the report with cheers, and a committee was appointed to carry out their portion of the contract, by breaking a certain number of acres on Arthur's place.

John Alden was made chairman of this committee, and the next day, accompanied by a plowman, with ox-team, he set out to begin.

He had not been on Arthur's place for some time, having no reason to suspect that anything was wrong. What was his surprise therefore, on nearing the timber to observe a thick smoke curling upward as if from a camp-fire.

He hastened forward, and in the thickest portion of the woods, where the branches of the trees were interwoven overhead, and there was an abrupt descent in the land, and a steep ridge rising beyond, he heard voices, a child's cry and a woman's angry tone. Nearer still, he discovered an irate mother in the act of administering salutary discipline to her refractory offspring. She ceased as he approached, and the white-headed offender made good his escape. The woman stared at the intruder a moment, and then resumed her work, which was evidently cooking the morning meal of pork and corn cakes over an open fire.

Behind her, in the side of the ridge, was a rudely constructed "dug-out," one of the upright kind, extending into the hill, with a frontage of boards, which must have been hauled there from some distance and deposited in the night-time to prevent discovery. A dark-haired, cross-eyed, vicious looking, middle-sized man sat on a tree which he had felled, smoking a pipe and watching the woman's movements with hungry-eyed interest.

"Halloa there, stranger!" said Alden.

The man took two or three long puffs, surveying John coolly before he deigned to reply:

"Halloa yourself."

Not to be outdone, as he had likewise his pipe, John seated himself opposite on the stump of another fallen tree, and also smoked awhile before asking:

"Where did you come from?"

He took his pipe from his mouth, expectorated two or three times, and then replied:

"Illinoy."

The woman, whose back was turned toward them now, turned right about face, placed her arms akimbo, and advancing a step or two, looked her lord and master defiantly in the eye and said: "T'aint so."

He did not correct his statement, however, but satisfied his conscience with a confidential wink toward John, and then calmly puffed away, awaiting the drawing out process with the serene complacency of a latter-day statesman, so Alden continued:

"How long have you been here?"

"Wal," scratching his head and expectorating: "Wal, nigh onto a month, I reckon."

His interrogator knew this to be a falsehood, and so did his truth-loving spouse, for she turned again angrily:

"Carr Withers, what's the good o'lyin', when the truth'll

do as well. It's flyin' right inter the face o' Providence. "Lemme see," counting on her fingers. "Monday, Tuesday, Wednesday, to-day's Thursday, hain't it? Jess four days we've bin in this hyer dog-goned place."

He laughed, a sort of chuckle, as if he rather enjoyed her obviously antagonistic feeling toward himself, and said apologetically:

"Bets didn't like this hyer move, not a bit; she don't like livin' in the woods away from her folks; but I say, when a man can git a good piece of land like this hyer, an licker an 'baccy thrown in, it's a woman's bounden duty to stand by him."

Bets' eye flashed fire, and she was about to oppose this interpretation of wifely duty, when Alden interposed:

"But this claim belongs to a friend of mine, Arthur Fairchild, who has gone to Ohio on business, and I promised to look after it and retain it for him."

Withers had resumed his pipe and former disinterested demeanor, and he now gave a tremendous whiff, watching the wavy line of smoke in its ascent with one eye, and observing Alden with the other, as he said:

"Promises are easy to make; the biggest job is keepin' on 'em."

"That's true. I keep mine nevertheless, and what's more, I am not the only man bound to take care of this claim. There's forty of us under oath to prevent any one jumping it, and I give you warning that you will have to leave. I shall report your presence immediately." John Alden spoke sharply, for he was irritated, and it brought his opponent to his feet, all the combativeness of his animal-like nature fully roused, his cross eyes scintillating sparks of fire in all directions, and with a fearful oath, he retorted:

"Stranger, thar's some folks as kin take oaths as well as others, an' thar's a thousan' or more of us boys swore by the

Eternal, to drive every last dog-goned Aberlition sneak outen this hyer Territory, an' we mean to do it too."

Here, Bets, seeing a conflict imminent, true to her woman's instinct, ranged herself on her husband's side, and came to the rescue, with:

" An ef you don't git out'en this quicker'n lightnin', I'll take every derned hair off'n your aberlition head, doggone ye."

Suffice it to say, the Free State man retreated before this combined assault, dreading the cat-like paws of Bets more than the sinewy muscles of her husband, but when at a safe distance, he ventured to say again: " This claim belongs to Arthur Fairchild, and we have promised to keep it for him until his return, which will take place in three or four weeks. As you have a family, I will give you a week to seek another place for them. At the end of that time if you still remain, we—" Bets advanced and he did not finish the sentence, but he heard the voice of Withers call out threateningly:

" The man who gits this hyer claim arter me, his friends 'll be sorry I didn't keep it. Wal they will."

Of course, John laid these facts before the Association, and they resolved to wait the week allotted, hoping that in the meantime Withers and his flock would depart in peace. But no. They drove off the man with his plow, obliging him to make double quick time with his oxen, in order to escape Bets' nimble feet and outstretched paws, to say nothing of her fluent speech. And then Withers went on hacking and destroying the best trees with the most outrageous disregard of economy, while Bets gave free scope to the belligerent spirit within her, alternately spanking her children, and railing at her husband, a species of connubial bliss to which he had no doubt become hardened, and but for which, his life would have sunk into a drear monotony.

At the end of the week the Association, in full force, and

well armed, paid the intruder a visit, and informed Wither that they had come to move him. He made no resistance, but quietly sat and smoked, only breaking his silence to interrupt occasionally the monologue of abuse showered upon them by his gifted spouse, with:

"Be still Bets, you ole fool you!" and when his lean horses were harnessed to his rickety old wagon, and his valuables piled on, even to the boards which formed the frontage of his dug-out, and when they had surmounted the load with his flaxen-haired children, and ordered him to get in and drive off, he mounted the bench with alacrity, and took the lines much to the disgust of Bets, who, clear grit to the last, refused to leave the premises until her husband threatened to drive off without her, and did actually move on some distance. But when those much abused children set up a heart-rending cry of "Mammy!" that cry which never fails to thrill the depths of a mother's heart, and break down the stoniest resolve, she made haste after them, climbed into the wagon, and Withers drove to the south until he had passed Alden's claim, and then turning to the west, crossed the creek and made his way to Calhoun, where he was evidently expected, and where he became a fixture, taking possession of Sile Hardiker's large building, keeping a hotel and dealing out whiskey and groceries from behind the bar, while Bets in the kitchen cultivated her talent for preparing corn-dodgers and frying pork.

Sile himself, having attained to the dignity and emoluments of justice of the peace, as a reward from the pro-slavery authorities for his distinguished services, built a somewhat neater, though smaller cabin for himself and his mother, who came to live with him.

Calhoun presently rejoiced in the addition of a blacksmith's shop, kept by one Kirby. It stood near the main road, a quarter of a mile from the "Withers' House," by which name the inn was now designated, and proved a very useful institution, saving many a long trip to Warsaw for repairs.

When the association had thus promptly ejected the interlopers, they decided to fulfill the remainder of their part of the contract at once, and proceeded with a will to the erection of a ten by twelve cabin.

Many hands make light work, and a few days were sufficient to complete it, and then Alden hired a man on his own responsibility, knowing that it was what Arthur would approve, to hew the rails for fencing the land, on which the patient plowman, with his strong-shouldered oxen, now unmolested, was turning the prairie-sod. He engaged the man to sleep in the cabin and then turned his attention to his own affairs, building a shelter for a cow and a calf which he had purchased, and putting up the fence for which he had already hewn the rails.

The long winter was nearly over, the long winter of lonely exile, and the springtime of nature, and of love, was returning with swift footsteps.

CHAPTER XIV.

A JOYFUL REUNION—A NEW LOVER—COL. DELANEY.

That pleasure, which, when dimly seen in the far off future we can calmly work and wait for, whose possession at some distant day we can look forward to with joyful anticipation, and yet lie down at night to dreamless, recuperative sleep, when brought nearer, almost within reach by slow-footed, yet ever onward-moving time, quickens the pulses and sends the blood bounding through the veins with wild impatience.

The hour approached, was almost at hand, for that glad reunion John Alden had resolutely put from him in the bright summer days, resolving not to drain the cup of joy to find the bitter dregs of humiliation in its depths, but rather to work and wait until his own house tree won by the patient labor of his own hands, should offer a protecting roof to his loved ones.

And as the time drew near the pent up stream of emotion so long forced to move sluggishly, o'erleaped its barriers. The days seemed interminable. His hitherto willing hands refused to perform their tasks. Even the excitement of the primary meetings incident to the coming election, awakened but a feeble interest in his mind.

Two letters had come for him. The burden of the first was:

"We will be in Lauderdale by the 1st of March. Be sure to meet us there. * * * AMY."

The other, from Arthur Fairchild, contained a draft, with which he requested his friend to purchase horses for him in Lauderdale.

"I have forwarded to your address, consigned to the firm Smith, Osgood & Co., with your household goods, a light spring wagon of my own."

Arthur also wrote:

"The ladies wish to camp out on their way up. Come prepared with necessary blankets, etc."

With an overflowing heart John Alden made arrangements for this journey, securing first a man to live in his cabin and hold his claim during his absence.

After a two days' journey, he stood one morning on the quay of the new city, Lauderdale, amidst countless boxes and bales of merchandise, having with the utmost difficulty made his way past innumerable teams of horses, oxen and mules, that stood drawn up as near as possible to the wharf, awaiting their loads of freight.

A representative of the firm Smith, Osgood & Co., whose warehouse for the storage of freight was yet the open prairie, though in imagination it loomed up in grand proportions in the near future, was with him, and by dint of patience and perseverance they found the boxes directed to John Alden's care. They were soon secured, the household goods placed in his wagon and sent forward to Walnut Grove, and Arthur's new spring wagon unboxed for use.

Alden then strolled along the one business street fronting the quay to find a resting-place for the night. The name "Temperance House" attracted his attention, and he entered one of the long row of one-story houses covered with huge signs.

As the name of "mine inn" implied, the only beverage found within its precincts was water, a bucket full of which stood at all times on the side table in the general sitting room with a tin dipper attached, for the use of the guests.

The latter were mostly Free State men, and allowed Alden to go and come as he liked, never so much as asking: "Are you sound on the goose?" a question he met at every turn on street and wharf.

He was given a single bed in a room where there were two other beds, each occupied by two persons, and standing so closely that there was scarcely room to pass between them.

Conveniences for the toilet were entirely wanting within the room, but, as was the democratic custom at that time and place, there was a board behind the house, forming a shelf, on which stood two large wash-basins filled with the muddy-looking waters of the Missouri, while a square foot of mirror, with comb and brush attached by means of a string, and a couple of crash towels swung on rollers near by, furnished all the bathing apparatus of the establishment, and which was in fact more than some of the guests made use of.

The house was provided with a long wooden porch across the front, whereon all day long, men sat with chairs tilted back, chewing tobacco, smoking and discussing the prospective value of town lots, and that never-failing topic of interest, the politics of the Territory. But the prevailing mood here was mild and temperate; no loud bluster, or bragging of personal prowess, nor brandishing of weapons, to keep a stranger in a state of perturbation, as at other places of resort in the place, and this disposed our friend John to eat without grumbling the "Johnny-cake" and bacon, set before him by "mine host," who prided himself on the excellence of his table arrangements. That John was unable to obtain any of the delicacies served, such as rice, pie, or apple sauce, was solely owing to his inability to acquire the sleight of hand process necessary to transfer them to his plate in the twinkling of an eye; the crowd that pressed in eagerly at the first announcement of dinner, being able to make a clear space in front of them, and resume their places on the porch, in five minutes by the watch.

As night came on, the ceaseless whiskey-drinking showed its fruits. The streets and numerous saloons were full of as base ruffians as ever disgraced humanity, and sounds of swearing, and carousing and gambling, fell on the ear unceasingly.

Now and then a pistol shot was heard, while cards were scattered all over the streets and whirled by the wind in every direction.

The better portion of the real settlers were building their houses some distance from the river, and out of sight and hearing of the unpleasant scenes and sounds. The city had been, like others, laid out with a view to future greatness, and lots in the business portion were already selling at fabulous prices, the trade of the plains, and the fitting out of government trains, assuring even the wariest capitalist, that this was no "ignis fatuus" blazing up for a moment to lead him on to loss and disappointment.

The next day Alden visited Fort Leavenworth, and found it beautifully situated on a lofty bluff overlooking the Missouri, and sufficiently elevated in position for its white stone walls and familiar flag to be seen for miles across the prairie. There was a feeling of security and retirement about the fort, which rendered a resort to it a relief after the turmoil and excitement of the settlement below, and which tempted him to remain. A stronger magnet however, attracted him to the city, and his business accomplished, which was to purchase horses for Arthur, he was soon on the wharf, attired in a new dark gray suit, a becoming hat, neat fitting, well polished boots, and seated in a stylish looking vehicle drawn by a pair of handsome blacks in new and shining harness, gazing anxiously down the "Great Muddy," for the expected boat.

Two, three hours passed away in patient waiting, and still no boat in sight. The weary, interminable afternoon and evening passed, and yet they came not. One or two boats laden with emigrants aroused his eager expectations as they came in sight, landed their freight and passengers, who went their way; but no Arthur, no Grace, no Amy, greeted his longing eyes, and it was not until the afternoon of the third day, that the Prairie Queen came in bearing her precious freight, and John descried on her deck as she slowly moved up to the landing, amid a group of ladies and gentlemen, first the manly form and blonde hair of Arthur, then recognized, not the form, for that had grown stouter and more staid than he remembered it, but the face, the pure, good, womanly face of Amy, with its tender brown eyes and sweet, expressive mouth, though there were lines of care which he had not in memory, and a slight mingling of silvery hairs amid those brown tresses, which he could not recall. The first plank put forth from the steamer to the landing bore John Alden like an impetuous young lover to her side.

Once more he held her in his arms, his dearly loved, his precious wife.

"Amy," he said in broken tones. "My love! Come what fate will to us, we will never again willingly be separated."

"No, John," she whispered with arms around his neck and head upon his bosom. "Never again."

Then Grace came—brown curls and roguish, laughing eyes, clear, white complexion, rosy cheeks and lips, a slender, graceful maiden, slightly taller than her mother. "Papa! oh, papa!" she cried joyfully, as with a loving embrace she was once more pressed to a fond father's heart.

Arthur came forward to shake hands and receive the "All's well!" which John communicated, and then the party realized that a duplicate scene had been transpiring near them between Col. Delaney and his daughter, who had come from South Carolina under her brother's care, to join him in the new home which he had chosen by reason of his appointment to a Federal office, and also because of his interest in the extension of slave limits.

GRACE ALDEN.

The Colonel was a tall, fine looking, dark-eyed man, whose gray hair gave an added dignity to his majestic appearance and haughty manner.

Miss Delaney was a handsome brunette, a little above the medium height, with a clear complexion, rosy cheeks, and large, liquid, melting black eyes. Indeed, the latter seemed to be a family characteristic, as they were noticeable in her brother, Roderick Delaney, a specimen of South Carolina chivalry, physically perfect, and with that easy carriage which marks the man accustomed to respectful homage.

He had a broad white forehead and jet-black waving hair, a nose slightly Roman, a well formed mouth and chin, giving a perfect profile, and then the crowning feature, those lustrous black eloquent eyes with long lashes. They were eyes which could express love, admiration, attention, respect, or scorn, loathing and defiance, at the owner's will.

Unlike his father, Roderick Delaney was affable and agreeable in his manner, with none of those haughty airs of condescension apparent in the bearing of the elder.

The younger man had but just returned from abroad, and his views were widened by culture, and the sharp edges of prejudice worn away by contact with equally positive minds of opposite opinions on many subjects, with whom he had associated under circumstances which compelled, at least, respectful consideration, and although still held to the support and defense of the pet institution of the South, by the force of early training and the ties of interest, his faith in its divinity had been rudely shaken.

Family greetings over, there were mutual introductions, by the travelers, who had become quite intimate on the ten days' journey, whose unusual length they explained laughingly, and in a fragmentary way.

"Have you been waiting long, papa?" inquired Grace.

"Yes,' John Alden replied, "three days."

"And I have been expecting you for a week," said Col. Delaney; "I could not imagine what detained you."

"You must charge it all to the low waters and the sand-bars, father; we were no sooner off one, than we ran on another," said Roderick.

"I think we shall have to dredge out this river when we settle up the Territory, and make it safely navigable," said practical Arthur.

"Oh! pray do not," cried Grace. "What should we do then for incidents of travel! How our diaries would suffer, and for my part, I rather enjoyed the novel sensation of a little danger."

"A sand-bar is not so dangerous as a snag, but both are execrable," said the Colonel.

"We became accustomed to the sand-bars, after a time or two," said Miss Delaney, "and knew in a moment what was wrong, when the boat with a great thump and shiver through all her timbers, came to a sudden stand-still."

"Yes," interrupted Grace, "and we knew we were all right, when the tired work hands after hours of toil gave a shout of triumph, as the great vessel, reared upon some cumbrous apparatus, all at once walked off into water like a schoolboy on stilts."

"Quite delightful, I allow for once or twice, but after ten or a dozen times in one trip it becomes monotonous," said Arthur.

"For my part," said young Delaney, in a low tone to Grace, by whose side he had taken his stand, "for my part, I could wish no better fate, than to spend my life travelling off and on sand-bars in such delightful company."

It was plain by the flush on Arthur's face that he had heard this speech, although he was apparently listening to Miss Delaney, as she remarked.

7

"We young folks managed to pass the time pleasantly enough, with our music and cards, and our moonlight promenades on deck; but Mrs. Alden must have found it extremely dull."

"Oh, no!" said Amy, "there was novelty enough in the incidents of the journey to make it interesting to me; besides, I found my position as chaperone to such a pleasant company of young people, a very agreeable one."

"Thank you, Madam," said the Colonel, with a very stately bow, and a glance at the group; "I presume they needed your espionage."

"Not at all! Not at all!" protested Amy. "I assure you, they were very well behaved."

By this time the way was clear for them to land. Col. Delaney, with true Southern hospitality, invited the Alden party to stop over night at his house in Lauderdale, and pointed out to them where it stood, on one of the hills back of the town.

Miss Delaney was also urgent, and appealed to Arthur with those expressive eyes of hers in such an eloquent manner that his refusal seemed almost uncourteous, politely couched though it was under the plea of hastening home on pressing business.

Amy also preferred carrying out the programme that had been planned, that of driving as far as possible that same evening, and camping out for the night.

And so they parted at the landing with many promises of correspondence and mutual visits from the young ladies, and calls from Roderick, who reminded the Aldens that, his colony being near, he should look up that way often, during the summer. At present he was intending to return to St. Louis, to meet a number of new recruits who were on the road.

"We shall outnumber you," said he to Arthur.

"Not a bit of it," replied the latter. "The few who are

coming from the North, now, are but a promise of those who will follow later in the season."

The Delaneys drove off in their fine carriage, with its colored coachman; and John Alden felt glad that, instead of his rough lumber wagon, he had a new, bright spring vehicle, with its nice harness and gay horses, toward which Arthur gave a glance of approval, as he assisted the ladies in.

And now our travelers left Lauderdale, and went westward at a rapid rate over the billowy prairie. The air was fresh and balmy, and the sky wonderfully clear, giving a long stretch to the vision, and disclosing in the distance on either side, the shapely hills, the conical, symmetrical mounds, and the gray bluffs encompassing the valleys, through which coursed gracefully the winding streams. The ladies could not restrain exclamations of delight; yet, remembering the wondrous beauty of the landscape in its autumnal garb, as contrasted with the bare-limbed trees with gnarled and knotty limbs and the dreary brown of the surface of Mother Earth at present, John Alden could not but wish the season was more advanced, and that spring had tinted the graceful slopes with green, and clothed the trees with foliage.

Arthur was driving, and seemed in high spirits, while Grace sat beside him, perfectly at her ease, and they kept up a running flow of sparkling conversation, gay comments on the travelers whom they met or passed, allusions to past events and persons far away; but not one word of those from whom they had parted so recently.

Amy and John were very still during that long drive— too happy, indeed, for words. Like shy young lovers, they only looked into each other's eyes, and clasped each other's hands in silence. The afternoon wore away, and twilight came and deepened into night, and when the moon and stars shone out in the deep blue sky, his arm unconsciously stole round her waist, and her dear head rested once more upon his bosom. There was no need to clothe their thoughts in words. Heart said to heart, "How precious is this love which time and absence only serve to deepen!"

At length they arrived at the camping ground which had been selected, and gaily set to work to make arrangements for the night.

Arthur attended to the horses, while Alden lighted the camp-fire, prepared the coffee, and spread upon the ground a white tablecloth, borrowed from Mrs. Langtry. Then he brought some material for luncheon which he had purchased in Lauderdale, at a restaurant, and Grace and her mother arranged it tastily, and made some additions of jelly and pickles from a basket of their own, and when all was ready they sat down to a pleasant meal. How many questions they had to ask, and how much they had to tell. When supper was over the young people strayed off for a moonlight walk, and Amy and John cleared up the supper dishes, disposed of the fragments, folded up the cloth, and re-arranged the provisions in the box to be ready for breakfast.

Interested as John Alden had become in Arthur's suit, he could not forbear asking Amy, as soon as Arthur and Grace were out of hearing:

"Are they engaged yet?"

"Oh, no!" with a shake of the head. "I'm afraid they are further away from that than ever."

"Why, how is that? Arthur was relying on this journey to give him the opportunity to make it all right."

"Yes, and so did I; but the Delaneys had taken passage on the same boat with us, and Roderick immediately recognized Arthur as a Kansas neighbor, and introduced him to his sister, and of course, then Arthur introduced him to us. I suppose that it was only natural that Mr. Delaney should prefer another young lady's society to that of his sister; at any rate, that is what he did."

"And did Grace seem to enjoy his society?"

"Indeed, she did; and I did not wonder at it, for, besides being handsome, he is a perfect master of the art of being agreeable, and he certainly spared no pains to make our tedious trip pass off pleasantly."

"Well," said John Alden, positively; "I don't want a Southerner for a son-in-law, no matter how handsome and interesting he is. They are all alike, conceited and overbearing, and the young man is no exception, I'll warrant. Beneath his suave manner you'll find the same domineering spirit. How did Arthur take it?"

"Oh, he bore himself bravely, and in fact, Miss Delaney was as charming as her brother, and took fully as much pains to make herself agreeable."

"The jade!" John interposed.

"And if I had not known just how Arthur felt, I might have supposed him equally interested in his companion."

"Good for him," John said, as the wanderers returned, and Grace came to him for a kiss in the old childish, affectionate manner which he remembered so well. He saw at once that they were too gay for betrothed lovers, and seemed to have enjoyed their walk and each other's society too well under the circumstances.

Both gentlemen were soon busy preparing for their night's rest in the open air. John had brought his tent and with some difficulty they arranged this to form a canopy over the wagon, in which they made a bed for the ladies, and then, wrapping themselves in blankets, they lay down beneath it, being thus sheltered from the dews of the night, which at this season of the year take the form of frost.

With the early dawn the party were up and away, and the next afternoon found them in their own home.

CHAPTER XV.

THE NEW HOME—TEA AT LANGTRY'S—VISIT TO WARSAW—BEAUTY'S COURT.

Never had the newness, the blank, uncultivated appearance of the wide-stretching prairie, so impressed itself upon Alden, as when, upon that March afternoon, approaching nearer and nearer, they came in sight of, and at last reached the rude cabin, bare and brown as the forest trees, fringing the creek to the west, and following the serpentine course of the river to the north of it. And as they halted at the door of the new home, the lack of symmetry in outline, the rough material, the contracted proportions, the lonely situation, every defect hitherto unnoticed or lightly passed over, stared at him mockingly, brought into full relief by the bright sunlight, and all at once, separately and aggregately imprinted upon his consciousness by his intense anxiety for a favorable first impression to be made.

Swift as a flash his thoughts went back to the home to which he had first carried his bride, and then to her father's house, commodious and beautiful, and for a moment he doubted the possibility of Amy's being contented in such a place. But he looked into her face, and the sunlight of happiness sparkled in her eyes. She gazed upon the rude walls and no shadow clouded the sunshine. She stepped over the door-sill as lightly, and trod the cottonwood floor as firmly, as though her footsteps fell on marble and velvet tapestry. She looked past the rough window-frames and out upon the landscape beyond.

"How lovely are the bare-limbed trees outlined against the blue sky, in this glorious sunshine."

She went up to the great stone fire-place, and, unnoting the rude masonry which stared at John from every wide, mud-plastered seam, she said:

"How cheerful this will be when the fire is crackling and sparkling on the hearth."

Then, seeing the ladder in the corner leading to the room above: "That must be your apartment, Gracie. You will find use for your calisthenic training in mounting to your chamber." And thus with everything. The glamour of love was breathed upon the scene, and every imperfection vanished, every beauty stood revealed.

Arthur went to work to build a fire, and Craig, the hired man, coming in from the field, assisted Alden to open the boxes, and arrange sleeping places for the night. The bedsteads were already prepared, and unpacking the bedding and making up the beds, was the work of a short time, although unrolling the quilts, and pillows, and feather beds brought to light numerous pieces of china, which Amy and Grace carefully ranged upon the shelves at the west side of the room.

And now came Mr. and Mrs. Langtry, with an invitation for the Aldens and Arthur to take supper with them.

In speaking of Mrs. Langtry to his wife, John had been careful not to say much in her praise, lest by raising Amy's expectations too high, he should defeat one of his dearest wishes, that a warm friendship and admiration should grow up between his friend's wife and his own; besides, he hardly thought it fair to forestall the pleasure of discovery, as many do, by heralding the good traits of an acquaintance, perhaps thus challenging a critical search for imperfections.

Whether this would have been so in Amy's case, determined as she was to see only good in everything, cannot be known. Certain it is, both she and Grace were delighted with their first caller, and accepted her invitation to tea, with pleasure. They were pleased, too, with her neat home which suggested possibilities in their own; but John Alden was glad in his heart that they had seen the cabin in all its naked ugliness, and treasured secretly those incontestable proofs of a devotion which could thus discover the bright side under the darkest possible exterior.

The tea was gotten up in Agnes' own inimitable style, and Amy and Grace said, laughingly, that they would be glad to take lessons of so accomplished a professor in the art of cooking by an open fire. Whereupon, Agnes assumed all the airs of an old settler, and gave the new-comers much valuable information concerning the pioneer style of domestic processes—the art of making one room answer for four or five, and one cooking utensil for half a dozen, trunks and boxes to serve for seats and storage closets at the same time, and above all, the secret of concocting favorite dishes without any of the usual ingredients, and devising new ones, dainty and appetizing, from unpromising, unpalatable material.

Then the conversation drifted to incidents of the outward journey. Notes were compared as to experiences by the way, pleasurable or otherwise.

Grace thought traveling by the steamer, even on the muddy waters of the Missouri, "Most delightful!" while Arthur voted the same "A bore!" and even Amy, "Rather preferred a railway."

Langtry hailed this difference of opinion as proof positive that all experiences are subjective, which conclusion was laughingly combated by the whole party.

Arthur gave a humorous account of his colonial agency, and from that the transition to politics and the condition of the Territory, was easy. They discussed the prospective institutions of the future State, with not a doubt but that they would be what they desired, so apparent was it already to those who had eyes to see, that the Northern immigrants would out-number those from the South.

Altogether it was a memorable evening, and is still looked upon as one of the bright spots in pioneer experience. Long they sat before the open fire, its cheerful light and genial warmth emblematic of the sympathetic hearts of the host and hostess, and then separated with heartfelt wishes for many repetitions of the same delightful intercourse.

Bright moonlight seems to retard the footsteps of young people the world over, even on a frosty night in March, and Arthur and Grace came on slowly, while the wedded lovers hastened to sit by their own hearthstone, full of the sweet, blissful consciousness of each other's presence.

The young lover, exultant with the assurance that loving he is loved in return, deems himself in the highest state of beatitude; yet is his joy as the murmuring brook to the deep river of rapture which overflows the soul when made sublimely conscious that years have but deepened and hallowed mutual attraction.

The first dawnings of that holy passion are no more to be compared to the love which has stood the test of time and absence, the trituration of petty differences, and daily commonplaces, and which, knowing all each other's imperfections, can look forward without shrinking to years of toil, and self-denial, amid uncongenial surroundings, than is the rushlight by which we can dimly discern each other's faces in the night, to the full glory of the noonday sun.

Craig had gone over to sleep with Garret, and thither Arthur also went when he had said "Good-night" to Grace at the cabin door, and she came in with the light step and sparkling face of happy girlhood, and ascended to her chamber.

With the morning light began a grand transformation scene. Amy within and spring without, stretched forth the wand of power, and beauty and loveliness reigned supreme.

A neat rag-carpet was laid upon the rough boarded floor, while the ground was covered with tender grass, and many-hued delicate wild flowers.

Amy hung pictures upon the brown cabin walls. Spring sent the gentle showers, and the trees clothed themselves in verdure, and stood outlined with bluff, and hill, and deep ravine, upon a background of green prairie, and deep blue sky. The merry birds sang songs among their branches, while within, sweet voices well-attuned, chanted in harmony with the notes of a guitar, touched by light fingers.

And withal, the daily work went on. The fields were already plowed—the seedtime was come. Nature smiles not upon the laggard. With resolute hand she points the hour, and he, who would gather the fruits of the harvest, must sow the seed in due season.

Amy had brought from Ohio a good selection of garden seeds, and north of the cabin, John spaded up a spot for a kitchen garden, and planting this they made their pastime, sowing radishes, lettuce, peas, onions, and later on, potatoes, melons, and various other vegetables.

She had also brought some young fruit trees, peach, apple and pear, carefully packed, and these John set out immediately, and the genial soil took the tender rootlets and germs to her bosom with a true motherly instinct, and they grew and thrived with a luxuriance unknown to them in their native climes.

About the house they planted honeysuckles and clematis, morning glory and wisteria, and lo! the log cabin became a vine-wreathed cottage.

Busy, happy, never-to-be-forgotten days, were these, full of work, and full of hope.

Occasionally, the threats of the border ruffians would come unbidden to John's mind, but they were resolutely put aside, and he said to himself: "Does not the same banner float over us here, beneath whose protecting folds we held life and property securely in the old home? We shall suffer no serious injury. A warm contest at the polls, and then all will be settled in our favor."

The second week after the arrival of Mrs. Alden and daughter in the Territory, they were happily introduced to society in Warsaw, and the event proved that they had not left all social pleasures behind.

The occasion was a visit from the Governor of the Territory, to the city of Warsaw. There was to be a political meeting in the afternoon, and a reception, with music and dancing, in the evening. A gay party, consisting of the Langtrys, Arthur and the Aldens, having resolved to make a gala day of the occasion, drove down in the morning, that they might have time to visit Mt. Olympus, and from its highest point give the ladies a view of the surrounding country, then to the "Pioneer House," taking dinner with Jake, "for old acquaintance' sake," although a rival establishment of fairer proportions and more inviting appearance, now stood by its side.

After dinner the ladies rested, while the gentlemen attended a meeting of the original town company, for the transaction of business; and then they all went to the political gathering.

Quite a number of ladies were present, it being characteristic of them from the first, to take a lively interest in affairs of state, and seats were furnished them, and in every way their presence made welcome. The whole Assembly numbered perhaps five hundred, and they cheered heartily, when, in an able and manly speech, Governor Reeves announced his determination to carry out the spirit of the organic act, and allow the majority of voters to determine the local institutions of the future State.

The Governor was a Democrat of Northern birth, and unable to read the organic act through Southern spectacles, and see in its provisions, a tacit promise of the Territory to the South.

Other speeches followed from Free State leaders, some quite conservative, and others, one of them from Langtry, quite radical in its tone, deploring the evils of slavery, and deprecating its further extension, after which the meeting adjourned, and most of those in attendance from the country, went to their homes.

A sufficient number remained, however, to fill to overflowing "Free State Hall," in the evening, where a newly organized band were displaying their skill on various instruments. It was a striking scene. Such a mingling of races and classes on the democratic plane of equality has seldom, if ever, been witnessed. The learned and the unlearned, the gentle and the loud-voiced, the courtly and the boorish, exchanged familiar greetings, and moved and mingled among each other in social unrestraint. And their costumes were as varied as their manners and their places of nativity. From the dress suit, kid gloves and polished boots, the styles descended with an easy gradation to flannel shirts, and stogas with pants tucked in, the wearers of which moved in the mazy figures of the dance, or discussed politics with equal "sang froid."

Among the ladies, Amy was pleased to find many of refinement and culture, with whom Agnes and herself were soon at home, and as for Grace, imagine, if you please, a handsome, sparkling young lady, not quite out of her teens, rather fond of admiration, the center of an admiring circle of intelligent and cultivated young men, the very flower of the youth of the country, having tended to this point, drawn by the magnet of excitement, and the possibility of political distinction.

When the music began, Arthur, as was his privilege, claimed Grace's hand for the first quadrille, but it was his last for that evening; one after another begged the honor of "just one set," until her mother, fearing undue fatigue, positively forbade another dance, and she took refuge from invitations by Amy's side, followed by a score of admirers, toward whom she bore herself with all the dignity of an American queen, contributing her share to the sallies of wit which went rebounding from side to side, striking here and hitting there, provoking audible smiles and counter-hits, until it was time to depart.

After this they had many visitors from Warsaw. The ladies and gentlemen came out to call, and inviting visits in return, making a round of social engagements which proved quite a relief to the monotony of country life. Another change, too, was brought about by the introduction of the feminine element into Alden's household—there were to be no more lazy Sundays. Amy had always been accustomed to attend church; in fact, she subscribed to the creed, with, perhaps, a few unconscious mental reservations, and Grace was soon invited to become a member of the choir, and as, like Longfellow's village blacksmith, John "loved to hear his daughter's voice," he went willingly, and Arthur was only too happy to drive around with his "restive blacks" each Sabbath morn, and carry them down to Warsaw in his wagon, himself the envied of a score of young men, any of whom would gladly have driven ten miles or more, to be able to escort to church the belle of the county. Not one of them but did frequently drive the eight miles from Warsaw to Walnut Grove, to be in attendance on "beauty's court," held as the evenings grew longer and warmer, in the open air, on the south side of Alden's cabin, while the political clique met at the same time for graver discussions on the east side, and the turbulent feelings generated by the latter party were often softened and moderated by the music of the young people's voices, mingled with the sweet tones of the guitar.

Arthur being made prime minister, and always allowed attendance on this squatter sovereign princess, seemed to be happy, and had not as yet tried to bind her by a promise.

"I am afraid to risk it now," said he to John. "I must bide my time. Of course it annoys me to see her smiles dispensed so graciously to others, but so long as they are widely diffused, I can bear it, rather than lose my share by attempting to intercept them all."

And he was right. It was much to be able to blend himself daily with all her enjoyments, to become a part, and a pleasant part of her life, to surround her at all times with an atmosphere of protection and appreciation, and to shower upon her little acts of kindness and love, which should speak for him with a thousand voices, when the auspicious moment for which he waited, should arrive.

CHAPTER XVI.

AN AMUSING VISITOR—BLUE LODGE SECRETS—GRACE ENTERTAINS THE SQUIRE.

Soon after the Alden ladies were settled in their cabin, they received a visitor to whom we, as did they, must give special attention.

As the insect, harmless in itself, sometimes deposits in the most carefully-tended garden the germ which develops into the parasite that fastens upon and destroys the fairest and the best, so did this woman, unconscious herself of the depths of wrong to which her ambition and perverted motherly instincts would lead her, come to them appealing for a little society, a little instruction, thus fastening herself upon those whose kind hearts never resisted the humblest appeal for sympathy. She was a wiry, active little woman of middle age, with crafty-looking black eyes, and black and gray hair, which she wore gathered into a knot on the back of her neck and placed in a net of scarlet chenille, that extended upward and almost covered her head, and was tied on one side with a heavy cord and tassels. Her dress was of bright blue woolen goods, the skirt gathered into the round waist, and spreading out full and flowing over a huge hooped skirt. She wore a large lace collar with a bright red bow at the throat, and an immense gold chain round her neck, to which was attached a large gold watch; from her ears hung heavy ear-rings, and her fingers were covered with showy rings, cotton gloves were on her hands, and her shoes—half high—disclosed with every tilt of the hoops gray, home-knit stockings.

She wore a shawl with stripes of many colors, and a hat gorgeous to behold, covered as it was with flowers, and ribbons, and plumes. Evidently she was gotten up with care, and expected to make an impression as a person of wealth and importance.

There was a self-satisfied look upon her face as she came toward the house, having been deposited a short distance off by her son, who, as soon as he had assisted her to alight, vaulted into his seat and drove rapidly away, without so much as a glance toward Amy, who went out to meet her, or Grace, who stood in the door-way.

"How air ye?" said she, coming forward.

"Quite well, I thank you. How are you?" replied Amy.

"Tolable peart, thank 'ee; but I wor gittin' powerful homesick and lonesome like, livin' up thar in Calhoun, with so many men swarin' and jawin' round, and no wimmen folks to speak on, and seein' you'uns drivin' by, lookin' so uncommon chirk, I jes' made up my mind to come over hyer and get acquainted. Sez I to Sile; sez I, (that's my son, an' I'm the widder Hardiker), 'Sile, sez I, 'taint no use talkin, I'm a goin' as sure as you live.' Men folks will do one't in a while; but for a stiddy diet, give me wimmen."

"I think so, too," said Amy, putting forth her hand to clasp the white gloved one; "and I am glad you have come." And as they came up to the door-step, and Grace gave way for them to enter, "This is my daughter Grace. Take the lady's hat and shawl, Grace; she has come to spend the day with us."

Pleased with this reception, the woman allowed Grace to assist in removing her hat, and then seated herself on a rocking chair, one of two which had been brought from Lauderdale, saying meanwhile, in reply to the introduction:

"Why, you don't say so! A right smart chance of a gal! A heap o' help to you, I reckon."

Mrs. Alden admitted Grace's general ability to make herself useful, and then the visitor flashed her sharp eyes about the room, seeming to take in at once its every detail.

"Powerful way now, Miss Alding, you Yankees hev o' gittin' up things. Some folks think 'taint no use hevin' a cabin slicked up an' kind o' purty an' stylish lookin'; but I've allers said, an I'll say it again, that it does one good to set an' look at 'em—them picters, I mean, an' them books an' white curtains. 'Tseems somehow as ef I'd got a leetle higher in the world. Did you make 'em?" pointing to the pictures, and looking at Grace.

"Not those on the walls; but I will show you some of mine," and Grace brought forth a portfolio of drawings and a few paintings done in water colors. The widow put on her spectacles, crossed one limb over the other, regardless of the tilt of her hoops, and settled herself to examine them, peering curiously at every piece.

"Cost a heap to learn this, I reckon!"

"Not a great deal to learn to do as well as this," said Grace. "I only took lessons one year."

"I reckon it's powerful hard to learn?"

"Why no, not so very, providing you have a talent for it."

"Jess so, jess so! That's what I've always bin a sayin'. Folks hain't alike no more'n critters. Some on 'em has faculty an' some on 'em has drive, an' a site on 'em haint good for nothin', unless, mebby, it's to set 'round and make trouble for other folks."

After the drawings and pictures, she scrutinized critically the daguerreotypes of all their friends, which Amy brought forth for her entertainment, then the books and the china, and when through with these, said:

"Lemme see your cloze!"

They both laughingly declared, that their wardrobes were

very plain, indeed, and hardly worthy of inspection; but she insisted, declaring that she wanted to know how the Northern ladies' dresses were made, that she might know how to make her own.

"Not that I do 'em myself. I've got a slave gal down in Missoury, that's a master hand at sewin', an' she could make 'em up complete, ef she had some one to learn her. Now you'd jist be the one to do it," said she, turning to Amy; "only I dassent bring her up here."

"Why not?" said Grace.

"La! gal, what a question! Why, yer own par, or Langtry over thar, 'ud run her right off under my nose; fact! That's why I came myself, to keep house long o' Sile. Ye see he's all the boy I've got, an' a mighty good boy he is, too; like his par—smooth an' easy, and lazy-like, only down to the bottom an' kind o' settled like, he's got his marm's grit, an' ef ye stir hard enough an' long enough, ye kin rile it all up, an' then thar's the devil to pay—beggin' parding, Miss Alding, I reckon you'uns don't use no sich words."

After dinner she grew even more communicative, dilating on her achievements in the past, and intentions for the future, in true frontier style. Evidently the little woman had an object in life, and she moved straight forward with a will toward the end in view.

"My ole man," said she, "had a few niggers an' a piece o' bottom land, most on it swamp, an' the way he run it wor a caution; didn't plant nothin' but corn, an' raised hogs, an' I vow! them hogs e't all the corn, an' them niggers e't all the hogs. I jawed, an' jawed; but t'want no use. A man ain't a goin' to be teached anything by a woman, partickler when the woman's his wife; an' so he sot thar, an' let 'em go on, plantin' the little patch year after year, an' sellin' off the extra nigs to get whisky an' terbacker, an' a kaliker dress or two fer me; an' Mary Jane Spears, she that was a Jonsing, goin' drest in silk, turnin' up her nose at me—wa'n't half so likely a gal as I woz nuther, an' Spears wouldn't a tuk up with her, nohow, ef he'd had any show long o' me.

"But as I wor sayin', thar my ole man sot in that thar swamp, until, as the preacher said at his funeral sarmount, he wor called by Providence to a better world. Wal, I reckon he wor; but the first thing I did, when I got to be the boss o' that thar plantation, for the ole fool hed sense enuff to make me Sile's guardeen, was to dreene that thar swamp. I didn't keer to get my call in the same way he had his'n," and the widow laughed, thinking this a good joke.

"But, as I wor tellin' ye, when I got that swamp land dreened, I made them niggers put it in corn, an' the corn land we put in terbacker. Made enuff the fust year to pay off the morgidge over which the ole man had groaned fer ten years; an' the second year, bought more land fer the surplus niggers to till. An' so on, an' so on, till now thar ain't another sich a plantation in Boone county. An' my Sile, he kin hold up his head with the best ov 'em; an' I'm goin' to hev what I want ef money kin buy it, an' I reckon 'taint much that money can't buy, an' what I want I'm goin' to hev, I don't keer what it costs."

"But why did you come to Kansas?" asked Grace, much interested.

"Wal, yer see, I didn't want Sile to come, in the fust place. I wor dead sot agin it, an' he wor dead for it, an' both on us strong in the mouth. 'Marm,' sez he, 'nigh about every young feller in the county's jined, an' I'm bound fer to jine.'"

"Joined what?" inquired Amy.

"Why, the Blue Lodge of course. Gen. Stringman, an' Col. Delaney, an' ole Dave Watkins, an' Dock Cornello, an' all the rest o' them big bugs, came roun' down in Boone county, makin' speeches an' ropin' in all them boys, gittin' them to swar to drive all the Yankees out'n this hyer Territory—writ it down in their own blood I've hern tell, that is, the boys made their mark to what them big bug fellers writ; most on 'em couldn't write theirselves. But my Sile now, he's got a eddication. He can read an' write, an' cipher too; an' he didn't hev no need o' thar whisky, nor their terbacker, an' sez I—'Sile,' sez I, 'what do you want to be a cat's paw fer them big bugs fer. It don't pay, sez I, when you hev whisky o' yer own.' An' somehow or 'nuther, stories will fly so fast, ole Dave an' the Kernel heard on't, how dead sot I woz agin it, an' how a lot o' the boys sed they wa'n't goin' over thar without Sile, nohow, an' ef you believe it! them two ole fellars cum to me, an' the Kernel, he's as slick an' as smooth as a skinned pig like, an' his tongue runs as easy—jest as easy as a steam saw-mill, an' sez he, 'Miss Hardiker, I'm sorry to hear you're opposed to the best interests of the country. You've got slaves, an' these Abolitionists have come down here to steal 'em away. Ef we don't go over thar an' drive 'em out, or go to the polls an' vote em down, we shan't have a nigger left, soon.'

"'An' Kernel,' sez I, 'sposin' my Sile goes over thar, an' some o' them Yankees draws a bead on him with a Sharp's rifle, what's the good o' hevin niggers then?'

"'Oh, thar's no danger o' that mum,' sez he, jest as perlite as if I wor a born lady. 'I don't ask your son to march in the rank an' file; what I want o' him is to go over thar, an' kind o' hold the ground like, an' let us know from time to time wot's goin' on, an' how the land lays. I want him to keep a depot of supplies, an' act as jestice o' the peace, too. He's jest the right temper for a 'squire—sort o' easy an' cool like, an' he's got the larnin.'

"'Squire! Jestice o' the peace! Jehosaphat! That brung me round. He must be ole Nick himself, I thought, or else how'd he know that wor my one weak pint? Ef I couldn't be Miss 'Squire Hardiker, I could be 'Squire Hardiker's marm. But I didn't like to give up too easy, an' so sez I:

"'You're quite sure they wont try no Sharp's rifles on him, Kernel?'

"'Not a bit of it,' sez he, 'they aint got no fight in 'em.'

"'An' ef he's a 'Squire in the Territory will he be a 'Squire in Missoury?'"

"'Why certainly,' sez he, larfin; 'I'm a Kernel in South Carliny, and of course, I'm a Kernel here, or anywhere in the United States.' Sez he, 'We give those common fellers, wot can't read or write, an' don't know nothin' about cipherin' a dollar a day, an' whisky, an' terbacker. But your son, madam, is a gentleman, an' a slave owner, an' I wouldn't insult him by offerin' him pay for pertectin' his own property.'

"'Wal,' sez I, 'you put it mighty plain Kernel, an' I'm one,' sez I, 'as when I see my duty clar, ain't a mite afeered o' doin' on it, an' you jist make out them papers, fa'r an' squar', an' I'll be bound ef I don't see as the new Squire is sot up in good style.'

"'Good,' sez he, 'less shake hands on it,' holding out a purty white hand as never done a day's work, for my bony fingers, an' givin' ov 'em a twist, an' a smilin'. An' the Kernel he kep' his word, an' I kep' mine. An' now he's goin' fur to do more nor he bargained, fer Sile's to be a member o' the legislater after next week. I guess some o' them big-bugs down in Missoury, as carried their heads so high over me, 'll be glad to bob a little after that. Ef we've got an office, an' we've got niggers, an' we've got money, I'd like to know what else we need to be on a ekality with any on 'em."

"What indeed?" said Grace, whereat her mother shook her head reprovingly, saying:

"But you cannot be sure of that office, until the election

day is over. Mr. Langtry is a candidate for the same position, and he has a great many friends, and you know success depends upon having the greatest number of votes."

"Now don't you believe it," said Mrs. Hardiker, putting her finger to her nose, tossing her head, and looking very knowing.

"Our fellers hain't a goin' to take any sich chances. Them ole long-heads o' Kernel Delaney, an ole Dave Watkins kin fix up the keards to win every time, you kin bet your eyes on that! I heerd the Kernel make a speech afore I come up hyer an 'Boys', sez he, 'they've bin pourin' o' thar men inter the Territory by hundreds. Air you goin' to set here smokin' your pipes, an' let 'em beat you all holler? No sir'ee! you've got too much grit for that. Most likely they could beat you on a fair count, but in a fair fight, boys, they'd be nowhar. An' I tell you now, ef you 'low them thar Aberlitionists to git control o' this hyer legislater, yer gone up. Yer high an' dry on a sand-bar, an' you won't git off till yer busted. This is yer time; you go over thar now, in mast, an' git yer grip on the body as makes the laws, an' ye kin make the Territory too hot to hold 'em. Boys,' sez he, kind o' smilin' in his pleasant way, 'that 'll be better'n shootin' on em, 'cause you'll have the fun o' standin by, an' crowin' over 'em, an' seein' 'em wriggle under pro-slave laws as they can't throw off, like a terbacker worm under a hot coal.' That's wot he said, only I can't put it into big words like his'n.

"But laws now! I'm afeerd I've bin an tole some ov the secrets," said she. "Howsumever, I never did swar to keep 'em. They didn't take wimmin folks in thar lodge, in a reglar way, but Lord! they might as well, 'cos we're bound to find out things anyhow, an' now yer mind, I tell yer, an' don't yer be skeert, wen ye see 'em comin'. They wont hurt ye, providin' yer quiet an' peaceable like; they're jist comin' to vote this time, an' when they've voted they'll take theirselves off ag'in."

During the afternoon the usually clear sky had become overcast with clouds. Suddenly the wind blew in gusts from the east, and the lightning flashed vividly portending a storm, and just as Sile drew up with his wagon at the cabin door the rain fell in torrents.

At first he stubbornly refused to accept an invitation to enter, but his mother pleaded "rheumatiz," as a reason for waiting until the shower was over, and he finally reluctantly consented to come in.

She introduced him first to "Mis Alding," and then to "Mis Alding's darter Grace," who, full of fun and mischief, took upon herself the onerous duty of entertaining him, asking him various questions, and marking the height to which the blood suffused his cheeks, and studying the various motions of his long, awkward limbs, and the twirling of his thumbs, while she uttered some commonplace remark and gazed at him sweetly with her innocent-looking eyes, and he vainly attempted, through timidity, and the natural defect of his organs of speech, to reply.

The widow seemed to take in the situation and enjoy it too, for she leaned over to Amy with an aside:

"Hain't she got 'im in a tight box though? Mighty peart gal that o' your'n," and then again, winking, "Never looked a gal in the face afore!"

The fact is, he did not look a gal in the face now, except surreptitiously, and when he thought she was looking in another direction, and the little witch observing this, forthwith managed to look away frequently, thus attracting his gaze, that she might suddenly flash the light of her pretty brown eyes full upon him, bringing the color to his sallow face, and turning his attention to the lines in the carpet.

The widow evidently looked upon this little episode as a

piece of educational discipline, which was good for her son, regarding it in much the same light as the nauseous doses for the benefit of his inner man, which many a time she had herself administered with resolute hand, yet, when it became positively painful, her motherly instinct was roused within her, and quick to devise relief.

"Show the Squire all them thar fine picters o' your'n, Miss Grace. He war allers mighty fond o' picters, used to put out his hands an' cry fur 'em on the circus bills afore he could talk."

And Grace brought forth her portfolio of drawings again, which seemed to make things move easier for the Squire. He looked on admiringly while his mother explained them to him one after another, with a wonderfully accurate memory.

By the time the shower had ceased, Sile sat quite easy in his chair, taking in the new sensation of neat surroundings, and the company of ladies, with a feeling somewhat akin to pleasure, though many degrees removed from ease.

When they came to leave, the widow freely expressed her enjoyment of the day, and added benignantly:

"You'uns ! ain't a bit stuck up, nor nothin', though I 'low to believe you could hold your own with the biggest bugs in Missoury," but when she invited them to visit her in return, Sile shook his head saying: "N-n-not yit, marm, g-g-git yer cabin fixed up fust," to which she replied: "Wal, that's so, we kin an' we will."

Mrs. Alden bade them come again, and not wait for her to return the call, then Sile picked the little woman up and lifted her to her seat in the wagon, and jumping in beside her, drove off to Calhoun.

CHAPTER XVII.

ELECTION DAY—LANGTRY IN DANGER.

Edward Langtry had received the nomination for member of the first Territorial Legislature, with feelings of gratification mingled with a sense of deep responsibility. He represented the most radical faction of the Free State men, and had never disguised or concealed his sentiments, but with his strict ideas of the duty of a representative, to represent his constituency, he deemed it necessary to declare anew that he believed the object for which they were then working, namely, the admission of Kansas to the Union as a free State, was but a step toward the consummation of the grandest event of the day and generation, the emancipation of the slaves.

He declared himself to be a member of that party which contended against slavery, not only beyond the limits of the Constitution, but within those limits. He believed in agitation—agitation as the very breath of the Republic, as necessary to its vigor and purity, as are the winds of heaven to a vital atmospheric condition.

Though gratified beyond measure that his friends and neighbors had selected him as their standard-bearer in the coming contest, he could not receive the banner without the privilege of bearing it in the van, and he scorned to accept a position, however honorable, which would restrict his freedom of speech and action. Then, with an eloquence born of deep devotion to a sacred cause, he painted a picture of the degradation, moral and physical, not only of the slaves, but of the poor whites, contrasting their condition with that of the Northern laborer—heir to the free schools, free press, and free speech of the North, and pointed in illustration to the settlements on either side, and the justice of the comments and the faithfulness of the portraiture could not be disputed, with ocular demonstration thus before them.

He was loudly cheered on the conclusion of this declaration of sentiments, and the nomination was confirmed, his constituency assuring him that they would trust his judgment not to hazard a present good by ill-timed efforts to secure that which he himself held to be attainable only by slow steps, and sure.

They then made out a list of all the voters in the Walnut Grove district, clas-ifying them as Free State, and pro-slave, and the summing up gave assurance of victory, though the contest would be closer than in other districts west of the border tier, and it was necessary that their full strength should be brought out.

Walnut Grove Colony, which extended along the eastern bank of the Areposa for several miles, with a few settlements on the opposite side, to the south of the ford, numbered, all told, ninety-eight voters, while the village of Calhoun and the surrounding claims occupied by pro-slavery men numbered thirty-six, Charleston, fifty, making a majority of twelve only, providing every Northern man voted, and voted the Free State ticket.

Their sympathies were all with Langtry at this time, but, in the two weeks following the nomination and preceding the election, they were visited privately by a number of leading pro-slavery men from other points, who urged the necessity of preserving the peace by voting for the pro-slavery candidate, or by staying away from the polls, declaring that the opposite course would bring destruction upon them from Missouri. Among these men was Major Jenkins, who worked hard to awaken a prejudice against Langtry, by calling him a woolly-headed Abolitionist, accusing him of stealing slaves, and urging, that, to follow his counsels, would deluge the land with blood, and perhaps rend the Union itself, in twain.

Langtry, however, patiently followed in his track, combating all his arguments, and portraying clearly the danger of electing a pro-slavery man to this first Assembly, which must adopt a code of laws, either in accordance with, or in opposition to, the principles of freedom and justice. Then, putting abstract arguments aside, he labored to convince each one, that to allow the introduction of slavery was inimical to his interests. Slaveholders must necessarily buy up the land in large tracts, to the exclusion of the poor man who only desires a homestead; the introduction of slave-labor invariably tends to lower the wages and degrade the status of the working man, and so on, with all the arguments which we, who have lived through the great contest, have learned so familiarly; and so convincing was his logic, that at a full meeting held three days before the election, every man announced his intention to stand by the Free State candidate, and to be on hand to deposit his ballot.

Then, just at the last moment, came confirmation of the truth of the information given by the widow Hardiker. A deep laid scheme was on foot to carry the election, despite the will of the majority of legal voters. Disappointed in their attempts to drive out the Free State men, and failing in their efforts to compete with the North in colonization, they had devised another scheme, astounding in its audacity, and capable of being conceived and carried into execution only by those in whom zeal for the perpetuation of a pet institution had outrun discretion.

For some months they had been organizing and enlisting men in the western counties of Missouri for the purpose of taking possession of the polls on election day, with the object of securing a Legislature, which should carry out their purposes, and, with executive officers already appointed, who were in entire sympathy with their design, their victory would be complete. In securing their migratory voters, they used all the tact of old politicians, seeming to understand by intuition the inducement necessary in each case, whether it was the promise of unlimited whiskey, a dollar a day, a petty office, or merely a little palaver.

By adroit speeches too, they raised the enthusiasm of their dupes to such a pitch, that many of them were really persuaded in their own minds, that it was a patriotic and praiseworthy undertaking.

By sending out small colonies to settle near Free State settlements, they were kept well informed of all their movements, and of the number of voters necessary to carry the election in each particular precinct; and at all these points, depots of provisions were established. Thus systematically did they proceed to defeat the provisions of the organic act. All who found it impossible to go on this expedition, were urged to show their patriotism by contributions of provisions and money, and such was the force of pro-slavery sentiment in western districts of Missouri, that no one dare refuse. Those who came, were, consequently, well provided for and in high spirits, considering the event in the light of a "lark." Their leaders were men belonging to what might be called superior classes, though the subdivisions were commanded by men of their own ilk, distinguished above their fellows by reason of their superior zeal and prowess, hence Zeke Fagin once more rode at the head of his men, swelling with a consciousness of his own greatness.

A large division of these invaders passed Alden's house on the afternoon of the 29th of March, an advance-guard of three hundred horsemen, followed by one hundred wagons, containing at least one thousand men, a nondescript set of fellows, "armed to the teeth," with pistols, bowie knives and guns, dressed in every variety of their native costume, flannel shirts, and pants in boots, with hat of felt or fur, from beneath which flowed long hair, unshorn, and in some degree unkempt, snaky-looking eyes of every hue; the only unvarying point of resemblance, a certain expression of countenance, indicating a lack of culture of the higher faculties and emotions.

As on a former occasion, they were provided with banners, whose mottoes: "War to the death!" "Knife to the hilt!" "Death to the white-livered Abolitionists," fitly expressed the sentiments of the members of the procession.

Here and there an inverted whiskey bottle crowned the pole of some particularly aggressive banner, and streamers of hemp waved suggestively in the air. A white ribbon had been adopted as a distinctive badge of membership by that powerful secret society, the "Blue Lodge," and every man in this procession, which wound its slow length along toward Calhoun, wore it proudly on his bosom.

At Calhoun they halted, three hundred of them going into camp for the night, and the remainder, after replenishing their exhausted jugs, whose emptiness made plain the reason of the unusual silence and dignity with which they pursued their course, continued on to Warsaw, where they encamped, as on a former occasion, beyond the ravine to the north of the town.

The voting place for Walnut Grove district was Calhoun, and Harley, John Alden and Arthur Fairchild had been appointed judges of the election. At a meeting hastily called, and held at Alden's house, after the procession from Missouri had moved on beyond the creek, there were many indications of a desire to avoid a conflict, many Free State men being in favor of abandoning the attempt to vote. But Arthur and Alden assured them that they meant to take their places at the polls, and enforce the law, which required that every voter should make oath that he was a resident of the Territory. This would, of course, rule out the invaders, and they urged every settler by all means to come up bravely and deposit his ballot, after the judges had thus borne the brunt of the battle. They all finally promised to do so, and it was resolved to proceed to the polls in a body for the sake of mutual protection.

Accordingly they were assembled early on the morning of the 30th, at the house nearest the ford, but to Alden's dismay only eighty men presented themselves; and after waiting as long as possible for the others, the eighty resolved to go on and do their duty, though defeat stared them in the face, even should only legal votes be cast. Of this fact their opponents did not seem aware. They had come to vote for their old crony, Sile Hardiker, at the bidding of their superiors, and they meant to do so, whether such illegal act were necessary to the end desired, or otherwise.

The polls were held in a small frame cabin used by the Squire as an office, and which stood on the open prairie at some distance from his residence, the grocery, and the other shanties which composed the town, and leaving their horses in the timber, the Free State men bent their steps thitherward.

The Squire himself recognized Arthur, Harley and Alden as the judges appointed, and opening the door, allowed them to pass in with a much more friendly "H-h-how," for the latter than he had hitherto vouchsafed.

They found chairs and a rough table provided, also a ballot box and poll books, which they took possession of, and prepared for use. They closed the door and locked it to prevent intrusion, and then removed a pane of glass from the window, that the ballots might be deposited in the box through the aperture. Their friends outside now began to come up, and Arthur administered the oath of residence, after which they deposited their ballots, and moved off. They had received some fifteen or twenty ballots, including their own, when a band of Missourians, headed by Zeke Fagin, moved up to the window, thrusting aside the Free State men who stood near, and offering their ballots, which had been printed in Missouri. Of course the judges refused to receive them, unless they could take the oath of residence. Zeke then appealed to the crowd, saying:

'Boys, we hev come here to vote. We hev sworn to vote, an' better men than these hyer dog-goned Abolitionists hev told us that we hev a right to vote ef we hev bin in the Territory five minutes. The very fact of our tendin' these hyer polls, shows that ef not actooal residents, we hev a sneakin' notion of bein' sich, some o' these hyer days. What air yer goin' to do about it?" 'Low these hyer low-lived cusses to back yer down, or jump 'em up yerselves?"

His men, who had all gathered about the little building, cheered this speech loudly, and cries of:

"Make 'em resign." "Make 'em resign." "Put in judges that will receive our votes," resounded with sufficient unanimity to indicate that they had been instructed in their parts beforehand, and Zeke, turning to the judges, continued: "Do yer hear that? them air our instructions, and, by G——d, we mean to kerry them out, and will ye step down now peaceable like, or shel we hev the pleasure of assistin' yer?" an attempt at pleasantry which brought cheers from his supporters.

The judges resolutely declined to be relieved of their duties, and then there was a rush at the window, which came in, sash and all, and lay in pieces upon the floor, and a half dozen guns were pointed at them through the opening. Then the building began to tilt, and rock from side to side, as if they had roused a small earthquake. A number of Zeke's men had

"HURRAY FOR MISSOURY."

placed a pry under one corner of the cabin, and it would soon have been a wreck, but for Sile Hardiker's presence within. He called out vehemently for them to desist, lest he himself should be injured, and for this reason also, the men at the window restrained their shots.

Zeke gave the judges still another opportunity to resign. When his men, swearing and blustering, had burst in the door, and stood with knives drawn and pistols cocked, demanding that these men receive their votes or resign, he took out his watch and arrogantly announced, that they had " five minutes to decide."

Arthur and Alden were silent, but Harley yielded, whereat the crowd cheered lustily, and Zeke announced:

" Only three minutes to decide."

"Good Heavens! Alden," said Harley, " you fellows are foolhardy. How can you expect to stand up against this mob? Give in now, and then protest against the whole thing afterward."

" Never!" said Alden firmly.

"Never," said Arthur, " will I willingly see the ballot box degraded!"

" Two minutes more in which to decide," said Zeke, pompously.

There was a dead silence in the room, save for the beating hearts which measured time, the ticking of the watch, and the occasional clicking of a pistol as it was cocked and deliberately aimed at their heads. Harley sat in despair, looking from his friends to the resolute face of Zeke, and then toward his creatures, upon whose countenances no lineaments of compassion stood revealed in the broad sunshine which came through the open door and window. All at once, a bright inspiration seized him. An involuntary smile spread over his face, and just as Zeke announced, "One minute more to decide," he seized the ballot box, and sprang toward the door, the movement of a single man having left the pathway clear, and suggested the idea. He swung the box over his head, and shouted: "Hurrah for Missoury." Involuntarily the crowd followed him, and attention was thus directed from the others for a moment, during which Long Sile picked Alden up in his powerful arms as if he had been a child, and depositing him outside in the midst of a circle of his own friends, ejaculated; "T-t-t-take this hyer f-feller home."

Arthur being thus left behind, grasped the poll books and some papers which lay on the table, putting the former under his coat, and with the latter in his hands, started for the door, followed by Zeke, who snatched the papers from him, allowing him to pass out. Anxious to retain the books, Arthur made for the creek near which the horses were tied; but Zeke had already discovered that the papers were valueless, and that the poll books were gone, and went tearing after him, followed by twenty or thirty of his men, all swearing in chorus. Of course they overtook and overpowered him, carrying back the books in triumph, and re-opening the polls. Harley consented to act with judges of their own selection, who received their votes without the unnecessary formality of an oath, thus electing Silas Hardiker, by a majority of three hundred and eighty pro-slavery votes, against twenty Free State votes cast for Edward Langtry, the latter being the number cast early in the morning, no Free State men being allowed even to approach the window, after they had taken possession.

In justice to Harley, it must be stated that he refused to sign the returns, until the words, "By lawful resident voters," were stricken out, which was done, and the returns made in that way.

Immediately after their ejection, the Free State men began to return to their homes. There was nothing to be gained by remaining. Eighty against three hundred and eighty was by far too much odds, even if they had been inclined to retake by violence, their position. Indignant and sore at heart, they went their ways by twos and threes, leaving Langtry and Alden alone upon the grounds, determined to be the last to depart.

They were walking slowly toward their horses, discussing the form of protest which they had determined to file within the four days' time allotted, when suddenly they became aware that their troubles were not over. A party of Missourians came yelping and hallooing after them, shouting that they were wanted at the polls. Unhesitatingly they turned to retrace their steps, thinking, perhaps, they had determined on some show of fairness, but no sooner had they reached the ground in front of the polls, than Langtry was suddenly seized by several strong men, one of whom was Major Jenkins, forcibly disarmed and placed upon a wagon which stood near, and with pistols pointing at him from all directions, commanded to make a speech.

"Make a speech, ye spalpeen!" called out Pat Malone, and the whole crowd, who had by this time taken considerable "spirits" on board, and were just in the mood for "a little fun," joined in the cry.

Seemingly nothing abashed, Langtry looked calmly about him, saying:

"I perceive that I am between Scylla and Charybdis."

"Hold on thar! don't call no names," shouted several voices.

"If I will not speak, I am threatened with death, and if I do speak, and give you my honest sentiments, you will certainly kill me. Is this America? Am I beneath the stars and stripes? but," pausing a moment, "I will speak, and I will tell you plainly, that you have this day lighted the torch which shall explode the mine beneath your feet. 'Whom the gods would destroy, they first make mad.' For long, long years, the voices of three million patient bondsmen have pleaded for deliverance, but the recital of their woes has fallen upon ears that would not hear. Men's eyes were closed that they might not see, but at last! at last! in your mad zeal you have struck a blow at the most sacred right of citizens of the Republic. You have violated the law and polluted the ballot box. To the measureless oppressions heaped upon the bowed head of the black, you have added invasion and overthrow of the constitutional rights of the white man, and I warn you that the tempest of his wrath shall cease not till we have become a homogeneous nation, till the clanking of the chains of no slave shall—" At this point Major Jenkins was no longer able to contain himself, and called out:

"Hang the d——d nigger stealer," and in a moment the passions of the border ruffians were all aflame.

"Cut his throat!" "Tear his heart out!" "Pull him to pieces!" "Shootin's too good for him," resounded from side to side. "Bring on your hemp," and dragging him from the wagon they moved toward the timber, the latter suggestion seeming to suit their fancy. But before this murderous design could be carried out, Roderick Delaney was seen galloping toward them.

"What does this mean?" demanded he. "What has this man done, that you thus menace him?"

There was authority in his tone before which they fell back in silence, and he repeated his question: "Of what is this man guilty?"

"Flung his d——d abolitionist sentiments in our teeth!" cried a number of assailants.

"Stole my niggers," said Jenkins.

Langtry turned and looked him full in the face, his own face white, and his teeth set with wrath, as he asserted positively:

"That's a lie!"

"No man mouths those words to me and lives," and the Major's pistol was aimed at Langtry's heart.

He stood within six feet of him, and a moment more would have been his last, but Roderick Delaney, with a quick motion sent the pistol flying beyond the crowd, and the bullet was discharged in the air, then turning to the assembly, who watched his every move intently, doggedly, but without daring to oppose him, he said:

"If I read correctly the orders of the right worthy president of the Blue Lodge, they were to take possession of the polls and vote for the candidate selected, avoiding all conflict. There must be no bloodshed. Release the man."

Instantly they released their hold on Langtry, and turned away, Jenkins muttering to himself of vengeance,—the others resorting to the consolatory influences of the jug.

Langtry thanked Roderick for this interference in his behalf, but the latter waved his hand lightly, saying: "I did but carry out my orders," then turning to Alden, he said:

"Mr. Alden, I hope you will believe me when I say that I do not approve of this sort of thing," and Langtry and Alden mounted their horses which were near, and turned their heads toward home. He joined them, continuing:

"I am in favor of straining every nerve to beat you honestly and fairly."

"And do you call this fair play," said Alden, "bringing men from another State to take possession of the polls and drive away legal voters?"

"I must say that I cannot fully justify it, and yet many of our leading men do, on the ground that it is impossible for us to bring in actual settlers as fast as you can, and we must therefore send in these fellows, as a sort of advance-guard to hold the country until they can come up, and to make such laws as shall protect their property when it is brought in.

"Why," said he, continuing, " to the Northwestern farmer it is a small matter to put his household goods and family into a wagon, and migrate westward in search of broader fields and richer harvests. The annual flow of this stream of immigration has been estimated at from two thousand to three thousand souls. To the Southerner, on the other hand, immigration means slow steps, attended with great expense in the removal of cumbersome machinery and a stock of slaves, and the introduction of a system ill adapted to the necessities of a new settlement."

"And why, then, make such an effort to introduce the institution into this Territory, for which it is so poorly fitted, and which was once held sacred to free institutions?"

"I will tell you," said he, "and I will tell you also, why you Northerners had better give it up peaceably, and retire to Nebraska."

Langtry had hitherto taken no part in the conversation, lagging behind a little, and listening in silence; but he now came up beside them, and said rather scornfully:

"Humph, indeed! and why? Please enlighten us."

"As to the first," said Roderick, quite unmindful of Langtry's tone, "it is a political as well as a national necessity. We must extend our territory that we may keep pace with the North in representation, and maintain our status in the general government. Then we must find in the newly-settled Territories a market for our slaves, which are increasing in numbers every year. Missouri alone has fifty thousand in that portion of her territory nearest Kansas. By estimating the average value of those slaves at six hundred dollars each, a very low figure, we have a sum total of thirty millions; a pretty little sum worth looking after. Now, should Kansas become a free State, it would be simply ruinous to the slave-holding interest of Missouri. The negroes have already, in numerous instances, been tampered with, and run off by

Abolitionists in the Territory; and such acts, with the stern retaliation which they must necessarily call forth, are calculated to produce a deadly feud between the Free State and pro-slave sections, which will deluge the land with blood, and perhaps rend the Union itself."

"And I tell you," said Langtry solemnly, "that this nation cannot pause in the presence of this great moral question, which is being pressed upon her for decision, to consult her safety. Safety never lies in the path of injustice. Justice, and not safety, should be the end of government. You of the South are impotent to turn back the advancing tide of civilization. It has swept on north of you, and west of you, prevented only by the barriers raised by the Constitution of the United States from rushing in upon you. And I tell you that, on the day when your rash hands shall tear down that bulwark, a tumultuous wave of freedom shall bear down upon the South, and carry off upon its triumphant crest every fetter. The spirit of freedom is in the air, it is around and above you, while beneath is a slumbering volcano, in which is treasured up the seething wrath generated by long years of oppression and wrong, and which ere long, will turn its fury upon the South, and scatter its social fabric to the four winds of heaven. A strict espionage over, and systematic repression of, the slave at present, subdues every appearance of insubordination."

"Oh, you mistake us entirely. Our slaves are our best friends. They are happy and comfortable, with plenty to eat, and no care for the future. Now, my man Cæsar was asked a short time ago, by a meddlesome Free State man, if he did not wish to be free, and his answer was, "Why, de Lord bless you, massa, no. Slavery might be bad for white man, but it's good enough for niggas."

"You were present at the time?"

"Yes."

"And other pro-slavery friends?"

"Yes; a half dozen of us, and we got the laugh on the meddlesome Northerner."

"But your negro's testimony was worth just nothing at all. Do you suppose he would have dared speak the truth before you, his master, when experience had taught him that the master is stern, strong, and relentless,—that the punishment for insubordination, however slight, is cruel and barbarous, extending at times even to the taking of life?"

"Do you mean to insinuate, sir, that I am an inhuman and barbarous master?" said Roderick, with the Southern fire in his eye.

"I insinuate nothing personal," said the other. "It is of the system I complain. That system which has induced in the negro the broken submission of despair, and in the white race a domineering spirit, a proneness to violence, and a distrust or habitual forgetfulness of law, and of civilized customs under exciting circumstances."

"You are hard upon us, Mr.—?"

"Langtry," suggested John, remembering that the young Southerner had not yet learned the name of the man whose life he had saved, and who continued: "And herein lies the danger in the conflict that must ensue. We, of the North, are a law-abiding people, and we have great respect for the sacredness of human life. We shall never be the aggressors, but we hold in reserve the right of self-defence, only to be exercised in the supreme moment when it shall be necessary to preserve our lives and property from destruction."

At this point in the discussion Langtry was obliged to turn off in the direction of his own home, and it was well, for both were becoming more excited every moment, and it would have been a difficult matter for them to preserve much longer the appearance of calmness.

As he disappeared in the distance, Roderick turned to John Alden with a smile.

"I have not yet inquired after the health of Mrs. Alden and your daughter?"

"They are both quite well, and would no doubt be happy to have a call from you."

"I was about to ask your permission to call; I have many messages from my sister for them;" then, as a turn of the road brought them in sight of the house: "I must confess that the claim of a Northern man may be recognized at a glance by its neat surroundings. I hope the example will incite some of our poor fellows to do likewise. Believe me, I had a philanthropic, as well as a selfish, design at heart when I induced the men of my colony to come here. In the South there was no hope for them; land was high and labor degrading, but by coming here, at least they can have what they call a 'white man's chance.'"

"And yet you would have them vote to inflict the same degrading system on this new Territory, and thus rob themselves of that chance?"

He put out his hand deprecatingly: "No more argument just now please, Mr. Alden," and they rode in silence to the cabin door.

CHAPTER XVIII.

RODERICK AT THE CABIN—POLITICAL GATHERING—AGNES AND AMY.

Under other circumstances John Alden would not have given Roderick Delaney an invitation to his home—loyalty to Arthur and his intense interest in Arthur's suit with Grace forbade a warm reception to one who might prove a dangerous rival, even had he not conceived a prejudice against the young man on account of his Southern birth. He knew that letters had been exchanged between Grace and Mabel Delaney, and that Amy expected Mr. Delaney would call when business brought him to Charleston, but it was exceedingly distasteful to John that the visit should be made on his own invitation. But the young man's gallant conduct of the morning toward his friend Langtry called for at least politeness in return, so John yielded gracefully to the inevitable. He threw open the cabin-door, and then paused, to allow his guest to enter first. Amy was near the open fireplace, intent on the preparation of dinner. She wore a large gingham apron over her dark dress, and her face was somewhat flushed with the heat, and yet she came forward immediately, while no shadow of false shame at her appearance or occupation dimmed the hospitable smile with which she greeted her guest, graciously extending the hand of welcome. She did not hesitate, either, to express her joy at her husband's safe return, while Grace and Arthur were exchanging courtesies with the visitor.

The latter had gone directly home after his discomfiture at

the polls, and Grace had beguiled him into a game of chess, in which they had become quite absorbed. On Alden and Delaney's sudden entrance, rising simultaneously, the chessboard, which they had held upon their knees, fell to the floor, and the kings and the queens, the knights and the castles, as in many a game of life thus suddenly ended, lay ingloriously mingled with the pawns. A flush of pleasure rose to the cheek of Grace Alden, and a happy light was in her eye, as she extended the hand of welcome. But Arthur's face, and John Alden had learned to read it well, reflected all the annoyance he himself had felt, and there was a peculiar dryness in the tones of his voice as he replied to the familiar salutation of the young Southerner.

There was a striking contrast in the personal appearance and manners of these two young men—each a fair type of the ideas, as well as the personnel, of the section of country which he represented. The one, fair-haired, blue-eyed, with earnestness and devotion to principle visible in every lineament of his countenance, and energy, as well as grace, in every motion of his slight, active form; the other, deliberate of movement, as one for whom time waited, impulsive and pleasure-loving, yet capable of being roused to depths of feeling, but, as yet, carefully choosing the smooth walks of life and lingering in its pleasant vales—dark-eyed and ravenhaired—a genial smile upon his handsome face, and an easy dignity in the carriage of his tall, well-developed form.

He gave Grace a note from his sister, which she received with evident pleasure, and asked permission to read immediately.

Mrs. Alden had taken Mr. Delaney's hat, and John had brought him a chair, and then inquiries were in order concerning his sister, and all smiled to hear that the young lady liked her new home better than did Dinah, her negro maid, the latter pronouncing the invigorating Kansas breezes " powerful strong," and singing:

"Carry me back to Ole Virginny," with the pathos of true feeling. Then, of course, Roderick wanted to know if Amy and Grace were homesick.

"No, indeed," replied Amy, "that would be impossible; we brought home with us."

"I should certainly say you had, Madam," said Roderick, politely, taking in with a comprehensive glance all the various evidences of taste and culture which gave a homelike appearance to the rudely-constructed, limited apartment.

"Oh, you misunderstood me," said Amy, apologetically, "I meant the fact that we are a united household, and that we brought the determination to be content. 'Home is where the heart is,' you know."

"And both were necessary to the result which we see before us," was the graceful reply.

Grace here looked up from her note to say that so far she had not yet exhausted the novelties and varieties of the situation. Perhaps when they began to be an old story, she, too, might long to be carried back to old scenes and friends.

"Never fear, my daughter," said her father, "in a country filling up so rapidly with young men as this is, and with such vast capabilities of development, you will always find new subjects of interest."

"Now, papa!" said she blushing, "you are too bad. You know I do not care for—for—"

"Flirting," said John; "not a bit of it."

"Dinner has been waiting for you a long time," interposed Amy, "and if you excuse me a few moments it shall be served at once."

The table, which stood in the center of the room, was already dressed with snowy cloth and necessary china and silver, and soon an extra plate was placed for the guest, the substantial food transferred from its place before the fire to the table, and all sat down to partake.

Arthur said little; he was full of the events of the morning, and could not at once throw off his feelings and enter into the lighter themes to which Mr. Delaney steered the conversation, avoiding with dexterous skill the slightest allusion to anything which could possibly bring up the great question in dispute between them. He was an interesting talker and could give a tone, even to remarks on the weather, and the climate and soil of Kansas, calculated to bring a smile to one's face, provoking a retort whose wit surprised even the one who uttered it, and drawing out some latent thought which needed this vivifying power to bring it to life.

Grace thought Kansas sunsets were magnificent, and Roderick had seen no fairer sight in foreign climes, nor limned by the old masters' hands, than nature pictured for the dwellers on the prairie, on many a summer eve, "when," said he, "the sky becomes a deep, dark, unfathomable blue, and the pillared clouds a mass of crimson and purple, fringed with gold, are moving gently hither and thither, dividing and subdividing into flakes of many brilliant hues, then modulating slowly into tints of unspeakable softness, where, above the bare bluffs, the horizon becomes a line of flame, gradually fading out as the sun descends, and stars one by one come out in the firmament, and day has faded into night."

"There is for me more beauty in a noble human action, than in any combination of material things," said Arthur.

"Is there not an intimate connection between the two?" asked Amy, "and does not what is common to them both, their perfectness and harmony with the divinest aspirations of the soul, constitute their beauty?"

"True, and the embodiment of both is the highest degree of art," said Roderick, and then he described some of the statues, and pictures, and noticeable features of the beautiful architecture which he had seen in lands beyond the sea, intermingling little sketches of personal adventure which called forth the "chorus of conversation," a hearty laugh. And ere long Alden found himself telling a laughable story of the mining camp, which had almost slipped his mind, and in response to hearty encores, another, and another.

"Why, papa," cried Grace, "you should have told us all these things before. I supposed you experienced nothing but trouble, and hardship and sickness in California—"

"My dear," said John, "there is no sky so dark but that in it there are some bright spots; all you want is to look through a lens of sufficient magnifying power to disclose them."

It was surprising what a variety of topics they skimmed over in so short a time, very skillfully and resolutely avoiding the subject of slavery. Sometimes it seemed from the course the conversation was taking, that the next plunge would be upon that rock, but somehow the pilot gracefully and gently gave it a turn just at the point of danger, and they went sailing off again into the blue seas and sparkling waters of general topics and personal experiences. By the time the meal was over and they had risen from the table, Alden was in quite a genial frame of mind. For the time, the fact that his guest was a Southerner, and that he had not desired his presence, had faded from his thoughts, and he gave himself up unreservedly to the charm of Roderick's society.

As they rose, Delaney drew out a cigar case and proposed that they should seek some place outside and indulge in a little smoke. Of course that suited John, but Arthur declined—he did not smoke—and he was going down to Warsaw to learn how the election was passing off there.

Amy begged him to give up the idea, lest he should incur some danger, and turned to Grace to add her solicitations, but Grace had stepped to the book-shelf with Roderick, and they were intently examining a plate in a book of engravings, and she did not hear. Arthur had seen the motion and his eye rested for a moment on the pair, then laughing at the idea of danger, he departed.

Alden led the way to a seat outside, on the east of the cabin, where they could be shaded from the rays of the declining sun, and here with the broad, undulating prairie stretching to the right and left of them, and beyond the cabin the waving line of the little creek, marked by the timber with its foliage of tender green, separating them from the scenes of the morning, their radical feelings toned down by a sense of good fellowship and the soothing influences of the fragrant wreaths of smoke, they allowed themselves to drift gradually into the absorbing topic of the day.

Alden found his companion disposed to be reasonable, and yet he was unwilling to concede that the North was all right, and the South all wrong.

"Why," said he, "your anti-slavery orators who are rousing the North to a state of virtuous indignation against the sins of the South, look only at this question from a sentimental and emotional standpoint. They refuse to see, or at least they will not acknowledge the fact, that American slavery has done more toward the civilization of the negro, than all other agencies combined.

"That system is not surely all bad which in one or two centuries has transformed so many naked savages, upon whose liberty, when brought to our shores, clothing was an infringement, industry an outrage, and to whom marriage and the family relations were unknown, into a race of orderly, industrious people. Why, it was a heaven-born mercy to take the blacks of Congo or Ashantee from their pit of degradation and drive them into the cotton field, and teach them the first lessons of civilization with the whip of Saxon industry.

"Compulsory industry was the best form of compulsory education for them, and the only form, and yet you Northerners persist in ignoring all this, and regarding the slavery of the Southern States, as if it were a degradation of men otherwise equal, like your own white laborers, instead of being an elevation into industrial men and women, of creatures hitherto incapable of civilization."

All this John Alden acknowledged, and thought it a pity there were not leaders on both sides who could take a passionless view of this great subject.

"For," said he, "if the North is blind to the great advantage which slavery has conferred upon the subject race, the South is equally regardless, that having been a good thing in its day, is no reason why it should be extended indefinitely, and continued interminably; that, having inculcated the beneficence of the family relation, and awakened the tenderest of ties in the breast of the descendants of the imported negro, it is an outrage in pursuance of selfish interests, to ignore those feelings in the ruthless severance of family ties; and that, having fitted the race for freedom, and received the benefits of their labor during the years of tutelage, it is inexcusable, and indeed, inexpedient for the white race to continue him in that condition, when the humanitarian idea has given place entirely to selfish purposes."

"Oh, it's too soon! too soon by a century or two," said the young Southerner, giving a vigorous puff at his cigar, and running his hand through the locks of his long black hair. "Take off the shackles, remove the lash, and the negro will lapse back into savagery, forgetting all the lessons learned, just as the child does the letters of the alphabet, if allowed to stop the repetition of them, before they have become firmly fixed by repeated indurations upon the brain."

Any reply to this was prevented by the coming of the ladies, who now joined them with fancy work in hand, Gracie saying as they seated themselves:

"We've finished our prose lesson," meaning thereby that

the dinner table was cleared, and the dishes washed, "and have come out here for a little poetry."

"And is this the book you mean to read it from?" said Delaney, unrolling a mass of worsteds of various colors which had fallen to the ground beside her.

"Nay! they are but the cabalistic signs by which I shall hereafter call up the lines I read to-day. My book shall be the sky, the distant trees, the grass, the low wind's whisper, and you and papa."

"Oh, pray don't class me as poetry!" exclaimed John. "I am the very plainest and dryest of prose, a theological treatise, or something of that kind."

She laughed. "I won't open your pages then, but mamma will, and turning to Roderick: "What are you? I can't quite make out the letters on your title page. They are in a foreign language, I fancy."

"No, only good old English. I am a book of quotations." And as all smiled, "That's a fact, there's positively nothing original within my pages."

"Nothing? Are you sure?" looking at him archly; and as he nodded affirmation, "Pray, then, Sir Quotation Book, what have you to say on truth?"

> "Truth needs no color, with his color fixed,
> Beauty no pencil. Beauty's truth to lay."
> —*Shakespeare.*

was the ready reply.

"Hope?" said she, questioningly.

> "Hope is a lover's staff; I'll hence with that
> And manage it against despairing thoughts."
> —*Shakespeare.*

This he repeated with an earnest look which brought the blood surging to her face, and Amy took up the role of questioner:

"Now I'll ask for one on happiness."

"And I will give you a good old familiar one from Burns," said he with a smile and then repeated, with a good Scotch brogue—

> "It's nae in books, it's nae in lear,
>   To make us truly blest;
> If happiness has not her seat
>   And center in the breast,
> We may be wise, or rich, or great,
>   But never can be blest."

Thus they continued, for an hour or more, with this variation, that occasionally each of the others volunteered some remembered scrap, and when the sun was setting, Grace declared she had a sentiment for every square inch of her crochet-work, netted well into the web of memory.

By this time the sun had entirely disappeared, the short twilight was deepening into night, Delaney was taking his leave, and Mr. and Mrs. Langtry were seen approaching. Before Grace had finished the numerous and weighty messages which Roderick was to bear to Miss Mabel, the Langtrys were beside them. The gentlemen exchanged very civil bows, Mrs. Alden introduced Mr. Delaney to Mrs. Langtry, and she thanked him in her sweetest manner, for his interposition in behalf of her husband in the morning.

He turned it off hastily, saying it was nothing, nothing at all; and to Amy, " I have had a very pleasant afternoon;" to all, " Adieu," and was gone.

"Well," said John, turning to Langtry, "how do you feel by this time?"

"First rate," was the reply.

"Indeed! you do look pretty well for a defeated candidate."

"Not defeated yet, by a long shot," smiling.

"How do you make that out?"

"Easy enough. Do you suppose this election will hold

good? Of course not; we will enter a protest. The Governor will order a new election, and the United States troops will be sent to protect us in the exercise of our franchise."

"Don't be too sure of that. I will admit it is what would be done in any State north of Mason and Dixon's line; but you are out of the region of safe political predictions. You are launched on a sea of uncertainties, where even the compass of law is perverted, and no longer points with unerring directness to the polar star of justice. The Executive of the United States is with the slave power. The Governor will never be able to get control of the troops for our protection, even if he have backbone enough to order a new election."

"Well, we shall see; at any rate, they have done a good day's work in the cause of the emancipation of the slaves, and in the end we shall triumph, be the contest long or short. Let it come as they elect, gently as the summer breeze, or in the whirlwind of strife and passion and bloodshed."

One by one the members of the "Association" then dropped in for consultation, and helped themselves to seats. Our squatter sovereign had found it necessary to keep a pile of boards for use at these meetings, and they were laid upon logs placed at convenient distances, to serve as supports. The grounds soon presented somewhat of the appearance of a camp-meeting, with this difference, the attitudes assumed were not those of stiff-backed, puritanical election, nor yet of penitential devotion, but each man disposed of his limbs unrestrainedly in any or all directions most conducive to ease. Then, too, there was a liberal sprinkling of pipes throughout the assembly, and the air was redolent of tobacco fumes, nothing worse, except in rare cases.

A glance at the men was sufficient to decide which of them had families in the Territory. There was a well-dressed, well-fed look about those for whose welfare women cared, which plainly distinguished them from the flannel-shirted, collarless, forlorn-looking fellows who "bached."

Many and loud were the protestations of indignation at the events of the morning, each having " nursed his wrath to keep it warm." All were anxious to know what was to be done, and looked to Langtry and Alden for directions. Arthur's return from Warsaw was the signal for opening the meeting in due form, and as John Alden called the meeting to order, the talking, which had been carried on in little groups of three or four, suddenly ceased; and all listened attentively to his review of the events of the morning, and there was many a flashing eye and impatient gesture as he told of the indignities to which Langtry had been subjected. Then he called upon Arthur for a report from Warsaw, and the young man arose, stating that affairs had been managed in Warsaw much the same as at Walnut Grove. That the one thousand men who passed on beyond Calhoun on the day before the election, had camped that night over in the ravine north of the town. That they were well armed and supplied with two pieces of artillery—that they wore a badge of white ribbon, and brought election tickets which had been printed in Missouri —that they insisted upon voting without taking the oath as to residence; that they formed two long lines of guards in front of the polls, through which voters were marched up in single file, and then, as it was impossible for them to return the same way, an opening was made in the roof of the building, and voters passed out through and from the roof to the ground by means of ladders. That the leader, a Col. Ohmer, from Missouri, requested that the old men be allowed to vote first, as they were weary and anxious to get back to camp. And, most humiliating of all, that the representative for whom these perambulating voters had cast their ballots, was a semi-simpleton from Missouri, unable to articulate distinctly, whom they had picked up and used for the express purpose of deriding and humiliating the people of that Free State stronghold.

He stated, also, that numerous citizens of Warsaw had been driven off the grounds during the day, but that a number had been allowed to vote late in the afternoon, when most of the Missourians had returned to camp, but their votes numbered only two hundred and fifty-three, while the illegal votes cast amounted to eight hundred and two.

"And what do they propose to do about it?" was the question, as Arthur sat down after this recital.

He rose again to say that, "as far as he could learn, no definite plan had been determined upon, but that the general opinion was that the only course to be pursued was to protest within the four days allotted by the Governor for that purpose, and also to memorialize Congress on the subject."

Several exciting and eloquent speeches followed, and then a protest was written, affidavits made out and signed, and Arthur Fairchild appointed to present them to His Excellency the Governor. Soon after the Association adjourned, to assemble again at the call of the President.

Meanwhile, Agnes Langtry and Amy, who had retired to the house as the evening advanced, and the meeting outside assumed a political character, were making reports, comparing progress, and discussing methods on equally important subjects.

Agnes' white hen had hatched out ten dear little chickens, the first of the season, and it was so interesting to watch the fond mother strutting about surrounded by her little brood, and to hear her cluck! cluck! when she had scratched up some particularly delicate morsel of a worm.

Amy had two hens, the brown one with the black topknot, and the grey and white speckled one, which she expected to come off within a week. What should she feed the young chickens? Agnes thought corn-meal and water was the best, they didn't need much of anything for a day or two. How many eggs did Amy get a day? Only six, so many of the hens were determined to sit, and the family had used the eggs so there were none to give them; how to break them up she did not know, and then the perverse creatures all had such a fondness for the tender leaves of lettuce, just peeping above the ground.

Agnes said her chickens troubled the garden, too, but now that the election was over, perhaps she could get a place fenced off for them. She did not like to keep them shut up all day in a small coop, it seemed so cruel.

"So it is," said Amy, "and then they wouldn't lay if you did, and what should we do without eggs; they are our staple delicacy?"

"We care more for milk, but you can't imagine how dreadful it was to be without either, as we were when we first came to the Territory. What luck did you have with your bread?"

"Not first-rate; and we had Mr. Delaney here for dinner. I don't believe that yeast is good; or, perhaps, it is the flour that is poor. I'm sure I spared no pains in the making."

"What a fine-looking fellow Mr. Delaney is. I always did admire black eyes. Did you knead it up twice, and keep it warm?"

"Of course I did. I always keep my sponge warm. But do you like black eyes? I'm sure I prefer blue and true ones, like Arthur's. Are your flower seeds coming up?"

"Oh, yes; I meant to show them to you, when you were over yesterday; but you must come again to-morrow, and then I will give you a new recipe for pioneer cake. Only takes one egg, and you can make it of corn-meal when you are out of flour. Does Mr. Delaney live over in Charleston?"

"Oh, no; he only comes there occasionally, to look after the welfare of the colony from South Carolina. His home is in Lauderdale, but he is traveling most of the time. Do you use fruit in that cake?"

"Why, yes. I thought I told you I put in dried apples," and then Agnes told Amy of a poor family whom she had visited during the day where the mother was sick, and her three little children suffering for the want of care, while the discouraged father was endeavoring to bear up bravely under his heavy load of out-door work and in-door trouble.

In health it is easy to battle bravely with the ills of life, but many a one broken down completely under exposure, resulting from carelessness or ignorance of the necessary precautions to preserve health, had cause to thank Agnes Langtry and Amy Alden. It required just such cheerful, hopeful spirits as theirs to inspire the dispirited with courage to rise again; and also just such ingenuity and originality as that displayed in evolving fruit-cake from such unpromising materials as dried apples and corn-meal, to give variety to the daily food which supplied the force necessary to subdue and harmonize the discordant elements in this new environment.

John Alden was quite wakeful on this particular night, and his uneasiness was caused not alone by the existing political events of the morning, but by the book he had seen Grace reading in the evening, a new one, a book of poems, and by the delicate flush on her cheek and the light which he had seen in her eye when listening to Roderick Delaney.

He was not selfish enough to desire to carry out his own plans regardless of her feelings, but it did seem to him, as perhaps our own cherished plans seem to us all, that the path in life which his fancy had marked out for her, as the wife of Arthur Fairchild, was the one which led over the uplands, by shady paths and sunshiny dells. Of similar habits and tastes, there would be no wide divergence of inclinations and desires.

With means sufficient to make a fair beginning in life—with a home already chosen near her parents, what more could be desired? And, resolving that, while he could not stem the current, he would still use every means in his power to guide its course in consonance with his own wishes, he fell asleep.

CHAPTER XIX.

THE GOVERNOR'S MANSION—ARTHUR'S MISSION—THE PROPOSAL.

Arthur returned from his mission of protest in two days, with his ideas of the dignity of the gubernatorial office in the Territory somewhat modified, while his respect for the incumbent was materially increased.

"Now where," said he, "do you think I found the Governor of Kansas holding his official receptions?"

"In a seven-by-nine cabin," said Amy.

"On the open prairie, with the blue sky for a canopy," suggested Grace.

"Not quite so bad as that; but I found him occupying a room twenty feet square, in a rickety frame building, with an ill-hung door, through which the Kansas zephyrs play unceasingly. It has one window in the south, and two in the north, over which hang cheap tawdry chintz curtains, vexing the eye with their limp, colorless folds. A double curled maple poster, of ancient style, stands in one corner, on whose mattress of hay, covered with blue Mackinac blankets, the weary head, vexed with the cares of state, seeks repose, peacefully slumbering side by side, and snoring in concert with his private secretary, who shares his bed and board. A wash-stand that a fashionable Biddy would reject with scorn, furnished with a tin wash-basin and pitcher with broken mouth, stands opposite the bed; and above it hangs a deceitful looking-glass, sole ornament of the dilapidated walls, whose dust-begrimed surface reflected back such a conglomeration of ill-assorted features that I turned away in haste, lest suicidal intentions be developed there and then. In the center of the room stands a large table, whose blue Mackinac covering is in harmony with the bedspread, and this was literally covered with piles of public documents, newspapers, and writing material. A huge pile of law books lay on the uncarpeted floor, and, with a gallon of ink, the public documents aforesaid, and the Territorial seal—which occupied a conspicuous position—was all that reminded one of the power vested in the occupant of this primitive-looking apartment."

"Well, I should say," exclaimed Grace, "that His Excellency is the most *Democratic* Governor in the United States."

A laugh followed this pun, and then Arthur continued:

"But this is by no means the worst of it. There is such a pressure brought to bear upon the Governor by the slave power, acting through the national executive, that between this and his desire to act fairly by the Free State men he is bound to be crushed as between the upper and nether millstones."

"And what did he do with your protest?" was Alden's inquiry.

"Received it, of course; declared the acts of the Missouri invaders a base outrage on the rights of American citizens, and has ordered a new election to take place on the twenty-first of May, and in consequence, has incurred the deadly hatred of the pro-slavery party, who declare boldly, 'This infernal scoundrel will have to be hemped yet.'"

Before the March election the pro-slavery men had been suspicious of Governor Reeves, and feared that, weighed in the scales of pro-slavery propagandism, he would be found wanting; and now that he refused certificates of election to those whose seats had been contested, and ordered new elections in those districts, they declared open war against him. Their first move was to send a delegation of their leading men to try the virtues of persuasion, backed by threats, to induce him to disregard his own orders, and grant certificates of election to the victorious candidates of March 30. But persuasion and threats alike failed. The Governor was firm—he was determined to do impartial justice, so far as the power within him lay. Then they called a public meeting at the Shawnee Mission, and passed resolutions to this effect:

Resolved, That the right to order a new election, except in the case of a tie, or of a death or resignation, is not vested in the Governor by the organic act, and that consequently his order for a new election on the 21st of May, is null and void.

Resolved, That the Legislature itself upon organization must decide cases of contested election—that the pro-slavery men have elected a large majority of the members of that body, and therefore the interests of their party are safe, and all law-abiding citizens are requested not to attend the elections ordered, but to rely on the returns already made to sustain the claims of those whom they have chosen to represent them.

Copies of these resolutions were circulated in every district in the Territory, and, of course, conveyed to the political societies in Missouri, under whose orders the rank and file held themselves; and, when the 21st of May arrived, Langtry found himself elected to a seat in the House by the ninety Free State votes of his precinct, now increased to something over a hundred, but with the certainty of a contest before him if he endeavored to take his place.

From this contest, however, he had no intention of shrinking. Possessed of the true spirit of the reformer, he was ready to contend against all odds—to treasure up the smallest gain obtained, at whatever cost—to fall back, if beaten, only to take breath and resume his sturdy strokes at the wrong which waked his wrath. All considerations of self were swallowed up in devotion to the cause to which his soul had sworn fealty. There was for him no rest, no ease of body or mind while three millions of patient human beings clanked the chains of slavery. Their pleading faces were ever in his sight, their groans of agony in his ears, and all the beauty, and ease, and wealth in the world could not have tempted him to desist; nor could opposition or danger, or the fear of death, deter him in his course.

As the disagreeable news came into Warsaw and Walnut Grove that the elections of March 30 all over the Territory had been carried in the same fraudulent manner, and that but six districts had been able to protest in consequence of the short time allotted, or of ignorance of the manner of procedure, or in consequence of threats and intimidation, and even actual violence, used in the border counties, indignation ran high.

By invitation, the settlers of all the surrounding country met in Warsaw for consultation and discussion. There was a difference of opinion on many points, as is usual in such cases, but to all it was plain that it was the determination of the Pro-Slavery party to force that institution upon them, whether they desired it or not, and that it was necessary to take measures to protect themselves in some way against these aggressions. While one party contended that violence must be met with violence, the other was in favor of simply defensive measures.

A memorial was prepared for the Congress of the United States, praying for relief, and asking that a commission be appointed to investigate the election frauds. And it was also determined that, as the whole thing was a violent usurpation, no regard would be paid to any laws enacted by this Legislature, and that all its proceedings would be regarded as null and void.

Then, a gentleman from one of the cities on the Missouri River arose, and in a mild tone related the shameful proceedings of the ruffians on the border.

His voice grew tremulous; many of the audience were melted to tears, and others hardened to oaths, as he related the sufferings of a brave man in a city on the Missouri, who dared protest against the frauds of March 30. How he was torn from his family, and treated to a coat of tar and feathers; and of another, who, for the simple expression of his opinions, was set adrift on the Missouri River and forbidden to enter the Territory again; and how an editor on the Missouri border, in the town of Marksburg, for publishing, in very mild terms, his disapprobation of their proceedings, was subjected to insult and contumely, and would have been lynched upon the spot but for the interposition of his wife—a young and beautiful woman—who clung to him with such tenacity that they were forced to abandon their purpose, and content themselves with destroying his property—breaking up his press and throwing it into the Missouri River, and giving himself and family but a few hours to leave the place.

At this recital, excitement knew no bounds, and it was resolved that prudence required the Free State men to obtain arms, to form themselves into companies, and to drill, that they might defend their property and their lives. It was discovered that there was a sad lack of arms on the part of settlers from the North. Unaccustomed to decide difficulties or resent insults by the quick, sharp flash which admits of no appeal from its decisions, they were totally unprepared in this respect to cope with the frontiersman, who bristled with weapons from his belt to his boots; and it was thought advisable to send a committee to the East to obtain arms in as large quantities and on as favorable terms as possible, many of the best and bravest being unable to pay for them, unless allowed time.

Arthur Fairchild, having won the favorable notice of many, by a brilliant speech during the progress of the meeting, was elected a member of this committee, and furnished with credentials and instructions to many of the leading Abolitionists in Ohio, and other Northwestern States, while other gentlemen were sent on similar missions to the East.

The various settlements were instructed to form their own military companies for defense, elect their own officers, and then this convention adjourned.

Arthur was somewhat dazzled by the unexpected applause which had greeted his little speech.

But he had indeed spoken well, with all the enthusiasm of youth, with the fire in his eye which betokens a consciousness of strength to do battle, and an unwavering faith in the result. He could not foresee as did those further on in life, whom repeated failures, and half-won fields had tutored, the giants in the pathway, the sword suspended in air, the silken net of judicial chicanery, whose invisible web lay in wait to trip the feet of the unwary, the pitfalls of political delusion, the great shadow of fear which fell upon the land at the cry of disunion; nor yet the sorrow, the woe, the bloodshed, the destruction of the fairest and the best, which should come to both sides, ere the Gordian knot be cut, and the solution of the problem reached. Nay, his impulsive spirit leaped as did those of Langtry and many others, across the bloody chasm, and ranged the fair fields of universal freedom.

There was but one drawback to Arthur's elation at the appointment which had been given him. It was a great compliment indeed, to so young a man, to be selected for so important a mission, and one which a number coveted, and of course he appreciated that fact, and said so in appropriate words in acceptance of the trust. 'Tis true, in leaving at this time, he gave up all hopes of raising any crop, except the few acres of corn which he had put into the land broken by the Walnut Grove Association during his former absence. But having become possessed of the divine wrath of the reformer, the holy rage which crops up here and there, from time to time, in hearts which vibrate to the call of wronged humanity. —it was in the blood perhaps, descended as he was from old Puritan stock—there was naught for him, as for Langtry, but to put forth his hand to right the wrong which confronted him, at whatever cost.

But there was one obstacle in the way, one which an older man, or one less earnest in his nature would have brushed aside as trivial, of less account than the great cause which had engaged his services, of less account than that political distinction, the path to which this slight success had opened before him. But to Arthur Fairchild this other interest had grown with his growth, and was intertwined through every fiber of his being. It was his love for Grace, John Alden's daughter, she who seemed as unconscious of this deep devotion as of the air she breathed, so unobtrusive was it, so omnipresent, so pure.

With unexampled patience had he served and waited, determined not to imperil the happiness of his life by a hasty, importunate appeal; although it must have been unspeakably vexatious to give all and receive but a share of the smiles dispensed as graciously and as indiscriminately as the sun's rays upon all her attendant satellites. And then of late, he had noted what he feared most, a special interest awakened in another, that other a representative of the party against which himself and his friends were arrayed.

And the more he reflected, the more he felt sure, that he could not go single-hearted to his work, without at least an attempt to gain a word for his love to feed upon, a promise which would spur his faculties, released from this tension of uncertainty, to the utmost limits of their ability, and given which, he felt there was nothing on earth beyond his power to accomplish.

But a few days were allowed him to prepare for departure, and they were mostly spent in consultation with the Free

State leaders in Warsaw, that he might be able to represent the case understandingly, and state knowingly the intentions of his party for the future.

And each evening found a merry group assembled in Grace's court, on the south side of the cabin, to chat, to laugh, to sing, to linger in the moonlight, exchanging airy nothings which give a piquancy and zest to social intercourse, and he found no opportunity for the quiet and confidential talk for which he waited.

The last evening had come. The morrow would see him on his journey. He had been detained in Warsaw quite late, and returned to find visitors who lingered long. Who counts the hours when gentle breezes fan the brow, and silvery moonlight sparkles on the plain? when the dimly-defined outlines of hill and vale, of prairie, woods and stony bluff take on new shapes and hues of beauty?

But at last! at last they were gone, and Grace stood upon the doorstep, about to enter the house, when Arthur said:

"Grace! stay a moment, please, I have something to say to you.

"Grace," Arthur continued, as she turned toward him, "come and sit down here," placing her a chair in the moonlight, and one for himself near by, arranged so that he could look into her face. "You know that I leave in the morning and shall be gone more than a month."

"That is so! and you want any number of messages for those old time friends of ours," and then she ran on with a number of names, and some characteristic little speech of remembrance for each, to which he listened in silence, probably collecting his thoughts for the avowal which was to follow, for he did not seem to have heard, and at the conclusion of her chatter, said:

"Shall you miss me, Grace, when I am gone?"

"Why, what a question! Of course I shall; but I won't make a Niobe of myself, and dissolve away in tears."

Arthur got up hastily and walked away. The words and manner had cut him deeply, and years afterward they were to her a painful reminiscence. Even now, in a moment she realized that she had given him pain, and called out:

"There, Arthur, don't take what I say seriously. We have been jesting so much this evening that it seems impossible for me to get down to earnest conversation. Come back, please, and sit down, and let us have one more pleasant talk before you go." This with more feeling than she had yet displayed toward him, and of course he came, with his hand extended, and Grace laid hers within it, in token of reconciliation. She had risen, and as they stood there,'neath the silent sky, hand in hand, his earnest eyes looking into her beautiful face almost on a level with his own, had the love been mutual, had the deepest feelings of her nature responded to the surging passion which swayed his whole being, raging tumultuously beneath that calm exterior, maintained by the strongest effort of his will, a moment would have been sufficient for an understanding, a moment more, and the divinest joy vouchsafed to man would have swept over them as a flood-tide, leaving everlasting love and peace behind. But it was not so; one heart had struck the chords of love, the other vibrated but to friendship's tones.

"Then you do value my society a little?"

"Why, yes;" her penitential mood continuing, "a very great deal. I shall think of you every day. There, will that do, 'Sir Knight of the rueful countenance?'" and she looked up at him mischievously, withdrawing her hand, and seating herself again on the chair which he had at first placed for her.

"Now, let's talk of old times; I know you like that subject."

11

"I do, Grace; and why? Only because your image is interwoven with my earliest recollections. A smile from your brown eyes was sufficient reward for any achievement of my boyhood. To watch over you, to care for you, and to give you pleasure, has always been my first thought."

"I know it, Arthur. You have been very good to me, better than I deserve, for I fear I have often pained you, as to-night, with my light words. You are always so much in earnest."

"And never more than now, dear Grace, when I ask you to trust the happiness of your life with me. Give me the right to care for you, to protect you, and to love you always. Be my wife, Grace, my own dear, precious, loved and honored wife!"

She drew back in surprise.

"Oh, Arthur! Oh, my brother! this is sudden; this is unexpected. Let us be as we are! We are happy enough! Let us enjoy the present, and not seek to bind ourselves for the future."

He took a step or two from her, and then turned.

"Grace, I am already bound, hand and foot, with bands which have grown in strength with my stature. Every smile, every movement, every light word, every tear of yours, from the days of our childhood till now have but cemented those bonds, and they can be severed but with my life. Tell me," said he, coming back to her with quick step and vehement tone, "tell me, has a life-time of devotion no weight in the scale to offset a few flattering words from a fluent tongue, and the witchery of a pair of black eyes?"

Indignantly then she rose in her womanhood.

"What do you mean, Arthur Fairchild?" and she reached out her hand as if to put him from her, and turned toward the house; but he caught her in his arms and detained her, though she would not look at him.

"Oh, Grace! my little Grace! you cannot displace me from your heart thus easily. I know you cannot. Too often you have given your childish hands to my keeping. Too often have I borne you in my arms over the rough places in our way to school, as I fain would do now over the rough paths in life. Can you not see that you are all in all to me? Without you, there is no prize in the world worth gaining; and with you, there is no height to which I may not climb. Oh, Grace, I have longed for this hour, as the dungeoned prisoner longs for the sweet light of day. Oh, my playmate! my little love! Let me go again into my cell!—uncertainty was bliss compared to the darkness, the utter darkness, of this despair which has come upon me."

The agony of his tone melted her heart; she laid her head upon his shoulder, and her tears fell thick and fast.

"Oh, Arthur! My brother! I cannot make you thus unhappy. If I am indeed so dear to you; if my poor love is necessary to your happiness, to your life, it must be yours. Take it. Take me."

"Nay! nay! nay! nay!" and now the generous depths of his soul all stirred, he put her from him. He placed her gently on the chair.

"An empty chrysalis! A broken casket! I cannot accept the sacrifice. But," more cheerfully, "I will not take my answer now. You have fanned into flame the dying embers of hope—sweet pity is akin to love. I will wait! You must! Oh, you will come to me with love, and not pity in your tones."

He had seated himself beside her, and now she leaned forward and placed her hand on his.

"You are indeed a whole-souled, generous lover, Arthur, of whom any woman might be proud; but I—I am too light of thought—too frivolous, I fear. I am not capable of response to such deep affection."

"You are the sweetest, best, dearest, and fairest of women! I am not exacting, dear. I do not require measure for measure, but my wife must come to me of her own sweet will. I should be base, indeed, could I accept a promise drawn—almost forced—from you in a moment of excitement. You shall think of this in my absence; and remember, dear, a word, a look of encouragement from you on my return, will make me the happiest of men." He rose as he said this, came behind, and leaning over her chair, imprinted a kiss on her forehead.

"There, a brother's kiss; may the next one be a lover's."

For a long time the young girl sat there lost in thought, then rising, she passed slowly to her chamber.

The next morning they were both pale and silent at the breakfast table, and their eyes did not meet. Alden kept up a little conversation with Arthur on politics, which Amy interrupted occasionally with words of remembrance for old friends, and when the meal was over Amy and Grace bade him good-bye.

Mr. Alden was to drive down with Arthur to Warsaw, where, as on a former occasion, the latter meant to take the stage for Lauderdale.

On the way down Arthur confided to Alden much of the interview with Grace; and it was plain to be seen that, though not exultant, he was calmly hopeful and relieved in mind that the avowal so long contemplated had been made.

In fact, he could have chosen no better time for his appeal than on the eve of his absence. There were so many pleasant things they had shared in common, which, experienced afterward alone, she found had lost their flavor, and there were others which she must forego entirely in consequence of his absence.

Together they had explored the country for miles around;

there was not a mossy dell in the shade of the creek but they had learned its whereabouts—there was not a cave in its banks but they had traced its limits—or a bed of wild flowers, whether gorgeous in size and hue, or strange, shy, little, perfect blossoms of exquisite shape and delicate coloring, that they had not despoiled of its wealth to fill the vases in the house. There was not a cabin for miles around at which they had not called, and together they had driven to Warsaw to attend many social gatherings. Her parents had trusted Grace with Arthur as with a brother, and as they would not with a stranger. After his departure, as she could not drive out alone, and her father was very busy, she felt somewhat the constraint upon her freedom.

True, almost every evening was taken up by calls from one or more of the numerous young gentlemen who had made her acquaintance, and who were willing to ride a long way for the pleasure of a young lady's society, yet the homage of the many seemed to have lost its charm—the draught of red wine from a deeper still had dulled its flavor. My lady grew capricious. There were a number of aspirants for the position of prime minister in beauty's court, and they hesitated not to prefer their claims. But the standard was too high—one and all fell short of the requisites necessary. One was conceited, and talked too much of himself; another too reticent, seeming to avoid all mention of the past; another was too officious, and still another not attentive enough. One was too practical; another a dreamer; one sat on the edge of his chair and twirled his thumbs; another said, "Haeow" and "Naeow" and "Caeow," and so on, *ad infinitum;* till, last of all, though Grace would never allow him even to be numbered in the train, came Squire Hardiker, member-elect of the first Kansas Legislature, in a biled shirt and a pair of "store trousers," with boots, whose glossy surface betokened an awakening to the requirements of polite society,

SILE HARDIKER.

and an appreciation of the dignities to which their wearer had arrived.

He came at first in attendance upon his mother, whose anxiety to learn the " ways of quality " still continued, and whose volubility amused Grace so much that she encouraged her to frequent visits. She departed to Missouri soon, however, to make arrangements for building material to be transported to Calhoun for the erection of a house, which she declared should be " fit for a Squire and Member of the Legislater to live in." And she said when it was done she intended to bring over some of her " peartest niggers " to run the establishment, as by that time the Legislature would have rendered it safe for slaves to be brought in.

" I don't run no chances on my niggers," said she; " a nigger's worth a mighty nice little sum, and I don't keer to risk 'em."

After his mother's departure, Sile continued to make his appearance at Alden's cabin frequently, coming early in the evening and joining John as he was attending to the stock, sometimes lending a helping hand, and then sitting down for a friendly smoke. He seemed so good-natured and well-intentioned in his advances that Alden could not repulse him, especially after that occurrence of election morning. They could not suspect him of being a spy, as he invariably edged off when the Free Statesmen began to drop in, and found his way to the south side of the house, where he could look at Grace and fall heir to an occasional word or two which she graciously granted in return for the silent admiration which his eyes expressed.

Roderick Delaney did not come at this time; he, too, had gone off on some errand connected with the business of his party.

Had he come now, with his interesting conversation, his charming, deferential manner, and the novel sensations awakened by his presence, the result might have been different. The long days of Arthur's absence might have been bridged over with so fair a structure—suspended from such lofty towers—and with such bright, enticing views stretching far out into the future, that the past—the quiet past—with its sweet security, its loving dependence and confident trust, might never have been recalled—that longing for the unobtrusive, ever agreeable presence, which had, through constant association, become almost a part of herself, never have been awakened.

CHAPTER XX.

THE WIDOW—HER VISIT TO LAUDERDALE—A PRESENT
FOR GRACE—A FATHER'S ADVICE.

"Now, there comes Widow Hardiker, and I'm glad of it," said Grace, as the Aldens rose from the dinner-table one day near the end of June. A dinner-table whose *menu* no longer consisted of bacon and corn-bread solely, but which was now filled and running over with good things from the storehouse of nature, whose doors had opened wide at the first touch of the wand of labor.

There was sweet, crisp lettuce and tender radishes in scarlet coats, there were green peas, and beans, and beets, and onions, and potatoes, with dessert of wild gooseberries and plums, which latter were furnished gratis by the gracious mother in the woods near by. Appetizing food is not the sole foundation of human happiness and progress, but it is surely one of the pillars thereof. The blood supplied with rich material goes to each organ with accelerated force and volume, quickening the motion of the complicated machinery of brain and limbs, and producing the maximum of human achievement.

That toil which, under low diet, only the strongest effort of human will compelled, and which was drawing upon vitality for its motive power, under the stimulus of nutritious food, became a pleasure and a joy.

Then, too, those who had been in the country during the previous fall and early spring, and had labored diligently, now reaped the reward, not only in a bountiful supply for their own tables, but, so prolific was the rich new soil, a large surplus for disposal in the market of Warsaw, where the weekly visits which Langtry and Alden made with wagon-loads of garden produce were hailed as a godsend by the new-comers, and brought them a good price in hard cash. The money thus obtained was put into improvements on their claims, and comforts in their respective houses. Cooking stoves, with all their tin and iron accompaniments, took the place of the fireplace and Dutch oven, and each added a shed of rough lumber to his cabin, that he might not have to endure the heat of fire, in addition to that of the sun, in the summer now coming on.

Amy and Agnes were in good health and spirits, notwithstanding the constant toil necessary to carrying on their respective households, taking care of milk, and making butter. The latter process was almost like the coining of gold, not only in the appearance of the yellow pats, which resembled rich nuggets of the shining ore, but in the amount of cash returns yielded for all that could be spared from their own tables. Congeniality of calling makes work sweet, but even the most distasteful occupation can be made agreeable by prompt and adequate returns.

But the Widow Hardiker approached. Sile, having fastened his handsome chestnut horses, and also tied a pretty-looking bay pony with a glossy coat and long waving mane, on which was a new and stylish side-saddle, to a hitching-post, with more gallantry than on a former occasion, accompanied her to the house.

Amy and Grace went to the door, as Alden said:

"Well, every one to his taste. For my part, I can't see how you can endure the woman."

"We cannot well help ourselves," replied the gentle housewife. "She will come, and hospitality forbids us to turn her away, or even to treat her ungraciously."

"For my part," said Grace, "I like to have her come. She amuses me; she's as good as a comic character in a play."

"I'm afraid you'll find there's more tragedy than comedy in the depths of those malicious-looking eyes."

"Oh, papa! you're prejudiced. Why, she's the most open-hearted old creature I ever knew. She tells all she knows."

"Yes, and more too," said John, disappearing through the back door as the visitors were received at the front.

Sile merely said "H—h—how" to Amy, but extended his hand to Grace, a ceremony which, having once screwed up his courage to perform, he seemed loth to dispense with on any occasion; receiving her hand in return, he shook it with a slow movement in consonance with the usual motion of his long, lank, ungainly limbs; his languid eyes meanwhile warming up his usually expressionless face as they drank in her graceful image, and the musical tones of her " Good-morning, Squire Hardiker," fell on his ear.

Then he turned, his long strides bearing him to the wagon, a new one gaily painted, and surpassing Arthur's in style and finish, vaulted in, gathered up the reins, and drove away.

Amy turned to view the widow, who stood by her side gazing after her son with all a mother's expression of pride in her face, which changed as he disappeared in the distance into one of self-consciousness, and as " out of the abundance of the heart the mouth speaketh," when culture and refinement have not taught the speaker to restrain the expression of his emotions to fit times and seasons, her first words were:

"Wal, how'd ye like my rig?" pausing before the looking-glass to take in the reflection of herself, and allow Mrs. Alden and Grace to contemplate her attire in its full measure of completeness, before the removal of her hat and shawl should have shorn it of its crowning glory.

"Mrs. Hardiker," said Grace, surveying her from head to foot, "you're—you are simply immense;" and then she turned, pretending to move and at the same time clanging the strings of her guitar which stood in the corner, to drown the gurgling sounds of laughter which would not be suppressed.

"Wal, I thought so," was the pleased reply, "an' I reckon I've larned the paces, too," strutting across the floor her knees striking against her hoops as she walked with restrained gait, her pea-green silk dress, trimmed with black cotton lace, bobbing up and down at every step, disclosing the white stockings beyond the heights of her number seven prunella gaiters, which, owing to inevitable necessity, fashion producing none of more striking characteristics, were black and high, and plain.

"I kin put on the flourishes mighty pat, when I git all this hyer good harness on," continued she, tossing her head.

"Where did you get it?" asked Grace, turning toward her again with beaming face.

Amy was silent, for the inharmony between the wearer and her apparel grated on her feelings with a discord equal to that of the guitar strings, which Grace kept striking at intervals.

Nature had given her samples of the hues which could soften the deeply indented lines left by time and labor on her face, and tone down the harsh features and sallow complexion, in the mingled black and gray of the luxurious hair which graced her retreating forehead, when she had removed the dainty mixture of pink crepe and white lace, with a garniture of roses, and held it up for admiration:

"Now, this hyer bunnit I struck in Kansas City, saw it hangin' in a winder of a milliner shop, an' it tuk my fancy. Here, lem'me see it on you," and she put it on Grace's head.

Embodied spring, crowned with the graces and beauties

of June, could not be fairer than the oval face, with its clear cut, delicate outline, its large brown eyes beaming with mischievous expression, the transparent whiteness of the fine grained skin, through which the quick red flushes that mark the ebb and flow of the tides of feeling were plainly visible, the pinkish tint of the dimpled cheek, and the pearly teeth which the slightly parted rosy lips disclosed, set in the filmy frame of crepe and lace and roses.

The widow turned her from side to side, with a quick, nervous motion, and then held her off at arm's length, and gazed admiringly, ejaculating:

"Wal, I'll swan! Ef it looks like that on me, 'tain't no wonder the Kernel squinted at me, so kind o' pleased and tender like."

"What Colonel?" Amy said, controlling her risibles.

"Why, Kernel Delaney, of course. He's a widderer, buried his wife in South Carliny; his darter Mabel she keeps house for him. But he needn't be castin' sheeps' eyes at me. 'Tain't a goin' fer to do him no good, I hain't none o' your clingin' vines, an' don't allow to hang on to nobody, not ef I knows myself," and she seated herself in a rocking chair to the discomfiture of her crinoline, while Grace picked up the white crepe shawl that had fallen to the floor in her excitement, and placed it on the bed with the dainty head-dress, so charming in itself, and so unfortunate in its destiny.

"Tell you what, I've been ridin' a high hoss down thar! You kin bet on that! Them preachers may talk about bein' meek an' lowly in sperit, an' it goes down well enough, s'long as you hain't got nothin' to swell on. Ye kin tag along at the end o' the percession, ef yer ridin' a bony ole hoss, but jist you git mounted onto a high steppin, blooded critter, an' yer bound to come in with the music.

"I jist tell you what! Mis Squire Diggs, she that wor Mary Jane Spears, don't go turnin' up her nose an' flauntin' her peacock's tail ahead o' me, no more, you kin bet your eyes on that! 'Cause I'm one ahead; lands the same, niggers is even, or nigh about so. Squire's all right, but on member o' the Legislater, she's nowhar! an' when I come bouncin' in upon 'em down in Boone county, sort o' unexpected like, with all this good harness on," pluming herself, " they opened their eyes, you bet! as ef I wor a circus woman in her best rig, an' I felt as ef I wor swingin' 'round in a trapeze above their heads, but bimeby, I jest swung down easy-like, an' got onto a level with 'em, an' made myself to home for the sake o' ole times. 'Tain't so easy goin' it on the high strikes when ye hain't used to it," apologetically, and Grace here interposed:

"Did you get the plans for your house?"

" Yes, an' the lumber, got 'em in Lauderdale. The house is goin' fer to be a twin to Kernel Delaney's. What's the use o' tryin' to be quality, ef ye can't come up to the scratch an' shell out? an' ef ye want to do a thing right, go to them as knows how and larn, that's my doctrun."

" Did you visit the Colonel in his home?" inquired Amy.

" You bet! an' hired a hack fer to ride in, too. You don't ketch me footin' it like pore folks when I've got the spondulicks," and she rattled a steel bead purse of the kind then in vogue, with an air of satisfaction.

" Most things kin be got when you've got the yaller boys. Git them fust, an' you're all right. But," and she crossed her feet, and endeavored to readjust her hoops, " as I wor tellin' ye, I wor druv up to the Kernel's in style, an' knocked at the door with my parasol handle, an' soon it wor opened by a white-headed nigger, all dressed up in a blue coat with brass buttons onto it.

"'Good!' sez I, to myself. 'Thar's a wrinkle fur ye, Susannah Hardiker, jist put that in your heel. Thar's ole nigger Steve, that hain't bin wuth a picayune in the corn field this five year, ye kin rig him up to tend door. 'Is your master in?' sez I.

"'Yes'm,' said he, bowin' as polite as could be, 'but he's engaged.'

"'Lord,' sez I, 'that don't trouble me a mite, I didn't come on that kind o' business; jist you step in an' say the widder Hardiker would like to see im.'

"'But he's engaged,' sez he, bowin lower'n ever, 'an' I don't think it will be possible for him to see you this mornin.'

"'Lord a massy! Can't he leave her a minnit, to see a woman on business? Must be all fired sweet on her, fur an ole widderer, older'n I be. She needn't be skeert, I hain't set my cap fer anybody in fifteen years—I go it alone, every time! an' don't git euchred, nuther,' said I, an' I 'low I must a spoke up tolable loud-like, fer a door opened to the fur side o' the hall, an' the Kernel himself, with ole Dave Watkins, an' Governor Harlan, an' five or six other ole cocks cum struttin out.

"'What's all this noise about?' said the Kernel, an' as the ole nig lit out, I spoke up fur myself: 'I'm the widder Hardiker of Boone county,' sez I, 'an' I cum here fur to see you an' that cussed nigger 'lowed I couldn't nohow, 'cos you wor ingaged, as ef that wor any reason for not seein' a woman on business.'

"'The nigger was mistaken, Madam,' said old Dave, afore the Kernel had time to answer me. 'The Kernel is still in the market,' an' with that they all larfed, an' it sort o' riled me.

"'He kin stay there for all me,' sez I, 'I hain't dealin' in that breed o' cattle. Only yer blooded stock's good enough for my plantation.'

"'Sich as my friend General Watkins here,' said the Kernel. The larf war on t'other side now, an' the Kernel tole me to come in the parlor an' set down, an' he looked at me so kind o' sweet-like, as he said:

"'I wor lookin' for you in Boone county last month, but didn't find you.'

"'No,' sez I, 'I stay up in the Territory, mostly, long o' Sile.'

"'With the Yanks,' sez he smilin'. 'Wal, they seem to have brightened you up. Really, now, you are a lookin' young an' hansom,' an' I'll swar ef the ole coot didn't look at me, so admirin' like, an' me a widder, an' him a widderer, that I felt streaked all over.

"'It's all owin' to you, Kernel,' sez I, 'you gin the ball a start when you made Sile a Squire, an' now thar's no tellin' whar it will stop.'

"'No tellin' at all,' sez he; 'your son may be Governor of Kansas yit; always pervidin' his friends kin hev the runnin' o' things.'

"'Wal,' sez I, 'they've got the upper hand now, and they're blamed fools if they don't keep it.'

"'Of course, Madam,' said he. 'We've elected our men to the Legislater, an' now we must stan' by 'em, an' see that they are 'lowed to meet, an' then we must help them to enforce the laws they pass; an' to do this we must have money. How many slaves did I understand you to say you possessed, Madam?'

"'A hundred,' sez I, 'most all on 'em able-bodied.'

"'Then,' sez he, 'I should say the price o' two on 'em, vally'in ov 'em low; say, six hundred dollars apiece, would be a fair contribution from you.'

"I wuz sort o' dazed like at that, an' said nothin'; but he went on so kind o' perswadin' an' sorry like, sayin' as how he'd staked his whole fortune in the cause, an' ef we didn't come up to the scratch an' help him out he wor a ruined man, that I giv in at last, an' set my mark to a order for the money."

" The grasping old fellow," said Grace, "that was too much to ask of you."

" I dunno," said she, swinging her foot and smiling complacently, " mebbe t'war a leetle high; an' then agin, mebbe t'want; an' I 'low, as the Kernel said, t'wor better to give the price o' two to help him to save the rest, than to hev the Yanks overrunnin' the country an' turnin' 'em all loose."

" But they wouldn't do that," said Grace. " They do not intend to interfere with Missouri, at all."

The widow put her thumb to her nose, and wriggled her fingers in a way most disagreeable to Amy, but at which Grace laughed heartily.

" D'yer see anythin' green in my eye?"

" Only the reflection of your dress," said Grace; of which remark she took no cognizance, but went on:

" Mebbe *you* wouldn't—'low to say, you wouldn't. You're young enough to larn the vally o' niggers; but there's that rantin' fellow, Langtry, over thar, an' that peaked-nosed white young skeezicks, I see round here a while ago, they'd make no bones o' doin' it," tossing her head viciously; " but they're both on 'em spotted."

Grace would have taken up the cudgel for her absent friends, but Amy shook her head.

In a war of words with the widow, Grace would have been worsted at the first onset, so her mother discreetly recalled the subject of her former dissertations, by inquiring:

"And did the Colonel show you his house?"

" And were you introduced to Miss Mabel?" said Grace.

" You bet!" was the reply. " I didn't take no shine to her though, stuck up thing! The Kernel he called her, an' set her to show me over the house, an' then he went back inter the room whar the men folks wor, an' what did the hussy do but call a nigger—the same ole feller, with a white head, as did the door tendin'—an' she told him to wait on me; sed she wor engaged; reckon it runs in the family."

"And did you see the house?" said she.

"Yes, sir-ee! I wor riled at first, an' most a mind to git up an' git; an' then it struck me I'd stan' a better chance o' peekin' into things, with the ole nig guidin' of me than that stuck up thing. Hain't nigh onto as good lookin' as you," to Grace. "An as for keepin' house, golly soggers! but things is wasted over thar! I'd like to have the trainin' o' them niggers for one while, but I wouldn't like to run the Kernel—No!" said she emphatically, shaking her head, and dangling the red chenille tassels of her hair net; "not ef he cum on his bended knees to ask me."

The picture suggested of the haughty, aristocratic-looking Col. Delaney on his knees to the wearer of that pea-green silk, was too much for Grace's equanimity, and she laughed merrily.

"And did you like the house?" Amy inquired.

"Wal, yes, I reckon it will do. I've got a picter of it here. The Kernel he writ down on a card the name of a man as built his'n, an I went to him, an' he made this picter for me," drawing from her pocket the plan for a neat-looking frame building, somewhat Southern in style; "an' the same feller give me a bill for the lumber as would be needed, an' I tuk it to the board yard an' got it shipped, and then I cum on home, an' brought somethin' for you."

"For me?" said Grace in surprise.

"Yes, for you. You didn't s'pose I wor goin' off to Lauderdale an' Kansas City, to say nothin' o' Boone county, an' not bring back anythin' for the purtiest gal in the Territory; got the best manners, too, by a long shot!"

Grace blushed a rosy red at this point, conscious of the many times she had laughed at and mimicked the speaker, although she had, in her presence, treated her with respect, out of consideration for her feelings.

"But, thar now, that pony 's slippin' off his bridle!" and the widow, who had glanced out of the window, started for the door, followed by Grace, whose young feet bounded on ahead, and she righted the bridle, and patted the pretty, gentle creature, saying, as the visitor came up:

"What a perfect little beauty she is. Where did you get her?"

"Down at my farm in Missoury. There's mighty good blood in that thar pony. She's high strung, but she's gentle as a lamb—like yourself, Miss Grace. You git on an' try how you like her."

Grace had been accustomed to riding in her Ohio home, and it required little persuasion to induce her to mount the gentle animal, who turned hither and thither at her bidding, and skimmed over the prairie as lightly as a bird upon the wing.

"Oh, Mrs. Hardiker!" cried she, coming back, "she is too lovely! Did you bring her for your own use?"

"No; I brung her for you."

"For me!" exclaimed the astonished girl, "for me! Oh, but that is too much. Squire Hardiker will not, perhaps, be willing."

"Don't you be skeert. You kin bet your eyes on him, every time! You see t'wor jest this way. We wor settin up, me 'an him, the night afore I went; him a smokin an' me a dippin, an' sez I, 'Sile, that's a mighty peart gal o' Alden's;' an' sez he, in his stutterin' kind of a way, 'Th—th—th—that's so, by golly!' an' sez I, 'She's allurs treated me white, an' I'd like to bring her a ring, or a chain, or a ornament o' some kind when I come back.'"

"'N—n—no,' sez he, 'she won't like that so well as one o' them blooded ponies; the one I b—b—broke last spring fur instants, an' ye know it's a standin' thar now, eatin' its own head off.'"

"Why, is it vicious?" interrupted Grace.

"Lord, no! I meant eatin' its wuth in hay, an' oats, an' corn, an' sez he, 'You go the whole hog or nothin'. You jest git the chipperest side-saddle in Lauderdale, put it on the pony, an' give it to the young lady.'

"'As a present from you?' sez I.

"'N—n—no,' sez he; 'from yourself.'"

"Oh, I'm afraid papa will not allow me to keep her. I'll ride off to him now, and ask him," and away Grace went flying over the prairie—the gentle creature obedient to the slightest pull at the rein—and brought up by the side of her father, while Mrs. Hardiker and Amy returned to the house.

Presently Grace came back, smiling, to say that her father had compromised the matter with her, by allowing her to accept the pony as a loan, to be returned in the fall, or sooner if Mrs. Hardiker should desire.

"Good enough," said the widow with a peculiar sparkle in her black eyes. "An' me, an' you, an' Sile aint worth shucks ef we can't fix up a plan for headin' off the old man, an' 'lowin' you to keep the pony fer good."

Sile came at tea-time to carry his mother home. Amy invited them to stay to supper, and they did so. Grace having accepted a favor was, as in duty bound, exceedingly gracious to them during the meal, and also throughout the evening which followed. She discussed with them the plans for building the new house, and gave her opinion unreservedly as to furnishing it, and they took their leave at nine o'clock in a good humor with themselves, and of course with all the world beside.

A few days after this visit, they came again one afternoon in their new spring wagon, to beg of Grace and Amy to ride over with them to Calhoun, and assist in selecting a site for the new residence.

"I jist 'lowed," said the widow to Grace, "I'd better

come over an' git you to come an' tell us whar it oughter set, an' which way you'd like to hev the front-door open—that is, if you wor me."

Amy was busy, and could not possibly go. She doubted whether Grace ought to go without permission from her father, and he had gone to Warsaw. But Mrs. Hardiker insisted, the day was fine, and Grace thought she should like to have just one ride after those spirited chestnuts, so her mother finally yielded, and they drove off with her in triumph.

A beautiful spot was selected as a site for the new house, on a gentle eminence within the limits of Calhoun, and they decided in favor of a south front. When this was attended to, the widow got out at her own cabin, and left Sile to drive home with Grace alone, at which her father was indignant. Of course he brought her home safely, and she said she had really enjoyed the drive and her own chat—for Sile said nothing—but sat listening with mouth and ears open to every word of hers, and skillfully guiding his horses as they flew over the ground with the speed of the wind, concluding her speech with—

" Now, papa, what harm is there in my riding a few miles with that great awkward Sile Hardiker? I shan't fall in love with him; to quote the widow, 'You kin bet your eyes on that.'"

" Oh, fie, Grace!" said Alden impatiently. " Don't use slang, it's vile stuff to come from the lips of a lady. Come here, my daughter." He had thrown himself upon the bed, being quite weary after his morning's work and afternoon ride. She sat down on a chair beside him, her hat still in her hand, and her face flushed with the exhilaration of that rapid ride.

" What is it, papa mine?'

" Well, my dear, it is my opinion Sile Hardiker and his mother are very much in love with you."

"It won't do them any good, or me much harm, I'm thinking. I'm already 'bespoke.'"

"Aha! engaged, are you. When did you arrive at that dignity, and which one of all the gay Lotharios who dance attendance on my squatter sovereign princess is to win the prize?"

"Now papa," said she, tossing her head saucily, "don't tease. You know very well whom you want me to marry."

"Humph, and pray how long since you divined, Miss Wiseacre, that I wanted you to marry anybody?"

"Oh, I can put this and that together, as well as the next one. I did not see it, however, until since Arthur spoke to me; but"—and she leaned over and looked at him earnestly—"I am not mistaken. You do wish it, do you not?"

"Well, and if I do, what of it? Parents' wishes in this respect are not often regarded," said John, testily. "Do you not love him?"

"I do not know."

"Don't know! Well, that is a happy-go-lucky state of affairs. I advise you to find out before it is too late."

"That is just what I've been trying to do. I have talked with mamma and Mrs. Langtry."

"Oh, ho! been holding a consultation over the matter, have you?"

"Not exactly," with a shrug of the shoulders, indicating annoyance, "but Agnes was giving me a history of her life, and I merely inquired how she knew that Mr. Langtry was the man she wanted to marry."

"Aha! what a cunning diplomatist it is. And what did she tell you!"

"She smiled, and said her own heart told her plainly enough."

"And what said mamma?'

"Why, mamma told me about the same thing—but—." and

she hesitated a little, "I think perhaps I am different. My happiness is dependent upon the feelings of those about me. I've tried it many a time, this having my own way in spite of everything, and it was always the same. The coveted pleasure was like apples of Sodom, sure to turn to dust and ashes in my mouth." She laid her head upon her father's bosom as she spoke, stifling a little sob, and he could not but caress the gentle face.

"You have learned that lesson young, my daughter, but you were always wise beyond your years;" — and then, as she did not speak —" if your mother and myself desire your union with Arthur, and I will own to you that it has long been the dearest wish of my heart, it is because we believe it would be for your own good. He is of a good family, and is noble and earnest, he is true-hearted, he is brave, and what is better than all else, my dear, he loves you devotedly. We are in no haste to give you up; this cabin would be a dreary place without you. But, if it were Arthur who wooed you away, if your home were near our own, where we could see you every day, where we could witness the increasing happiness which such a union could not fail to bring, we should feel that we had indeed not lost a daughter, but that we had gained a son, one who would become the prop of our declining years."

She raised her head and looked him in the face, her pure soul shining from her eyes.

"Papa, it shall be as you wish; I know you are right."

John took the hands which she reached forth, tenderly in his own, continuing:

"We are wiser than you are, my dear. We have lived more years and seen more of life, and it has been my experience that there is no happy marriage that is not based on mutual respect as well as congeniality of tastes. With your inherited sense of justice, and the strong influences which have surrounded you from your youth up, I think you could not truly love one whose interests and whose education led him to trample on the rights, and build his own prosperity on the wrongs of others."

"You mean Roderick Delaney, papa. He has never spoken to me of love; I do not give my heart unasked."

"In that case, my dear, if the precious treasure of first love is still within your keeping, give it to him whose soul longs for it as the most sacred trust under heaven, and who will guard it jealously, as the one priceless jewel in his crown of life."

"Papa," said she, rising and smiling through the tears which dimmed her eyes, "I may only *think* I love Arthur, but I *know* you do."

CHAPTER XXI.

THE FIRST LEGISLATURE.

Toward the end of June the current of travel set in toward Pawnee, the paper city on the verge of civilization which had been designated by the Governor as the Territorial capital, and consequently the place of meeting for the newly-elected Legislature.

Pawnee was situated one mile east of Fort Riley, and within two miles of the formation of the Kansas River by the junction of the Smoky Hill and Republican Forks.

Immediately upon the location of the capital at this point the erection of buildings for the accommodation of the Territorial officers, and the Legislature had been begun, and they were at this time in a half-way state of development.

Built of the native limestome, the foundations were laid firm and solid, the walls rose broad and high, they were roofed in and floored, but at this stage work had ceased, and they were unplastered and without doors and windows.

Thither now the wise Solons of the Territory were hastening, many of them from beyond the muddy waters of the Kaw. Hither also on the morning of the 30th of June, Langtry and Alden, accompanied by several others from Walnut Grove settlement, who were determined to see their legally elected representative through, in his endeavor to take his rightful place in the law-making body, turned their faces.

Sweet Agnes wore a face shadowed with apprehension, on that fair June morning, as she said "Good-bye," and saw with tearful eyes her husband depart on what to him was a mission of duty and patriotism.

"Now do be careful, Edward, and please say nothing to offend the Missourians," was her parting injunction.

"I must speak my mind, Agnes, come what will, but do not fear, there's more bluster than bite in those fellows. I shall come back safe, and George will care for you well in my absence."

George was a younger brother of Edward Langtry's, who had recently come to the Territory, and he had promised to remain with Agnes during the absence of her husband, as a protection, and also to carry on the farm work, which was assuming quite a forward shape. He had likewise agreed to look after Alden's stock and carry his farm produce with Langtry's to the market, and Amy and Grace thought they could manage the rest for a short time.

As for the travelers, they carried an abundant supply of provisions for a number of days' absence, feed for the horses when they should stop during the day, and picket ropes by which they could allow them to graze on the luxuriant grass of the prairies during the night. Better than all, set free from the daily routine of labor which had bound them down for months, their spirits rose with a bound to the highest pitch of enthusiasm. As Alden and Langtry passed by Calhoun on their way to Warsaw, they could see Sile Hardiker's team drawn up in front of his cabin door, and himself and Zeke Fagin making preparations for a start, and soon they came following on behind, until our friends reached Warsaw, where they halted, and the Calhounites passed on ahead.

They were joined here, after a little delay, by the representative elected from Warsaw on the 21st of May, and also by a number of leading Free State men, and formed quite a procession as they wound their way over hill and dale along the south bank of the Kaw.

Twelve miles from Warsaw they reached a pro-slavery settlement called Lecompton, then consisting of a few cabins and dugouts, but afterward famous as the capital of the Territory, and the place where was originated the famous Pro-Slavery Constitution which bore its name. Still journeying westward from grove to thicket, over creek and prairie, now descending the precipitous sides of a ravine, then mounting the opposite bank, and now following a trail over an ocean of waving grass and flowers, they reached Topeka; the neatness and thriftiness of whose small number of collocated cabins indicated plainly the line of heredity of their owners, and also gave promise of the development which has since resulted.

Here they were ferried over the river on a large flat-boat by a flaxen-haired, muscular Charon, whose motive power was his own right arm—that power brought to bear with the least loss, and in the right direction, by an arrangement of posts and ropes and pulleys, which enabled him to guide his boat at will, 'gainst wind and tide, toward either bank.

Safely over, they pursued their way along the north bank of the Kaw, and several miles further on came upon a settlement of Kaw Indians and half-breeds—the remnants of a tribe long in Kansas, and who once claimed as their hunting grounds all those vast and wide-stretching prairies. Less than a year since they had roamed the prairies at will— now the circle of restriction was fast closing round them.

And now the way lay over high and rolling prairie; gentle undulations, alternating with wide level sweeps, and brilliant with the mingled hues of grass and flowers.

Here and there nestled the little brown cabins of the settlers—stray waifs of human life cast by the waves of progress far out on this illimitable expanse, whose lines of grandeur and grace, whose wealth of coloring, and profusion of form, whose clear, pure atmosphere and unrivaled skies bespoke the impartial hand of nature, who scatters her gifts regardless alike of appreciation or of use.

Arrived at Pawnee, our friends found most of the legislators already assembled. They found them, also, something after the style of the electors who placed them in power—big-booted, long-haired, hard-featured, and well-armed.

There were exceptions, no doubt; but, as a general rule, even those professional and business men who at home went well-clad, had on this occasion, as in a play, assumed the costume suited to their part, and went masquerading in bright blue and red shirts, which gave a picturesqueness to the scene—the unusual scene—of legislators assembled for the grave purpose of making laws for an enlightened people, building their own camp fires, and preparing the food for their own evening meal.

One of the unfinished buildings had been fitted up for use as a hotel, or rather eating-house, but, for reasons of their own, they preferred to camp.

And it was a scene worthy of remembrance. Three rough stone buildings, without windows or doors, standing in the midst of a plain, which reached from the tree-fringed river to the distant line of bluffs, whose grey tops could be distinctly seen in the distance.

Here and there, clustered in little groups of six or seven, were encamped the Kansas law-makers. The smoke of the camp fires slowly curling upward in the calm air of the summer evening, while within the limits of the encampment the atmosphere was redolent of the fumes from frying bacon and steaming coffee, which, with the contents of the jug, at intervals passed freely round, formed the chief elements of the evening meal.

The morning of the 2d of July dawned fresh and fair, and the Legislature proceeded to organize. The Territorial officers, among whom was Col. Delaney, with their books, papers, and other paraphernalia of office, occupied one building; the Council assembled in another, and still another was set apart for the meetings of the lower House, and toward the latter, Langtry and Alden bent their footsteps.

Owing to ignorance of parliamentary law among the majority of its members, as well as the difficulty of reconciling the various conflicting interests, much delay ensued, and the day was consumed in effecting an organization by the election of Dr. William H. Stringman, a violent pro-slavery man and resident of a border settlement, as Speaker of the House, and Rev. Thomas Jimson as President of the Council.

A slight acquaintance was sufficient to convince the Walnut Grove men that other districts had been even more hardly used than their own. More than a two-thirds majority of the members they found to be not even temporary residents of the Territory. This mattered little, however, as all were controlled by a small knot of politicians, representatives of the slave interest, and guiding spirits of the Blue Lodge, which had bound its members by fearful oaths to vote, as well as act, in accordance with their will.

There had been but one Free State man elected to the Council, and that body made short work of expelling him, and giving his seat to his pro-slave competitor; and, on the morning of the 3d, the lower House also proceeded to purge itself of opposing elements. This required more time, as there were five contesting members present, with papers, evidence, and affidavits, which necessitated, at least, a show of examination. On the morning of the 4th, however, the whole matter was summed up by Mr. Langtry in a clear and concise manner, his audience sitting impassively, with faces as impenetrable as the sphinxes of Egypt, and as unimpressible. His well-grounded facts, his forcible arguments, and his flowers of speech, alike came back to him with a hollow sound, as if projected against an adamantine rock, and immediately on his conclusion, without attempting to confute him, they gave a unanimous reply in the shape of a resolution to admit the members elected on the 30th of March; alleging that they were the rightful members, inasmuch as the Governor had, in their opinion, no right under the organic act to order an election, except in case of death or resignation.

Langtry hardly expected to be received as a member; and yet he could not but entertain some measure of hope for that which he earnestly desired, and he did most earnestly wish for a right to record his vote as a protest against the measures which he anticipated they had in view.

And now there still remained one Free State man in the Legislative body—the representative from New Boston—whom there was not the slightest pretext for displacing, he having been elected in March; but, finding himself alone and surrounded by a group of invaders who had no right to legislate for the Territory, he offered his resignation, which was received with shouts and yells of applause; and soon after this dignified body adjourned, and during the remainder of the day and evening amused themselves with shooting at a mark, games of cards, etc.

Alden suggested taking shelter for the night in the stone hotel, although the sky was clear, and a myriad silent stars looked down with eyes undimmed upon the scene of revelry transpiring in honor of the anniversary of American Independence.

"I am an old weather prophet," said he; "and there are certain signs in the air, insignificant in themselves, but sufficient when taken together, to indicate a coming storm."

Acting upon this advice, the Walnut Grove party selected the most sheltered spot in the undivided second story of the stone hotel, and, spreading down their blankets, were soon asleep, to be awakened suddenly, when the watches of the night had gained the wee small hours, by a deafening clap of thunder, followed by a low, continuous muttering mingled with the wild wailing of the wind, and the sound of rain pouring down in torrents, while the continuous flashes of the forked lightning, which darted hither and thither across the angry sky, illuminated the whole country round with the brilliance of noonday, disclosing to their vision the wise Solons of Kansas, with their beds upon their backs, scampering from their camping grounds to the stone buildings for protection from the elements.

There was considerable swearing done, and a number of collisions between irascible members of the different parties. But the morning's sunshine dispelled the clouds from the heavens and from their tempers, and they proceeded to business.

Alden and Langtry were interested in observing the conduct of the member from Walnut Grove, and noticed that he compared favorably with the average, having at least discretion to keep silent the unwieldy tongue within his half-open mouth, which praiseworthy quality, Alden suggested, " He must have inherited from his father."

The member from Warsaw was a semi-idiot, whom the border ruffians had picked up on the outskirts of the place, and voted for with many a hurrah, for the express purpose of mortifying the radical citizens of that Free State burg. He had frequently to be called to order, his defective, disagreeable manner of speech being unendurable to his colleagues.

Being now duly organized, their next step was to appoint Territorial officers, and they scrupled not to appoint their followers to every place of authority or emolument in the Territory, even the most petty.

Many of these appointees, among whom was Zeke Fagin, who received the office of Sheriff of Hamilton county

—which included the settlements of **Walnut Grove** and **Warsaw**—were residents of Missouri, and were only induced to take up their temporary residence in the Territory by the gift of offices conferring authority or material reward. And this done, they deliberately proceeded to adjourn the Legislature to the Shawnee Mission, abandoning the seat of government which had been duly designated by the proper power, for a place near the Missouri border, ostensibly in consequence of insufficient shelter, but really for the accommodation of the members who wished to return to their homes at night after having spent the day in adapting the laws of Missouri to the Territory of Kansas.

This act of adjournment the Governor vetoed, but with many threats of hanging, lynching, and removing His Excellency in various ways, they passed it by a two-thirds vote over his veto, and forthwith took up their line of march for home. Likewise, so did our friends, reaching Walnut Grove about noon on the 7th, to Mrs. Langtry's great relief, and to the joy of Alden's family.

CHAPTER XXII.

THE FOURTH OF JULY—RODERICK AND MABEL DELANEY—
ARTHUR'S RETURN—OF HER OWN FREE WILL.

The people of Warsaw were making grand preparations for celebrating the Fourth of July. Invitations had been sent to all the surrounding settlements, both Free State and pro-slave, to unite with them in doing honor to the nation's birthday. Nor had the red men been forgotten. The Delawares and Shawnees, being near, and sufficiently civilized, as was thought, to understand and appreciate, had also been requested to take part in the procession and exercises.

Preparations from the first went on with an enthusiasm unknown in older communities where celebrations, processions, and pageants have grown to be an old story. Every one was willing to contribute his or her mite of money, or talent, or labor, for the entertainment of the expected assembly, or the completion of the arrangements, esteeming it an honor to be called even to the humblest service in the behest of the committee, and by the evening of the 2d nearly everything was in readiness.

About two miles from Warsaw, on the banks of the Areposa, whose course here reached the nearest approach to the town, a grove had been cleared of underbrush, a speaker's stand erected and handsomely decorated with evergreens and flags, seats of rough lumber had been constructed around it, and a long table of the same material had been built. The programme of exercises was arranged and in the hands of the printer; the various speakers had been notified and accepted their appointments, the toasts with their replies were in readiness, and the music had been rehearsed until all was as nearly perfect as possible. Grace, who was a member of the musical coterie, had remained in Warsaw with a friend several days, for the purpose of attending rehearsals, and Mrs. Alden had been down one day to assist in decorating the stage. It now only remained for the busy housewives to exert their culinary skill to produce from the limited resources of many households a bountiful and appetizing display for the long dinner-table, and the 3d of July had been set apart for that purpose.

> "You must wake, and call me early,
> Call me early, mother dear,"

sang Grace, as she retired on the evening of the 2d.

"Indeed I will," rejoined Mrs. Alden, "for it will be much pleasanter to finish our work in the cool of the morning, and be able to take a nap in the afternoon, with the cheering sense of duty done, than to be worrying over our preparations all day."

And early indeed they began, for the mists were still lingering on valley and plain, and the first faint tints of rosy dawn just peeping above the distant horizon, when they arose.

There was light bread to knead, and rolls to make out, chickens to dress and prepare for roasting; there was milk to strain and put away, and butter to churn; there were doughnuts to fry and pies to bake, and gold and silver cake to make and to frost, and the house to put in order. But everything had been well planned beforehand, and all arrangements worked to a charm that morning, as things sometimes will, and sometimes will not, to the vexation of housekeepers. But this was a "red letter" day, and by 10 o'clock the kitchen table was a perfect mass of good things, all finished except the frosting of the cake, and Grace sat on a high stool with a

MABEL DELANEY.

dish of egg-froth on her lap, flourishing an egg-beater in her hand, as she whipped the snowy foam, and mingled the white sugar and flavoring. Mrs. Alden stood at the sink performing the less poetic but equally necessary duty of washing up the plates, and cups, the bowls and spoons, the pots, and kettles, and pans, which had been used in these culinary operations.

There was a knock at the door! Who could it be?

They looked at each other in dismay; neither felt in trim for visitors, but there was no escape. The way to the upper chamber lay through the front room, and the front door was partially open to admit the morning air. Grace wore a light calico dress with a neat frill of lace around the neck, her hair had been well arranged when she arose, and was gathered in a braid at the back, and tied with a blue ribbon.

"You look well enough, my dear, go on," said Amy, as a second knock, louder than the first, was heard, and Grace obediently put down the dish and beater, removed her apron, and went to the door.

Mrs. Alden, pausing to listen, heard:

"Why, Mabel Delaney!"

"Why, Grace Alden!" and a dozen kisses were given and received between them, while a gentleman's voice, which she recognized as that of Roderick Delaney, said:

"Good-morning, Miss Alden."

Amy's first thought was that of the housekeeper:

"How glad I am that we have so much cooking done; we can entertain them without much labor, and still have a bountiful supply for the picnic dinner to-morrow." Then she washed her hands, brushed her hair a little, removed her work-apron and went in to learn that Miss Delaney had come, escorted by her brother, on that long-promised visit. Mrs. Alden shook hands with them, and assured Miss Mabel that she was very glad to see her, as indeed she was, for the young lady, though brought up in luxury, and surrounded by all that wealth could bring of comfort and adornment, had sufficient culture to perceive that refinement of character is compatible with narrow and humble surroundings, and, while she resisted with all the hauteur of a Southern aristocrat, any assumption of equality by moneyed coarseness, as in the case of widow Hardiker, she at once perceived and acknowledged the social standing of Grace and Mrs. Alden, and not once during her stay did she by word or look indicate that she observed any lack in their accommodations, and to their limited quarters, submitted as gracefully as if she had been accustomed to a cabin her life long.

"When the cat's away the mice will play," said she, "and papa having gone away back in the Territory to attend a meeting of the Legislature, Roderick and I thought we would follow suit and run up here to spend the Fourth with you."

"We hear you are making grand preparations for the celebration," said Roderick.

"There will be nothing grand about it in any sense of the word," replied Amy, "but the fact that it is the first celebration of our national holiday which these prairies have known, will make it interesting."

"And now that you have come," said Grace to Mabel, "I am sure that we shall have a good time."

"When did you return?" inquired Mrs. Alden of Roderick; "we understood you had gone to South Carolina."

"So I did, but came back last week, and now think I shall remain during the summer."

After a few more courteous speeches, Roderick Delaney arose, saying that he had business at Calhoun and at Warsaw, but would return early the next morning, and hoped to have the pleasure of carrying Mrs. Alden and Grace to the celebration, having brought the family carriage for that purpose.

"That is," said he, looking at Grace, "if you have no previous engagement."

They had none; Grace had refused several invitations to go alone with gentlemen, and the tacit agreement she and her mother made to ride with George and Agnes Langtry, in no wise interfered with their acceptance of this offer. Soon after Mr. Delancy took his leave, and Mrs. Alden went into the kitchen to finish the morning's work and prepare dinner, which happily was a very small affair, with so much in readiness. Of course, she excused Grace from any further attention to household duties for the day, so, after changing her dress, that young lady brought down her fancy work, and Miss Mabel took from her portmanteau some fleecy wool work which employed her fingers, while the two tongues ran briskly, occasional snatches of the conversation reaching Amy's ears as she busied herself in the kitchen. She heard Mabel ask:

"Where is Mr. Fairchild?"

"In Ohio," was Grace's reply, "unless indeed, he is on his way here. He went on business which should have been finished by this time."

"Your cousin, is he?"

"No, only an old friend."

"Do you know I think him very handsome? I always did like blondes."

"On the principle of the attraction of opposites," said Grace, "you are such a perfect brunette."

"No," with a little laugh, "I think it is on the principle that forbidden fruit is always the sweetest."

"And why is Arthur forbidden, pray?" queried Grace, with just a little blush.

"Oh," said Mabel, "papa would never consent to my marrying a Northern man. We have such different views you know, unless indeed he could be made to abjure all his principles on the subject of slavery, for my sake."

"And in that case you wouldn't want him," laughed Grace.

"Why not! I like what I like—and perhaps it would please me to have so much power over him. Papa has some grand scheme in his head," continued she, " of a great slaveholding nation to be established on this continent, after the manner of the ancient republics, with the negro race to perform all the drudgery of existence, while the whites devote themselves to the higher pursuits of the arts, literature, science, and statesmanship."

"Well, I should say, as in the old fable of the stoning of the frogs in the pond, that it might be fun for us, but death to the blacks."

"Roderick says it wouldn't be good for us. He says that coming to Kansas has opened his eyes, and he sees a hundred flaws in the fair fabric which he had been taught to revere as perfect."

To this, Grace made no reply, and presently Miss Delaney inquired:

"Are there many young people up this way?"

"A great many young men, but few young ladies."

"Will they have dancing to-morrow?"

"Not until evening; it is too warm in the middle of the day, even in the woods."

And thus they chatted on, darting from one subject to another, as the birds do from branch to branch—now soaring aloft to the domain of poetry and art, and anon descending to fancy work and fashions.

After dinner they went upstairs for an afternoon *siesta*, descending again, at tea-time, fresh and fair, in the light, fleecy robes of summer, and with sparkling eyes and merry voices.

After a lunch, all went outside to enjoy the cool breezes, which invariably come with the setting sun.

And now another glad surprise awaited them. With the

lengthening of the shadows and the falling of the dew, there came a distant footstep, growing nearer—nearer still—then a shadowy form appeared, coming toward them in the twilight. A moment more:

"'Tis Arthur!—yes, 'tis Arthur!—he is here." Grace sprang up with a glad cry, and then, remembering the presence of her visitor, restrained somewhat the exuberance of her joy; and Mrs. Alden was the first to grasp him by the hand with words of greeting, then Grace, and then Miss Delaney.

He had arrived in Warsaw by the evening's stage, engaged a man with a team, to bring him up to his own claim, and had passed by while they were at tea.

"Did he not want some supper?" Amy inquired.

"No; he had eaten while in Warsaw, and had no need of anything to-night."

Now, a shadow had fallen upon his face, and the smile with which he had first come toward them had faded, and he had assumed his most reticent and unresponsive mood. It was impossible, however, to resist long the fascinations of Miss Delaney, so frank and pleasing were her manners, so brilliant her wit, so easy the flow of her conversation.

It was as if her whole nature had been warmed and mellowed by the tropical sun, until it had become the source of life-giving light and heat.

And as for Grace, gayer even than her wont, she laughed and talked, she played on the guitar and sang; and the trio, so far as outward appearances could indicate, passed a very pleasant evening.

At parting, Miss Delaney inquired of Arthur, "If he were going to the celebration in the morning?"

"Indeed I am," was the reply. "I hastened my return for that purpose, and I will drive over in the morning to carry you all down to Warsaw. Shall I not, Grace?" looking at her directly, but Miss Mabel answered:

"You're too late! You can't have Grace, for she promised brother Roderick this morning to ride with him, and so did Mrs. Alden."

"Too late, am I!" looking at Grace, who only blushed and gave an affirmative nod, and he turned away, with some light remark. Then, as if the thought struck him, he said to Miss Delaney:

"And how is it with you? Did you promise Mr. Delaney also?"

"He did not ask me," said she, playfully.

"Well, then, Miss Delaney, can I have the pleasure of escorting you to the celebration to-morrow?"

"With the greatest pleasure, Mr. Fairchild," bowing; and then, "It is better to be second choice than no choice at all," looking mischievously at Grace, and soon after Arthur took his leave.

Morning dawned with a cloudy sky—a pleasant fact in itself—for the rays of the summer sun are vastly more agreeable when tempered by an intervening mass of vapor.

"If," as the girls said, "we could but be sure that it would remain in suspense, and not come showering down to the disarrangement of our attire and plans."

But they would not allow fears of rain to detain them, and were in readiness, as girls usually are, when, at 8 o'clock, Roderick Delaney drove up with his carriage; and at the same moment, from an opposite direction, came Arthur with his wagon.

A slight shade of disappointment was visible on the face of Miss Mabel, as she noted that the back seat in the vehicle was already filled by George and Mrs. Langtry. She said nothing, however, and received politely an introduction to them, given by Arthur, who had alighted, and said "Good-morning" to all, and who then assisted her to a seat beside himself, while Grace and Mrs. Alden entered the carriage with Roderick, and the provisions were stored away in both vehicles.

The carriage was easy and comfortable, the roads were in good condition, and the horses trotted swiftly along. On either side of the way might be seen small oases of waving corn, which betokened the ready hands of earnest workers.

Roderick Delaney was in his most pleasing mood, and the slight shadow of unrest which a look of sad reproach from Arthur had cast over the sunshiny nature of Grace, gradually lifted, and Mrs. Alden and she both partook of the irresistible contagion of his cheerfulness.

As they neared Warsaw they found teams of every description, from the light buggy to the heavy wagon drawn by strong-shouldered oxen, decorated with waving branches of green leaves and flowers, and gay with ribbons and flags, pouring in from every direction, and by 10 o'clock from fifteen hundred to two thousand people were assembled on the principal avenue. The newly-organized military were drawn up in line, and a lady stepped forward on a platform erected for the purpose, and gracefully presented to them a beautiful American flag; to be borne, she said, "Where the battle for the right is thickest."

It was accepted by a member of the company, with thanks for the honor conferred; and then, headed by the band, the military led the way, and the long procession of wagons and carriages, and men and women on horseback, formed in line, and followed to the grove, situated about two miles from the town.

After the reading of the Declaration of Independence and the singing of the national hymn,

"My country, 'tis of thee,"

followed the oration of the day by the Free State leader, Dr. Francis Rulison. It was a masterly speech, delivered in the

Doctor's clear, cool, unimpassioned tones, and produced a wonderful effect; many of those present, immigrants from Southern States, hearing, for the first time, a concise statement of the arguments against slave labor. Then the Doctor read extracts from speeches and letters of Southern men of education and influence, delivered and written at various times and places, forming a complete condemnation of the system, and that from their own mouths; after which, the subject of the position of Kansas, in regard to the encroachments of a neighboring State, was touched upon, and the firm determination expressed to assert and maintain the right of American citizens upon the national territory.

The orator was in earnest. This regnant calmness was but the restrained power of a soul which comprehended the greatness of the crisis which was upon the land. He discerned the hidden rocks upon which shallow counsels would have wrecked the bark, the rapids upon which a rash precipitation would have plunged it, and he saw as well, the open sea beyond, to which firmness and moderation and patience would lead, when the gathering storm had been weathered.

Roderick Delaney had listened with a thoughtful expression on his face, while the speaker made point after point in favor of making Kansas a Free State; but that expression now changed to one of rapturous delight when, at its close, the clear voice of Grace rang out with surprising sweetness in the " Star Spangled Banner," the full choir joining in the chorus.

She had stepped forward a little as she began to sing, and stood beneath the arch of evergreen, a vision of girlish loveliness, simply clad, in a dress of white Swiss muslin, tucked to the waist, a sash of blue, blue ribbons at her throat, and a blue tie confining the long brown hair which was drawn back in waving ripples from her forehead, and hung in a heavy braid.

The brown eyes sparkling, and the trills of song gushing forth on the still summer air, seemed to reach the depths of Roderick Delaney's heart. He stood as one entranced, listening till the last note died away. Arthur Fairchild, too, listened, but his attention was divided between the young Southerner and Grace. His eyes wandered from one to the other as if seeking to divine their feelings, or to perceive any exchange of glances or recognition between them; but there was none. Grace seemed perfectly unconscious of everything but the words and melody of the song to which she was endeavoring to give expression.

Next in order came speeches of welcome to the whites, from the chiefs of the Shawnees and Delawares.

" They were glad to see the white man coming, not with the hatchet and sounds of war, but bringing the sweet fruits of peace and civilization."

Then followed Whittier's gem of a Kansas song, written expressly for emigrants from the North.

The words had been printed on slips of paper, distributed among those assembled, and as the air was a familiar one, many voices joined the choir in singing:

> " We cross the prairies as of old
> The Pilgrims crossed the sea,
> To make the West, as they the East,
> The homestead of the free."

This closed the exercises for the morning, and Arthur stepped forward hastily to assist Grace in descending from the platform, but he was a moment too late. Roderick Delaney was before him, and Grace had accepted his proffered arm, and descended the steps before she saw Arthur, and then it was Mabel's voice saying, mockingly, " Too late again, Mr. Fairchild," which attracted her attention, and she heard and felt what Mabel did not, the bitterness in his voice as he replied, " Yes, it seems so; my fate, it appears." He turned away toward a group of gentlemen who were conversing at some little distance, found Mr. Benty, took a short walk with him, and evidently came to some understanding with the gentleman from Boston, for soon after, giving him an introduction to Miss Delaney, Arthur disappeared. Mr. Benty was a very agreeable gentleman, and his attentions, as well as those of several others to whom she was now introduced, seemed fully to console Mabel for this desertion by her escort. A number of pleasant ladies had joined Mrs. Alden's group, among them the intelligent and lovely wife of Dr. Rulison, and together they stood chatting, while the busy Marthas of the occasion, unfolding the tablecloths, and uncovering the well-filled baskets, placed their contents upon the long table.

"Why, there's that horrid woman who called at our house in Lauderdale, some time ago," said Mabel to Grace.

"Ah, where?"

"Under that large tree, to the right of the stage. Horror! she's coming this way!"

And, looking in the direction indicated, Grace and her mother recognized at the same moment Mrs. Hardiker in her pea-green silk and pink crepe bonnet making her way toward them as fast as her stays and her hoops would permit.

"Oh," said Grace, "that is a neighbor of ours;" and to Roderick, who was laughing at the incongruity of the dress and the wearer, "A product of your Southern institutions, Mr. Delaney. How do you like the style?"

"Abnormal, I assure you," was his reply, and at this moment, the widow, whose restless, piercing eyes had been wandering over the group, espied Grace, and darted down upon her as upon some recovered treasure.

"Wal, here ye air at last! I've been lookin' for ye high an' low ever sence the singin' was done. Why, the land sakes! Mr. Delaney! Whar did you come from, and with

Grace, too! Whar's yer mar?" to Grace. Amy came forward to speak to her, just as Mabel Delaney deliberately turned her back. The quick eyes of the widow had caught the motion, and, tossing her head with a don't-care sort of air, she ejaculated:

"She needn't be skeert. I wouldn't tech her with a ten-foot pole."

Her voice was loud and coarse in its tones, and of course attracted the attention of the group, though they were too well-bred to laugh, on Mabel's account, who, with Mr. Benty, now moved off to some distance.

"Interdoose me to the quality," said the widow, in a stage whisper. Mrs. Alden hesitated a moment, hardly knowing whether it would be agreeable to the ladies, but, with the utmost ease and coolness, Grace turned to the company:

"Ladies and gentlemen," said she, "allow me to introduce to you a neighbor and friend of ours—Mrs. Hardiker—*the mother of our member of the Legislature.*" Of course the ladies bowed, and the widow proceeded to make herself "to hum with 'em."

"Powerful crowd here to-day; 'pears a'most like circus day in Boone county, with sich a comin' an' goin', an' the music a playin'."

"Yes, indeed; quite a large gathering for a new country," replied some one.

"I wor bound fur to cum. I allers like to tend all the goins' on—never missed a circus yet, as I knows on."

"Glad you did. We were anxious to have all the settlers unite with us in this celebration, regardless of their political affiliations," said Mrs. Rulison, good-naturedly.

This was sufficient encouragement for the widow, and she proceeded with a monologue of her experiences and opinions, which amused the company highly; even including

Miss Mabel, who, with her escort, presently returned to learn the cause of the shouts of laughter, which greeted her comical utterances and ludicrous manner when "ridin' on her high hoss."

When a fine-looking gentleman who loved fun, and enjoyed the study of new types, offered her his escort to the dinner table, the widow felt that her debut in Warsaw society was indeed a success. She had achieved an intimacy with the highest, at a bound, and the pink crepe hat, and the pea-green silk, were valued accordingly as accessories to this delightful consummation, and perhaps they were; the whole is made up of minute portions, each indispensable in its place.

Roderick gave his arm to Mrs. Alden and Grace, and they took their places at the table only to fill their plates and move away to find seats at some distance, thus giving place to others.

Liberal as the provision of table room had been, it was insufficient to accommodate all.

Quite a number of friends soon joined their group, and it was interesting to sit and watch the crowd, they differed so widely in appearance, costume, gait and manners. Besides, there were Indians, most of whom were gaily dressed in bead-trimmed mantles, feathers and moccasins, an eager expression lighting up their saturnine countenances, as their eyes rested on the variety and delicacy of the food prepared for the guests at " the white man's feast."

Grace's usual score of admirers were clustered round Mabel, while her brother with his imperious air seemed satisfied by monopolizing Grace. But he could not keep her thoughts from straying; though he exerted himself more than he had ever done, her eyes would go wandering off, and even the most brilliant sallies of wit failed to provoke the wonted repartee, the burden of reply falling to Mrs. Langtry and Mrs. Alden.

With a mother's instinct Amy divined her daughter's

thoughts, and her own sympathies also went out to the one who was groping his way miserably, and in the cold and darkness, when the lifting of the slight shadow of misunderstanding would restore him to warmth, and light, and love. When the dinner was over and the dishes returned to the table, a member of the committee of arrangements approached Mr. Delaney with a request that he would reply to an impromptu toast, and the two moved off together, to consult.

Mrs. Alden whispered to Grace: "Let us go and find him" —and aloud to Mrs. Langtry: "If Mr. Delaney returns before we do, take good care of him." Grace arose hastily, put her arm within her mother's, and they moved away in the direction Arthur had taken more than an hour before.

"He should not be so impatient, mamma," said Grace. "I have had no opportunity to speak to him. He ought to see that."

"Of course he ought, my dear, and I presume he does. I do not think he went away in a spirit of resentment, but only because he misunderstood your relations with Mr. Delaney, and could bear no longer to see you with him, and himself, as it seemed, put on one side completely."

"If he only knew how unhappy I have been all the morning," said Grace, still hurrying on.

"Tell him so then, and it will be all right. Arthur is too generous to wish you to be unhappy."

"And I am sure I cannot be happy when he is miserable," said Grace.

"There is a beautiful dell up here, somewhere—we have visited it several times in search of flowers. I think, perhaps, we shall find him there;" and she led the way down by the creek, along a little path which wound through the thick underbrush and heavy growth of young plum trees, to a ravine which had been spanned by a fallen tree, and there, beyond, in a more open space, where the grass was green and the flowers starting up in clusters, where the birds were darting hither and thither with a little note of pain or affright at his presence, stood Arthur, leaning his weight heavily upon a low branch of a large tree. His face was turned from them, but his whole attitude was that of despair, his head bowed down as if crushed with the weight of a heavy blow.

One glance was enough for the tender heart of Grace. Love hath a thousand forms of attraction. Sweet pity, true respect, a deep sense of the value of the unchangeable affection which had long lain like a precious jewel at her feet, tender memories of the past, a thousand pleasures shared in common, all impelled her toward him with swift feet. Her light steps passed quickly over nature's foot-bridge at which Amy halted.

"Arthur!" she called.

He turned, his face lighted up at the sound of her voice.

"Arthur! I am come to you of my own free will."

He stood erect. The electric thrill of hope once more animated his form. His unstrung nerves recovered their tension. Despair fell away like a cast off garment, as he stepped forward to meet her, and opened his arms.

And the sun shone out with brilliant flash, illuminating the whole atmosphere, the birds broke forth in a carol of gladness, the waters of the little creek rippled sweet music, and amid the leaves of the trees shimmering in the sunshine, the winds murmured soft and low: "Love is joy, love is joy."

Mrs. Alden turned, and found her way back alone to the company. Mrs. Langtry was with Mabel, and Roderick Delaney was on the stand in the midst of a brilliant reply to a sentiment concerning the perpetuity of the American Union, which was received with rounds of applause.

Mrs. Hardiker, her passion for the direction of affairs strong within her, superintended, with well-received officiousness, the removing of the remains of the dinner and the repacking of the dishes; and when Mr. Delaney had concluded, said to Mrs. Alden who had returned, and was collecting her own dishes and replacing them in the baskets:

"Thar ain't much diffrunce 'atween we'uns an' you'uns, 'ceptin' the grammer, an' I reckon that don't count for much," and Amy agreed with her.

Perhaps an hour, perhaps more, elapsed, before Grace and Arthur returned, and there was a smile on both faces, a look of peace on Arthur's, as if the angel of hope had cast her joyous spell upon him, and as for Grace, the old light-hearted, merry mood had returned to her. She was again at one with those nearest and dearest to her.

And now there were no more misunderstandings. When Arthur Fairchild received from Grace Alden's own lips the assurance that his happiness was dearer to her than that of any other, there was no room for doubt or jealousy in his breast. The demons were cast out, and nevermore found resting place therein.

When Roderick Delaney came toward them, with others, to rally the runaways, did some subtle influence convey to him the fact that there was a change in their relations? Perhaps so, for hereafter, although he redoubled his attentions to Grace, as one grasps for a possession which is being borne beyond his sight, there was a tacit acknowledgement of Arthur's right to share in her smiles. Yet, this might have been only because Arthur claimed that as a right, which he had hitherto, in Mr. Delaney's presence, suffered to go by default.

Mabel was happy, surrounded by admirers, and pressed with invitations to dance. She was in her element, nor did it detract from her pleasure that she was enabled to punish Arthur for his desertion of the morning, by saying "engaged," when he preferred a request for a quadrille.

And so the evening, and in fact, the night, passed away;

the first faint approaches of the dawn being heralded by rosy fingers in the east, when our party reached home after the long drive. Having dissipated the restful hours of night, they were fain to borrow of the day that they might settle the scores of nature with their weary frames.

Mabel remained with the Aldens until the morning of the 6th; both Roderick and Arthur coming in to spend the evening of the 5th. Mr. Benty came also, his Boston reserve seeming to be completely melted by the witching manners of this Southern beauty. Agnes and Amy enjoyed the evening as much as did the young people. Mrs. Alden's own youth came back to her in the bonny loveliness of her daughter.

CHAPTER XXIII.

PREPARATIONS FOR THE WEDDING—THE BOGUS LEGIS-
LATURE—THE JEWELED HAND THAT MOVES THE
PUPPETS—RODERICK IN OPPOSITION—CAPITAL OF-
FENCES—TESTS FOR JURORS—LEGISLATION INDORSED
BY SUPREME COURT—LANGTRY'S CIRCULAR.

And now, for a brief happy time, the current of life with the Aldens moved on in waves as gentle and as smoothly-flowing as the bright waters of the placid river changing its course with every undulation of the land, and bearing its modest offering to the sea. So bright were the skies above them, so genial the atmosphere of the little home which they had reared in this new land, so radiant the future with its promises of a competence, that it was to John and Amy as if they had drank of the elixir of life, whose reviving power had not only permeated and renewed every atom of their bodies, but restored the old-time spirit of buoyancy to their souls.

Together, one in purpose as in heart, a mutual confidence and trust, born of trial and separation, and far surpassing in depth and fervency the passion of youth, possessed them; broad lands, their very own, with smiling wheat-fields, a small earnest of great things to come, already ripening for the harvest; their only child, their joy, their blessing, about to be wedded to one whom they could receive with pride and heartfelt satisfaction as a son, what could they ask for more! The time for the union had with one consent been set for the coming autumn. Arthur's parents had been written to, and

SHAWNEE WATER WORKS.

a cordial approval and congratulations received. They also mentioned a modest sum, which was at his disposal, sufficient to enable him to build a comfortable house for his bride, and put his claim in good working order.

A mind at ease has a wonderful tendency to develop working power. Doubt restrains. Hope allures, but certainty of reward removes all pressure, and mind and body spring to their allotted task with faculties in the full plenitude of their powers. In the sunshine of assured love, Arthur Fairchild discovered a strength of purpose, a concentration of will and energy, before which difficulties melted away as the mists before the rising sun. A lime-kiln, long contemplated, soon rose on his claim, and was in successful operation. A stone-quarry was opened on a bluff to the south, where the white building stone lay invitingly near the surface, and men were at work quarrying stone for his new house; for, after many consultations with the young mistress that was to be, it was decided that it should be of stone, substantially built, and in such a shape that additions could be readily made. Breaking was begun, that the sod might be turned over and exposed to the mellowing rays of the sun and air, to be in readiness for fall plowing and seeding. Nor was this all; his exuberant energies, overflowing the narrow bound of selfish interests, carried their freshness and zeal to the field of politics, and the Free State cause had no more eloquent or more fearless advocate.

But at present, the star of love was in the ascendant. The long bright days of July and August were full of happy work, and the glorious evenings, when the deep blue vault of heaven was iridescent with a million diamond points, or when the fair moon rode in stately magnificence o'er a tranquil sky, illuminating the landscape with a silvery radiance, and the south wind, balmy and cool, tempered the heat of day and recuperated the wasted energies—these evenings were sacred to the quiet joys of affection.

But now and then there vibrated upon this harmony a strain of discord from without, which rasped the nerves and stirred the fountains of indignation to their depths; a wail from homeless settlers on the west, the smoke of whose burning cabins rose like a cloud in the clear sky, the flames lit by the hand of Zeke Fagin, who alleged, to certain Missouri friends of his, a prior right to the claims, and enforced that right with the torch of the incendiary.

From the East, through Langtry, on whom the spell of a high mission lay heavily, dwarfing all minor interests, came the tale of a mockery of justice. He had gone to Shawnee Mission, after a day or two spent at home, drawn thither irresistibly as the moth to the candle, by a strong interest in the action of the Legislature, and letters came from time to time to Alden, and to the Association, containing a full account of the proceedings.

He wrote:

"When I look around upon the countenances of the men assembled here to give the laws and form the institutions of this embryo State of ours; when I listen to their conversation, and learn the motives which govern them, it is hard to realize that we are still within the limits of our own country, whose political ideal, we have supposed, was equal rights and protection to all her citizens, or that we are within the dominion of that law which was founded upon a recognition of the sacredness and inviolability of human rights. What can more forcibly illustrate the profound debasement to which the slave system tends, than the fact that those usurping legislators confidently expect that an adoption of a rigid and barbarous slave-code will effectually banish from the Territory all Abolitionists, and bar the entrance of those yet to come? To them their present advantage seems the completest victory. It remains to be seen whether their expectations are built upon enduring foundations. * * * *

"That they work under special and systematic direction may be clearly inferred from the fact, that within the past week this body of men, picked up mostly from the servile and uneducated classes, have accomplished more work than any legislative Assembly ever known to history, having given to the Territory a code of laws which will occupy in the printed volume, more than a thousand octavo pages. The "modus operandi" by which this was accomplished, however, somewhat dims the luster of the achievement; they having adopted with a few exceptions, the statutes of their own State, merely directing—by the passage of resolutions to that effect—that, wherever the words State of Missouri were found, the copy should read Territory of Kansas.

"The *few exceptions* are still occupying their time and attention, and yourself and the Association may rest assured that I will give you early and correct information as to the result.

"LANGTRY."

Two days later he wrote as follows:

"'They are progressing with their work; the statutes which they have enacted in relation to slavery, would not be tolerated by their own State of Missouri. Mark you! they have made it felony to utter a word against the institution, and the penalty for thus offending, penal servitude from two to five years, the convict to drag a heavy ball and chain affixed to the ankle, and to labor on the public roads, or in the service of individuals at the fixed price of fifty cents *per diem.*

"For greater offences against the slave property, they have provided a severer penalty. For instance, to aid in any rebellion of slaves, to assist any slaves to escape from their masters, to bring any book or tract calculated to excite rebellion on the part of slaves, free negroes, or mulattoes, to carry out of the Territory a slave belonging to another, or to assist the same, are all capital offences, to be punished with death.

"It remains to be seen how men from the North, where the battle of free speech and free press has long since been fought and won, will bear this. Will they discontinue the newspapers from their old homes, burn up their copies of Uncle Tom's Cabin, and destroy the poems of Whittier? Will they see the slave driven by the lash of the master to labor on these fertile prairies, see his scars, and hear his groans; will they witness the sundering of family ties and see marriage made a mockery, and their lips be sealed? I answer, No! as well might they try to chain the winds which sweep resistlessly over these prairies, as to bid us keep silence in the presence of this great sin. * * * * *

"Are the politicians our masters, that they may lay their fingers on our lips at will? Nay, we shall but echo with one voice, the words of him, who twenty years ago, said: 'I am in earnest, I will not excuse, I will not retreat a single inch; and I will be heard,' and whose eloquent appeals have since then taken this country by the four corners and shaken it until railroad and steamboat, homes and halls of legislation resound with discussion of the great question upon which these puny lawgivers bid the people of Kansas be silent.

"Also, they have enacted, in order, I suppose, that persons accused of violating the statutes in relation to offences against slave property, may obtain justice,

"Section No. 13, which reads thus: 'No person who is conscientiously opposed to holding slaves, or who does not admit the right to hold slaves in the Territory, shall sit as a juror on the trial of any prosecution in which the right to hold any person in slavery is involved; nor in any cause in which any injury done to, or committed by any slave, is in issue; nor in any criminal proceeding for the violation of any law enacted for the protection of slave property, and for the punishment of crime committed against the right to such property.'

"Thus, at one blow, they have demolished that ancient bulwark of freedom which has ever been a stumbling block in the path of tyrants.

"Unjust and oppressive laws may be passed, officers may be found who will execute those enactments, but, if before a charge can be brought against a man, beyond a trifle, a jury of twelve unprejudiced men must indict him for the offence, and then before he can be punished twelve of his peers, unprejudiced against him, must say with one accord: 'He is guilty,' he is measurably free from oppression.

"But how will it be with us in this Territory of Kansas, when we have allowed this tide of aggression to sweep away this last safeguard.

"Already we have judges, whose sympathies, interests and feelings, are strongly enlisted against us; the sheriffs and other officers appointed by this Legislature, are all most resolute adherents of the pro-slavery cause, and lest any one of a different stamp should by any possibility creep in, they have instituted a test, contrary to the Constitution of the United States, demanding of every candidate for office that he subscribe to an oath, 'solemnly swearing upon the holy evangelists of Almighty God,' that he will support or sustain the provisions of the Act of Congress entitled 'An act to organize the Territory of Kansas and Nebraska,' and the provisions of the law commonly known as the 'fugitive slave law.'

"With courts and juries organized for the conviction of Free State men, of felonious offences, whose highest turpitude consists in the exercise of the commonest rights of citizens, and obedience to the impulses of human feelings, could human ingenuity exert itself in politics to the creation of a more diabolical scheme?

"LANGTRY."

Again:

"Another week of law-making has passed, another week I have sat and watched their movements, discerning, I think, the one hand which touches the keys, and guided by subtle instinct, strikes ever the correct note which wakes the passions of ruder minds, and compels them to do his bidding. Ambition, material interest, and the inherited prejudices of several generations of pro-slavery progenitors, joined with a rare insight into men's motives, and disregard of such old-fashioned virtues as truth, equity and justice, when they stand as obstacles in his path, combine to make Col. Delaney the leader of his party in the Territory. In the confidence of the government at Washington, trusted by the Southern leaders, admired, almost worshiped by the great servile body of men who make up the rank and file, what shall hinder him from accession to the highest office in the gift of the State, should he succeed in fastening slavery upon us, a measure which I believe is meant but as an entering wedge to open the way by which their cherished institution shall be carried into all the territory belonging to the United States, and from thence into the States themselves. So much have they marked out, and the master of ceremonies sits serenely, smiling and watching—his large black eyes bent, now here, now there, noting every movement of his puppets, his long, slim, jeweled hand running nervously through the locks of his iron gray hair, when hesitation or faltering appears on some point where the way has not been accurately laid out, but coming to the rescue swiftly by suggestions to the member who sits at his side, and acts as mouthpiece.

"The young man, his son, in whom must have reappeared the spirit of some revolutionary ancestor, is here too, the greater part of the time, and listens with undisguised amazement, and freely expresses his disapproval of their proceedings, and the Colonel regards with no little apprehension this rebellion against his paternal rule. I was an unwilling and unseen witness to an interview between them, in which the son remonstrated against the passage of the law in regard to jurors. He used arguments drawn from reason and history, and pointed to the utter impossibility of Americans who had drank deeply from the fountains of political liberty, submitting to such a regime of despotism, but his words made no impression, and then he declared:

"'You are mad! These men from the North are no meek negroes that they should thus lie down and allow you to tread upon them; they will never bear it. They will rebel.'

"The reply came in contemptuous tones:

"'I wish they would. We ask nothing better. We can meet and

vanquish them with force where we fail in argument; they having the appeal to sentiment and emotion on their side. But they will never do it! They are a nation of traders, with the almighty dollar for their God. The very mention of a war with the best customers of their shops and factories, causes them to cringe, and shrink, and press to their bosoms their precious money boxes.'

"'Father! you mistake them entirely,' said Roderick; 'they are industrious and energetic. They love gain, I will allow, and they love law and order, but they love justice and freedom more. There are those among them who would venture all things for the liberty of a depised race, but they are held back by others who can see no wrong, feel no injustice until it touches themselves in life or property, and *these* even, you will arouse by this outrage upon their brethren, who have sought new homes in the Territory, trusting to the laws of their country for protection. I beg of you, to stop and consider, before you carry your aggressive measures so far that the whole world will look on aghast.'

"The elder Delaney turned upon the younger with a sneer: 'I believe you are become a white-livered Abolitionist. Such language ill becomes a man in whom the blood of many generations of South Carolina's proudest sons flows unsullied.'

"'Nay!' said the younger, gravely, and with deference: 'It is because I would preserve untainted the blood of noble patriots of our native State who fought so bravely for sweet liberty, that I thus protest against this desecration of the rights of free-born American citizens.'

"Col. Delaney's voice was husky, and his face pale at white heat with anger, as he replied:

"'You had better join the Kansas Legion at once. We want no such half-hearted followers in our ranks.'

"'Perhaps I will,' and the young man turned on his heels, the victor, at least in self-control. LANGTRY."

A week later he wrote again:

"They are now engaged in drawing up a memorial to Congress, praying to remove Governor Reeves, he having added to his former offences against them, by declaring all their proceedings irregular and void, on the ground of their removal from the place designated as the Capitol, and also having replied to the committee appointed to call upon him, who used such mild means of remonstrance as threats of hanging, shooting, and other forms of death:

"'Gentlemen, two or three can assassinate me, but a legion can not compel me to do that which my conscience does not approve.'

"Such a man will never answer their purposes, and so they will request his removal on some trumped up charge of speculating in lands. All honor to this brave Governor from the Keystone State. Let our people remember this man, too honest to be bribed with place or power, and too courageous to be intimidated.

"That their enactments passed over the Governor's veto may not lack sanction, they have resorted to a high-handed judicial expedient. Without waiting for cases to arise under their laws by which to ascertain their validity, they have submitted the most obnoxious of them to the consideration of the Supreme Court, that body with a wise forethought being convened in this place at the present time. The result I will give you anon. LANGTRY."

Still a week later, he writes:

" As might have been expected, overlooking the fact that there was no case before them, that they were prejudging any case which might arise under the statutes, that the party who might be interested was thus condemned without a hearing, and that the whole proceeding was irregular and extra judicial, the Supreme Judge and one of his associates, the other dissenting, decided in favor of these enactments, and against the Governor's veto, and bolstered up a lengthy and confused legal opinion on the subject, by the following superb piece of irony:

"'In reaching this determination, we (the judges) have been influenced in no small degree, by our high appreciation of the constituent elements of your honorable bodies, thoroughly satisfied as we are, that in the great requisites of intelligence, and public virtue, the legislative Assembly of Kansas will compare favorably with any other.'

" Imagine if you can, the sardonic grin with which your worthy justices penned this indorsement of your Legislature, and the cheers and yells with which the last named body received it. A legislative assembly, many of whose members live in Missouri, who spend the nights in wild revels in Westport, and who are often found in a state of bibulous insensibility through the day here, who have robbed the public of security by imposing their minions upon us to execute the laws, receiving the eulogium of the Supreme Court. Could servility bend lower?

" No wonder that, having thus received absolution in advance, they have proceeded to gather together all possible spoils, and parcel them out among themselves and their supporters. They have passed over a hundred and forty pages of acts of incorporation, by virtue of which joint stock companies are called into being, and charters given to railway, mining, insurance, landholding and other companies, to toll bridges, ferries, plank roads, even universities, beyond all we may require for many years; and then, oh, immaculate body which has impeached a Governor for speculating in lands! not only repaid themselves by dividing the lion's share of the stock in these various concerns, but by a judicious introduction of other names into their grants, bound to themselves four or five hundred individuals, who, as favored grantees, have become interested in upholding the laws upon which the legality of their grants depend.

"They have located our future capitol at Lecompton, the most inconvenient and inaccessible place they could have selected, but the settlers in that vicinity are mostly pro-slavery, and it is affirmed that the 'members' have received from the town company liberal grants of town lots as the price of their votes, a good speculation on the part of the latter, as a large sum of money will be expended in public buildings.

"With the passage of a few measures of less importance, this body will adjourn, and it becomes our duty as citizens to take into consideration the question, whether or not we will acknowledge it as a legally-elected body, and its enactments binding, or repudiate the whole thing as bogus, and a fraud upon our rights. I inclose herewith some of my reasons for considering it the part of wisdom to pursue the latter course, and the Association may, if it see fit, put them in print, and use the same for a circular in calling a convention of the people.

"EDWARD LANGTRY."

This was done immediately, and large numbers of copies distributed with the call for a convention to be held at White Springs on Sept. 5, this call having originated with the people of Warsaw, at a meeting held in that place, during the latter part of August.

In this circular Langtry recounted in full the circumstances of the election of the members of the Legislature by fraud and violence on the 30th of March, and then reviewed, as in his letters, the most obnoxious of their acts, declaring them illegal and void, and not binding upon the conscience of any man, not only because enacted by a body of usurpers, but as violations in themselves of the principles of justice which should be the supreme law. He discussed the propriety of resisting their enforcement, not by violence, unless the same was necessary by failure of all other means, but by an inauguration of measures looking to the formation of a State Government. This, he said, was a measure which could be adopted with propriety at any stage in the affairs of the Territory, and one which the present exigency called for as a remedy that would meet the case, and restore authority to the people of Kansas. He discussed with eloquence the necessity of preserving the rights of free speech, free press, and trial by jury, as three safeguards of society, which could not safely be allowed to be infringed; and also the sin of obeying any law which conflicted with the laws of God, as in the case of the Fugitive Slave Law, an oath to support which must be taken, under this bogus code, by any officer, juror, or voter in the Territory; and he compared this code to the famous edicts of Philip of Spain, an attempt to enforce which deluged with blood and almost depopulated the Netherlands.

The fearless character of this man may be seen in the fact that he signed his full name, Edward Langtry, to this document, well knowing that it would bring upon him the furious imprecations of the pro-slavery men, and perhaps the secret vengeance of the Blue Lodge.

CHAPTER XXIV.

RODERICK'S DISAPPOINTMENT—CONVENTION AT WARSAW —AGNES' APPEAL.

Roderick Delaney came twice to visit the Aldens during the session of the Legislature. The first time in a gay, happy mood, laughing and jesting, quoting poetry and sentiment, and discussing politics with Alden; neither of them belonging to the most radical type of their respective parties, they could talk issues over without becoming excited, a fact so uncommon at that time, that they chuckled over it not a little, and took to themselves great credit for fairness and impartiality.

He came in a two-horse buggy, and at sunset asked Grace to take a short drive with him, and she consented. They were gone perhaps an hour, and on their return they all sat out of doors in the starlight until a late hour. The conversation was light, and very general. Delaney at last took his leave, and Amy, having bread to knead, or something of that kind to attend to, went into the house, leaving Grace and her father alone.

"Papa," said she, rising from her seat and coming to stand behind his chair with her arms around his neck; "papa, I want you to do me a favor."

"Well, what is it, Grace? Out with it."

"The next time Mr. Delaney comes, I want you to tell him—not abruptly, you know—but in some round-about way, and yet so that he may be sure of it, that Arthur and I are engaged."

"I will do so, certainly," and then taking her hands and turning so as to get a glimpse of her face, "Afraid, eh?"

"No! oh, no!" said she quickly, "but I think it due to Mr. Delaney, as well as to Arthur, that he should know that our relations have changed—that I am not free to receive his attentions."

"And you do not want the pleasure of refusing him? I thought my girl was a little bit of a coquette."

"You must not form rash judgments on short acquaintance, papa. It is not prudent," said she, archly. "And now will you do as I bid you? Arthur's generous confidence toward me since our engagement has bound me to the utmost loyalty."

"Yes, I will. I think myself it will be best." She kissed him good-night, and was gone, and, for the first time a doubt suggested itself to John Alden whether he had done right in swaying his daughter's inclinations by so much as a hair's breadth. He talked it over with Amy, after they had retired, and she quieted his apprehensions by her certainty that Grace was perfectly happy in her new relations, which were most assuredly promising, so far as human prevision could penetrate the future.

Roderick Delaney came again toward the latter part of August. It was early in the evening, and Amy and Grace were still busy with some housework which detained them within doors.

Mrs. Langtry was with them, and the sound of their cheerful voices could be heard where John sat, on the east side of the house, in the shade of a morning glory vine which, having been planted in the spring, had grown up with almost the rapidity of Jonah's gourd, covering a rude trellis, completely. As usual, when alone and idle, John was enjoying his pipe.

Roderick having fastened his horse, joined him, offering

his cigar-case, but, content with his pipe, John declined, offering in return a rustic seat and a light, which Roderick accepted.

It was soon plain to John that the young man had something to communicate, for his manner was restless and nervous, unlike his generally unruffled tone. After a few commonplace remarks, and while Alden was still revolving in his mind the question of how best to approach the communication Grace had requested him to make, the young Southerner plunged at once into his own affairs, with:

"Mr. Alden, I came expressly to speak to you this evening, on two subjects which deeply concern me."

"Ah," said John, questioningly.

"Yes; and I shall speak to you first, while we are free from interruption, of that which is nearest my heart—your daughter—"

"Stop! One moment, Mr. Delaney! Before you go on let me give you a message with which I am charged. It is this; my daughter is engaged to Arthur Fairchild, with the consent of parents on both sides, and the marriage will take place in November."

Roderick's face was slightly turned from Alden, so that he could not see the play of emotion, but it was sometime before he spoke. John had not intended to be so abrupt; in fact, he had spent much thought on ways and means of delivering this communication in a gentle and delicate manner, but the young man's looks, his earnest mention of her name, made plain to him that, if a declaration of his affection for her was to be prevented, it must be done at once.

When at last Roderick Delaney spoke it was calmly, yet with visible effort:

"I had feared as much; yet, as long as there is one straw of hope a drowning man will catch at it, and I will not try to conceal from you that I am deeply disappointed. Blind that I was, not to see it from the first. No man could be with her constantly and not worship the ground she walks on."

A pause, during which he arose and walked to and fro, saying at last:

"Fairchild seems a good enough fellow, too."

"He is one among ten thousand," said Alden warmly; "and he has waited more years than Jacob waited for Rachel. But now that question is disposed of, let us consider the other."

"Disposing of the first," said Roderick hastily, and somewhat gloomily, "has settled the other also. I will leave the country. I will go back to Europe."

"Why! What has occurred?"

"Simply this: My father and I have disagreed. For the first time in my life a serious difference has arisen between us, and if I remain here it must become an open rupture."

"Not—about—not my daughter, I hope?"

"No; I do not think he would interfere with me in an affair of this kind; and I have as yet had no occasion to mention it to him. Now, of course, there is none. It is this vexed question of slavery which has come between us."

"'A ferment,'" said John, quoting a well-known speaker, "'which is working in this body politic, and whose molecular motions will never subside until its entire substance shall have become homogeneous.'"

"Abolition cant! Don't quote it to me. You know that I believe that slavery is an institution ordained by the providence of God for the benefit of both whites and blacks, bringing to the former relief from drudgery, and leisure for the higher pursuits of life, and to the latter, protection, training, and development. This doctrine has been instilled into me from my youth up, as carefully—*more* carefully than the creed of my church. And as yet I see no reason to dispute it, but the trouble is here. I cannot see why we should force our institutions upon a body of free people who reject them, any more than we should impose our religious creed upon those who refuse it. The attempt strikes me as a return to the methods of the Dark Ages, and I am convinced it cannot succeed."

"Never!" said Alden, emphatically; but, without noting the interruption, Delaney continued:

"Through my father's solicitations, and a desire to benefit the poor whites of my native State, I became interested in the endeavor to colonize this Territory with men of Southern views, hoping thus to outnumber you, and obtain, fairly, under the provisions of the organic act, an enlargement of Southern boundaries, and thus that increase of political power which the South needs for her own preservation. But we have failed. I concede it, and I will never be instrumental in subverting the will of the majority, thus overturning the corner-stone of the liberties of my country.

"My father cannot be made to see this. He is an enthusiast in the cause of the South, and is carried by his zeal far beyond and above the realms of reason and prudence. I cannot soar with him, therefore I will take myself off, that the sight of his eldest son in opposition to himself shall not vex him."

With John Alden's idea of the duty of obedience to parents, influenced insensibly, perhaps, by the thought that Delaney's absence under the circumstances would be most agreeable to himself, he could not counsel him to do otherwise than take the course which his inclinations suggested. He was spared the necessity of saying much, however, by the coming of the ladies, who, contrary to their usual custom, did not linger on the south side, but joined the gentlemen on the east. The last lingering rays of the sun had faded below the horizon, leaving but the brilliant reflection of his light in gorgeous pillars of cloud, which shone like burnished gold, shading off into flakes of yellow and crimson and purple.

Grace came first, and, bowing to Mr. Delaney, took her place by her father, while Amy, after shaking hands with him warmly, seated herself on a bench near him, and Mrs. Langtry occupied a rustic chair carved from the stump of a large tree, which Roderick had vacated in his agitation.

So deeply had their own emotions been stirred, that the two men were unable to subside into commonplace, on the instant, and conversation flagged somewhat at first, but Amy always had a pleasant way of tiding over awkward pauses, and on this occasion she playfully put in motion the surface waters, allowing the deeper currents time to subside. It was simply done; a housekeeping anecdote or two, a little Warsaw gossip, some good-natured remarks about the widow Hardiker, who had been over during the day, arrayed in an entirely new suit of pink organdy, gorgeous to behold, some affectionate inquiries about Miss Mabel, in which Grace joined, cleared the atmosphere, and the rebound of repressed feeling was such that after awhile they were even gayer than usual, Mrs. Langtry participating in the general good cheer with a buoyancy unknown to her of late, her husband's absence having plunged her into the deepest gloom. He was her sunshine, and, like the flowers, she drooped when the life-giving rays were withdrawn. But the time was at hand for his return, and she brightened up in consequence. Roderick, too, was able to give her assurances of his safety, having seen him only the evening previous.

In the midst of this easy chat came Arthur Fairchild, and then, as often happens, on the introduction of a new element into a social circle, a stiffness again fell upon the group, though he came with a pleasant greeting for Roderick Delaney, and an unconscious glance of love and admiration for Grace's upturned face, as he seated himself at her side, a look which paled the face of the young Southerner, as for a moment a tide of envy and jealousy, and a sense of disappointment surged over him.

They had changed places, these two, and it required all the self-control which the strong will of Roderick could summon to his aid, to accept, with calmness and dignity, the situation which had so lately been forced upon him. He succeeded, however, meeting with graceful hauteur the smiling complacency which a consciousness of being preferred, had infused into Arthur's manner.

Arthur had just returned from Warsaw, having been there to attend a meeting called to take into consideration the political situation. Disputes ending in violence were at this time common all over the Territory, and several street brawls had recently occurred in Warsaw, much to the chagrin of her people. He had carried Langtry's letters, except the last, which, with the circular, had not yet arrived from Shawnee, to be read at the meeting, and Mrs. Langtry, whose interest in the Free State cause was second only to that of her husband, began to inquire of him as to the proceedings.

He replied that there was manifested a general disposition to repudiate the bogus legislature, and resist the enforcement of its laws, reports of the most obnoxious of them having been read and commented upon, and that her husband's letters had been read and received with enthusiasm.

"But did they not decide upon any measures, any plan of action?" inquired Agnes, with a woman's eagerness for something tangible.

"Nothing, really they decided nothing; of course a meeting of the citizens of one county could accomplish nothing decisive. But they have issued a call for a convention to be held at White Springs, on the 5th of next month, to which representatives from every part of the Territory will be invited, for the express purpose of discussing and devising a plan of action."

Roderick Delaney having listened with interest and implied approval to this, Agnes ventured to say to him:

"You will attend this meeting, will you not?"

He hesitated a moment, the attention of all being thus called to himself, and then said:

"I hardly think I shall be in the Territory at that time. I hope to be on my way to Europe before many days."

"To Europe! leave the Territory at this time, when the presence of every true man is required in the solution of this vexed problem? I cannot understand such a move on your part, Mr. Delaney."

"It is to escape the tumult and turmoil of passions I go, Mrs. Langtry," said the young man, thus pressed to the wall. "I shall put the sea between this tempest in a teapot and myself, and remain away until it has subsided."

"And thus shirk the responsibility of your own acts. Oh, Mr. Delaney! where is your patriotism that you can thus say, 'Let others take care of my country, it matters not to me?'" cried this blue-eyed mentor, whose perception of duty was ever clear, and whose brave, impulsive spirit led her, seeing the path, to point it out without hesitation.

Delaney's eyes had been fixed on Grace from the moment of his announcement of his determination to leave the country; and his watchfulness had been rewarded by a little start of surprise, but he turned at this questioning of his patriotism.

"I seem to have no lot nor part in this contest, Mrs. Langtry. I cannot go to extremes with either party. I stand on a central ridge in the battlefield, within range of the guns on both sides, and the safest way is to move off until the battle is over."

"The safest," said she, in scornful tones, "but the true patriot—the true man—considers not ease nor safety, when principles are in danger. I had thought you made of better material, Mr. Delaney," and then, as he made no reply, "Nothing for you to do! nothing! Is it nothing, that you can stand upon your middle ground, and by your force of will, hold in restraint the aggressive zeal of the one party, and by your fairness and moderation assure the other that there is still a point in common whereon they can meet and settle their difficulties without bloodshed?" In her earnestness she had risen and stood before him, putting forth her hand as if in entreaty, and Roderick listened in silence to this new view of the situation — which, in his chagrin and personal disappointment, he had failed to see. But, thus adjured, though in the presence of his rival — in the presence of the woman he loved and had failed to win, he was still noble enough to perceive and acknowledge its force. He listened until she had ceased to speak, and then rising, and reaching forth his hand, he grasped hers. His voice was husky with emotion, and there were tears in the eyes of the witnesses of that scene beneath the silent stars, as he said, "I thank you, fair mentor, for this clear showing of my duty. Into the breach between the two, where misunderstanding and blame from both parties, where danger and no glory awaits, my pathway lies, and at your bidding I will try to walk therein. Good-night to all," and in a moment he had turned to go. John Alden went with him to where his horse was tied, shook him warmly by the hand, and bade him come again. "I will," said he, "when I can," and was gone. When Alden returned to the house, the little group had dispersed. Grace and Arthur had walked home with Mrs. Langtry, and Amy was busy in the house with some preparation for breakfast.

CHAPTER XXV.

WHITE SPRINGS—A WARNING TO LANGTRY.

The Convention at White Springs was a great success in numbers, in enthusiasm, and in its effect upon the future movements of the Free State party, there and then regularly organized.

One hundred regularly elected delegates were present, and they represented every district and settlement in the Territory. The meeting was held in the open air, no building being found large enough to contain the large number assembled.

The first proceeding of this Convention was to repudiate the acts and doings of the late Legislature.

Then the circular written by Edward Langtry was read and approved, and a call issued for another convention to be held two weeks later, whose express object should be to determine whether the suggestion there made, that measures should be inaugurated to organize a State government, should be acted upon.

The mere mention of a State government called forth the wildest enthusiasm.

But the most important act of this Convention, and the one which rendered it a starting point of the party, was the nomination of a delegate to Congress. The bogus Legislature had made provision for an election to take place on the 1st of October, but having declared that body and all its acts illegal, and as the qualifications required of voters in the shape of test oaths and taxes were irregular and oppressive, it was determined to hold an election on a different day.

After prescribing rules for the government of the election, and electing an executive committee of seven, the Convention proceeded to the nomination of a candidate.

Edward Langtry rose, and in an eloquent speech narrated the brave acts, and enumerated the wrongs of ex-Governor Reeves, who had been superseded by Governor Harlan, and whom he said he wished to put in nomination for the office of delegate to Congress. As he paused, a deep silence for a moment pervaded the assembly. Every man drew a long breath, as if he for one instant considered the importance of the step which they were taking, a step which might be held as treason by the usurping party; but the next instant the air was rent with cries, "Reeves! Reeves! three times three for Reeves and the right!"

The nomination was seconded, and immediately afterward Reeves was nominated by acclamation.

He was a man of erect and determined aspect, with hair slightly grey, and had hitherto been more apt to listen than to commit himself by words; but now that his connection with the government had ceased, and the weight of oppressive authority was lifted, he felt free to express his convictions, as he had ever been prompt to act on them. He accepted the nomination, which was a practical indorsement of his course, in a speech of unusual fervor, and the enthusiasm became almost ungovernable, the settlers gathering about him at its close, with warmest greetings.

When order was again restored, a platform was proposed, and was finally adopted, after much discussion and warm debate, it being found almost impossible to harmonize into a homogeneous body the widely differing elements with but the one point in common—a desire to make Kansas a Free State.

The first resolution invited men of all parties to join in the movement.

The second denounced non-resident voters, no matter where from.

The third declared the policy to be that which should make Kansas a Free State.

The fourth expressed a determination to make reasonable provision for slaves then present in the Territory.

The fifth, over which there was much discussion, and which bid fair at even this early day to divide the party, declared that no negro, bond or free, should be permitted to come into the Territory.

This was the notorious black law feature, and, in conjunction with the sixth, which repudiated the charge of Abolitionism as affixed to the Free State party, was objected to by Langtry and others, whose sympathies were wide enough to take in all humanity, without regard to color or previous condition, and they expressed this feeling unreservedly; but, finally, on the principle that half a loaf is better than no bread, and inasmuch as the results of the Convention taken as a whole, were a great step forward for the cause in which they had long borne the burden and the heat of the day, they determined to be satisfied.

And so, too, were the border ruffians. Every step taken by the Free State settlers in opposition to the government was hailed with joy as leading toward an open rupture, which might make possible that movement which had long been promised them—an armed invasion of the Territory.

Returning home after the adjournment, Edward Langtry found his wife in a state of extreme trepidation. She had passed a sleepless night of anxiety and terror, on his account, and not without reason, our friends felt, upon hearing her story, which she related in tears.

It was nearly bedtime on the evening of the 5th, a dark, cloudy night, and she sat alone in the house, George having gone to the barn to attend to the horses. It was warm, and close, and still, save for the shrill notes of Bob White, which could be heard at intervals in the direction of the timber. She was thinking of her husband, and how happy and prosperous they might be, but for the unsettled condition of the Territory, and his active interest in politics; and yet she could not blame him. It would be base indeed to sacrifice his lifelong principles, to ease and security, even if the sacrifice would insure their safety. Suddenly the form of a man appeared in the doorway, which stood open for the admission of air.

"Whisht! is it alone yez are?" said a low voice.

She started up in affright, but controlled herself with a strong effort, as she replied:

"Brother George is somewhere near; I can call him. Do you wish to see him?"

"No," said the intruder, still in the same whispered tone. "It's yerself I wud be afther spakin' to; the blissed leddy that yez are, and Pat Malone wud have the heart of a rock, an' he saw sorrow comin' to that shwate face, an' niver shpoke a word o' warnin' to yez."

"Why, what do you mean, Mr. Malone?" said Agnes, coming forward, recognizing him as one whose family she had taken care of during the season of sickness in the early spring, and for whom she had since done many a little kindness in an unobtrusive manner.

"I mean, leddy, that I'm commanded to 'take care' of yer husband, mum, an' by me troth I'll do that same,'" said he with a very perceptible twinkle in his eye, enjoying the play upon the words, "take care," with all an Irishman's sense of humor.

"But can he not take care of himself?" said Agnes, still mystified, and yet with a deepening of that sense of danger which had long haunted her.

Pat made no reply, but drew from the pocket of his blue

jeans pants a paper, which he placed in Agnes' hand, and stood in silence while she read.

"GENERAL ORDER NO. 1. Blue Lodge No. 10, S. of S.

"Mark every leader of this obnoxious Abolition party and exterminate him. Neither give nor take quarter. The time has come when all qualms of conscience as to violating state or national laws must be disregarded, as your rights and property are in danger. It is enough that the slaveholding interest wills it, from which there is no appeal.

"Special Order No. 15. Blue Lodge No. 10, S. of S.

"To Pat Malone,—A member in good and regular standing of Blue Lodge No. 10, S. of S.

"*Whereas*, one Edward Langtry of Walnut Grove, has in various ways proven himself the deadly enemy of our institutions, the success of the objects for which we have banded ourselves together, and the triumph of our cause, demand that he be taken care of.

"Special Order No. 16, Blue Lodge No. 10, S. of S.

"To Pat Malone is delegated the execution of Special Order No. 15. If not executed within thirty days, the solemn oaths taken by said Pat Malone to obey all orders of the executive committee of the S. of S. shall be declared violated, and himself be given over to the vengeance due, under the laws of the lodge of which he is a member.

(Signed) W. H. MARKS, Sec."

Agnes read the paper through with a blanched face, and then sank into a chair, overcome with terror.

"But you will not do this wrong? You will not obey this order?" she sobbed appealingly.

"Not if it coshts me life, leddy. Pat Malone niver forgits sich kindness as yours; but it's not long they'll wait for the likes o' me, and so if you could be afther persuadin' of 'im to sell out and move away, it would be healthier for 'im, I'm thinkin'. It's lavin' I'll be myself afore long; but kape the sacret, pl'ase, or I'll niver get away wid a head on me shoulders;" but George's footsteps were heard, and Pat disappeared as silently as he had come, and with a weight upon her heart which almost stifled its beating, Agnes retired to rest. To rest—if so we may name her tossing to and fro upon her couch, and starting up in affright from the visions of that medium state, between sleep and waking, which is peopled by fears with horrible specters and dragons, and over whose crags and abysses and frightful cliffs sweep dreadful storms, and from which she awoke pale and spiritless.

On her husband's arrival, she threw herself into his arms, and begged him to fly from the Territory—to abandon all they had gained; and to seek a home beyond the agony of fear, and out of the reach of cowardly assassins.

But he smiled incredulously at the idea of danger.

"I cannot think," said he, "that the leaders of this proslavery movement, men who have been in the Congress of the United States, and held high offices in their own States, would countenance assassination. This is all a made-up scheme to alarm me into moving away. Some one of these fellows, your friend Pat Malone himself, perhaps, wants to get possession of this claim, with all its nice improvements, when they have induced me to run away like a coward;" then, as she still clung to him, sobbing: "Come! this is unworthy of my brave little wife, who so lately advised a young Southerner concerning his duty. Where is your patriotism now? Summon it, my love. I must follow the dictates of my conscience and take my chances. You would yourself despise me, could I do otherwise."

Agnes knew this to be true, and acknowledged it in her calmer moments, but the clouds of apprehension had gathered in that once clear sky, and the girlish light-heartedness which had so brightened the cabin in the face of inconvenience and privation of every kind, was powerless to dispel them.

CHAPTER XXVI.

THE NEW HOUSE—SILE'S POPPIN'—RAGE AND JEALOUSY.

Silas Hardiker having gone from home to attend the session of the Legislature almost immediately after John Alden's suspicions as to the matrimonial nature of his attentions were aroused, and having remained away through the months of July and August, during which time the engagement of Grace and Arthur had taken place, and all preliminaries as to their marriage been arranged, Alden had given him no further thought as a possible suitor.

Grace had dismissed the suggestion at once as a "mere chimera of papa's imagination."

"You are so devoted an admirer of mine, papa, that you see a lover in every gentleman who happens to call a few times, eligible or ineligible. I'm not so conceited," said she, with a little toss of the head, "and as for Sile Hardiker making love to me, why the thought is too ridiculous for anything. He couldn't make a p-p-p-proposal if he tried from n-n-now till next fourth of July," mimicked she.

"Well, perhaps not," said John, quieted for the time, but on Sile's return he fell into the old habit of dropping in, early in the evening, smoking and talking with Alden about the crops, and later, awkwardly but unobtrusively, passing to the south side, where the young folks,—the ladies wrapped in shawls, reluctant to give up their social meetings in the open air—still lingered. Generally he sat in the shadow of the house, his chair tilted back until his head rested on the vine-covered logs, his long limbs swinging ungracefully, and his large hands wandering, now to his head, then down the sides of the chair, and anon into the depths of his breeches pockets, in search of a resting-place.

He seldom spoke, unless in reply to a direct question addressed to him by some one of the group, out of politeness, or a desire to witness the contortions of feature, and general muscular contractions necessary to bring forth an answer. But he could laugh without stuttering, and his hearty guffaw could be heard loud and long, when any little witty sally from Grace called forth the merriment of the company, and this note of applause, which was sure to follow, led her, it is to be feared, to unprecedented efforts at repartee.

John Alden watched him closely when not engaged with friends and neighbors who had graver subjects to discuss, as he became more and more anxious to know his object, but could discover nothing, and postponed from day to day his intention of questioning him, hoping that he came merely to pass away time, which hung heavily on his hands.

His mother came with him but once or twice during the early part of the month; latterly she had gone to Lauderdale and Kansas City to procure furniture for the new house, which had arisen, as if by magic, during the summer months, and now stood completed. On Grace's announcement of this fact at the breakfast table one morning, John could not but exclaim:

"Completed! well, I'm sorry for it. That woman needs some engrossing occupation to keep her out of mischief; Heaven knows what she'll be up to now!"

"Now, papa, you're too bad!" said Grace; "she tries so hard to improve, and, in fact, I think her earnest efforts are beginning to tell. She tones down her dress a little; don't she, mamma?"

"I wish she would tone down her voice a little," said John; "it is harsh and loud, besides, there is something suggestive of wickedness in it."

"Your old theory," said Amy.

"Yes, and you'll find it a correct one. There is no outward or audible sign so strongly indicative of character as the tones of the human voice, which, once heard, it needs but a quick ear and a clear and experienced perception to produce an accurate conclusion as to the general drift of a person's disposition and character; and, to one of thoughtful observation, such a conclusion is well nigh infallible. In this case, to my ear they are quite distinct, and run the whole gamut of selfishness, from a desire to appropriate everything which can in any way benefit herself, to unrelenting vengeance and unlimited capacity of persecution of those who fail to gratify her wishes, or who thwart her purposes."

"Well, all she wants of us is, to ' larn the ways of quality,' " said Grace, "and you know, papa, we are commanded to let our light shine."

"Very true, Miss; but you know, too, there is something in that same good Book about casting your pearls before swine."

"Lest they turn again and rend you," laughed she; "well, I hope she won't do that."

"But what would you have us do?" inquired Amy, with a troubled face. "I'm sure I don't enjoy her society, but when she comes so good-naturedly asking for information on certain points, and seems so desirous to improve, can we shut the door in her face?"

And here, as often happens with the wiseacre, Alden's wisdom was at fault. It is easy enough for the black bird of evil omen to flutter their wings and cry out danger, but only the eagle eye of omniscience, scouring the whole scene from above and beyond its perils, can point out the path of avoidance, if such path there be. So he only took up his hat to go to work, saying:

"Well, I don't know exactly what you had best do at

present, only try and prevent her misunderstanding your kindness, and interpreting it as a desire for closer relations."

To the great dismay of Mrs. Alden and Grace, after the expressed misgiving of Mr. Alden as to the reliability of their Missouri friends, which they had laughed at as only "father's prejudices," Sile made his appearance soon after noon of that same day, conveying an invitation from his mother, requesting them to come over and view the new house, and eat a 5 o'clock dinner. Mr. Alden was also invited, and Grace went out to the field where he was at work, as the envoy most likely to succeed in reconciling him to their going, and winning an acceptance of the invitation for himself.

She was gone some time, and her mother judged rightly in inferring that she found it difficult to persuade him to say yes.

He also found it difficult to put Grace off with no, and she finally came back with the intelligence that her papa had reluctantly consented to their going, and would come to escort them home soon after 5 o'clock, but that he resolutely refused to dine with the Hardikers, and they must excuse him as best they could.

This dampened the ladies' spirits somewhat, but they had promised long since to return the widow's numerous visits when the new house should be finished; besides, they were very curious to see the inside of it, so they made ready as quickly as possible. Arthur was absent at the time, attending the White Springs Convention, or they would have had an additional opposing element to contend with, which might have stayed them.

After a delightful drive, which they really enjoyed, they neared the new frame house. It was painted white, and towered above its fellows, though only relatively large, and would have passed unnoticed, save for newness, in any moderate-sized Northern village. Yet, there were few private residences of equal size in the Territory at that time, it being perhaps twenty-eight feet front, a piazza extending across the whole length, and a square cupola finishing off the roof. Its position was certainly very fine, and it was visible from a distance, in consequence of the eminence on which it stood.

They paused for a moment on the piazza to enjoy the view, the eye following involuntarily the waving lines of the creek on one side, and the more distant river on the other, the reflection of the afternoon sun bringing out in solid relief the gorgeous coloring of the many-hued trees which marked their courses, beyond which lowered in the clear atmosphere the bald bluffs capped with stone.

The hostess came forward to receive them, with a smirk of satisfaction and a voice whose tones disturbed the pleasant thoughts awakened by the lovely scene.

"How air you? You look right peart," and then she led the way into the parlor to the left of the hall, pausing a moment, that her guests might be properly impressed with its grandeur. A red and yellow, and white and blue carpet, a lounge covered with blue damask, six cane-seated chairs and two rockers, green 'paper blinds, shaded with lace curtains looped back with red ribbons, and a row of hideous lithographs in tawdry gilt frames, hung at equal altitudes and distances from each other on the white walls, with a stove and small table, comprised the furniture of the room.

"I reckon this ere'll do to bet on," she said.

"It certainly is *gorgeous*," replied Grace, while Amy remained silent, thinking that furnishings express character as well as voices, and then self-reprovingly, that, as this certainly expressed a striving upward for higher and better things, she might excuse it. But the widow interpreted her silence as occasioned by the bitter gnawings of jealousy, for she added, *sotto voce*, with a nudge, as she led the way into the spare bedroom back of the parlor, Grace remaining a moment behind:

"But I hain't puffed up nor nothin,' and ef you'll jine hands with me yer kin have a kinder sort o' half interest in this hyer set out."

Mrs. Alden made no reply, not knowing what to say, and Grace appearing at that moment, the widow, with a wink, excused her from answering.

The bedroom, as there was less occasion for the display of magnificent taste and the production of gorgeous effects, presented quite a comfortable and inviting appearance, notwithstanding the bed was surmounted by a quilt of wonderful design, worked out in blue, and red, and yellow, and green pieces of calico.

"This is my piney quilt; pineys an' sunflowers them air. Ain't it some on style? an' didn't cost nary red. Salome made it. She's the nigger sewin' woman I told you about. She's a stavin' hand at sewin'; did this hyer all after work hours."

"Poor Salome," thought Amy, as she looked at the many thousand neat stitches so deftly set. "It was probably a relief to her; a joy thus to work out her design in bright colors, as is the painting of the picture to the artist, and the song to the poet."

When Mrs. Alden and Grace had removed their wraps, she led them across the hall to a large empty room, the full length of the east side of the house.

"Now, this is what Kernel Delaney calls his library. You would know what to do with it," to Grace; "but we don't. Sile an' me don't make no pretensions to book larnin'. Sez Sile to me this mornin', sez he, 'Marm, there's jist one mounting as money won't move, an' that's larnin'.'"

"Not even niggers can do that for you," said Grace, a little maliciously.

"Wall, no," said she, pausing to look Grace directly in the face;—"but there's somebody I know of as kin, an' as I tole Sile, the niggers, an' the money, an' this fine house, oughter bring this yer person round," and as she led the way up stairs, "When a trade's on hand for what yer want, ye've got ter balance the scale, an' if it weighs down a leetle on my side, I don't keer, s'long's I git what I'm arter."

It was becoming plain to Amy what the widow's design was, but there was no escape until Mr. Alden came, and that would be after five o'clock. She could only try and ward off a direct understanding by resolutely refusing to take hints, and directing the conversation to different subjects. She looked at Grace, and found her seemingly unconscious. She could get no answering look. It was as well, perhaps, for the widow's sharp eyes were flashing from one to the other, as if to read their thoughts. Grace went to the window and called her mother's attention to the little cabins of the settlers nestling 'mid patches of corn-fields, the cattle grazing in small numbers here and there, and then to the sky of deep, dark, unfathomable blue, with heavy masses of white fleecy clouds pillowed in the east, and floating hither and thither in fragmentary fanciful shapes, lighted up by the rays of the sun now sinking rapidly in the west. They gazed admiringly and in silence, until Mrs. Hardiker's voice recalled them to the survey of the rooms, two of which were furnished in very good style, one for her own use and the other, she said, for her son, whose ample wardrobe occupied the closets, and whose profuse supply of jewelry was spread out upon the bureau. The two rooms across the hall and over the library were unfurnished.

"Ye see I've left somethin' fer somebody else to do," said she, with a knowing wink.

"I think you have done a great deal," said Grace.

"Yes, indeed," said Mrs. Alden, "and considering the

disadvantages we labor under in this new country, you have done it well."

They now descended to the parlor, and found Sile there, his chair tilted back and himself ready—after he had gone to the window and ejected the tobacco from his mouth out of deference to the visitors—to drink in every word of conversation, and every look and motion of Grace; and in his eyes Amy could now plainly enough discern a consuming passion.

Determined, if possible, to direct the conversation to general topics, Mrs. Alden began by inquiring concerning the acts of the Legislature, of which he gave his opinion in his broken way—

"F—f—fine lot o' fellers; h—h—had a r—r—rousin' good time down thar. P—passed lors? Y—y—yes, a dog-gon lot on 'em; m—m—mor'n a wagin' load. R—reckon t'war all right. K—k—kernel Delaney, an' ole D—D—Dave, an' D—D—Dock Cornello war thar runnin' things. N—n—no use'n us fellers t—t—troublin' ourselves a—a—about it, s'long's the ole l—l—long heads wor runnin'."

"But suppose they do not run things properly?" suggested Mrs. Alden.

He wriggled his hands about in the depths of his pockets, and "R—r—reckoned they knew what they war about; l—leastwise they oughter."

"They're commin' up here to-morrer, Guvnur an' all," said his mother, "an' I'm goin' ter do things up in style, you bet! They're both widderers—the Guvnur an' the Kernel,—an' Cornello he's an ole bach, an' if I hadn't made up my min' to go it alone, thar's no tellin' what might happen. He's a peart-lookin' ole feller, they tell me, an' Mrs. Guvnur Harlan' wouldn't soun' so bad; an' ef the name belonged to me, not to be sneezed at," said she, rising and strutting before the long looking-glass, at which Grace's risibilities could be restrained no longer, and she burst into a peal of laughter, in which Sile joined with his loud guffaw, almost upsetting his chair, as he said:

"D—d—darn it, marm! d—d—don't make a fool o' yerself!"

"I don't intend ter," said she snappishly, interpreting the reproof as meant for future guidance, rather than as applicable to her present manners.

"Didn't I say I meant to go it alone?" but, looking at Amy, "as I wor tellin' yer, they're commin', the Guvnur, an' the Kernel, an' ole Dave, an' Dock Cornello, an' Rev. Thomas Jimson, jist as many as kin sleep in the beds in this hyer house, 'lowin the Guvnur a bed to hisself. I can sleep 'em all well enough, but thar's the eatin' part. Sence I've saw you do it, so kinder easy and peart like, an' bin down ter Warsaw, an' took dinner with Mis' Dr. Rulison, I've got a sneakin' notion that our back country way o' settin' down, an' every feller pitchin' in, ain't 'zackly the style for this hyer set out."

"Have you been to see Mrs. Rulison?" inquired Grace in a surprised tone.

"You bet! Whar's the harm? I war interdoosed to her on the 4th of July, an' twar only manners to give her a call, so down I went, a month ago, with my best harness on, an' when I knocked she came to the door herself, reg'lar abolition style; a mighty peart-lookin' little critter she is, too, most up to you," with a toss of her head toward Grace, whereat the latter laughed, and Sile, as in duty bound, laughed also. "Leastwise she's as smilin' as a basket o' chips, an' not stuck up nuther. She asked me in, inquired about my family, an' I tole her that I was a widder an' hadn't only one son, an' he wor in the Legislater, an' that I hed hed a new house built, an' wanted to know how ter furnish it, an' she took me all over hern, an' tole me I might jist copy anything I wanted ter. An' then she asked me to stay to dinner, an' the table wor full o' people who had jist come inter the Territory, an' I wor a keepin' my eyes open to everything, an' I saw as how she waited on 'em jist as you do." Turning to Amy, " Now I'm mighty feered that's jist whar I'll git stuck to-morrer, with all them thar big bugs starin' at me, an' I wanted yer to come to-day an' kind o' post me up like.

"I've got a good cook—brung her up from Westport—got her cheap of the man who raised her, 'cos the dratted critter wor makin' a fool o' herself cryin' after her ole man wot hed bin sold South. She's pickin' up a little, an' gittin' kind o' peart agin' up here, but I'm mighty feered some o' the Yanks round the Grove will git hold on her an' ship her off to Nebrasky. None on 'em too good to do it," said she, rocking her chair violently for a few moments, then glancing up at her son, she arose, saying:

"Come, Miss Alden, please, inter the dinin'-room with me. I reckon them gals hez got the table all sot, an' you kin tell me ef it's all right on the goose; that's one reason why I wor partickler urgin' fer yer to cum to-day."

This was somewhat reassuring, and Mrs. Alden followed her cheerfully. Grace rose to come also, but Mrs. Hardiker turned to her:

"Oh, no, neow! yer jist stay here an' keep the Squire company till yer mar an' I git the dinner sot out in style, an' then we'll ask yer to step out."

"Shall we play we are your distinguished guests of to-morrow?" inquired Grace, laughingly.

"That's it, egzackly!" and then she led Amy out into the hall and back past the stairway to the door at the north, which led into the dining-room. They found the table with plates laid, and other accessories placed on it at random, in the awkward confusion into which ignorant or careless servants invariably fall. Mrs. Alden went toward it and re-arranged several dishes, placing things in their proper places, and called Mrs. Hardiker's attention to the change.

"Yas, I see," with a kind of a chuckle. "Set down, I want to tell yer," and she drew a chair away from the dining table for her visitor, and another for herself; "Sile's a-goin' ter pop—" leaning over and slapping Mrs. Alden familiarly on the knee, at which that lady involuntarily drew back.

"Ye needn't be skeer't; he'll do it all up right, jist now, an' then we'll all set down to dinner kind o' easy an' family like. I've bin eg'gin ov him on from the fust, an' t'wor mighty hard bringin' him up to the scratch; though, Lord knows, he's bilin' all over with love for that gal o' yourn, but you see he's so bashful-like, an' so feered she wouldn't hev him—an' he ain't no talker, nohow. But last night, when we wor settin' in this hyer house for the fust time, sez he to me, sez he:

"'Marm, I've sot my heart on that gal, an' 'pears like ef I don't git her I shall bust,' an' sez he, down in the mouth like, 'I don't bleeve she keers a mite for me.'

"'Lord,' sez I, 'Sile Hardiker, ye don't know nothin' 'bout gals, ef ye air a Squire. They won't fall inter yer mouth like ripe plums. Ye hain't so much as asked her. How'd ye know she don't keer fer ye? How does she know ye keer fer her, when all you do's look at her?'"

"That's so," said Mrs. Alden, interrupting her monologue; "I do not think Grace has ever suspected that he cared for her other than as a friend." But any suggestion of Amy's was as powerless to stop this outpouring as her feeble strength would have been to resist the torrent that pours down the mountain side, or the mill-wheel in its revolutions.

"That's jest what I told him; an', sez I, 'mebbe you'll hev to go on yer bended knees; gals is notional, an' likes to be coaxed—they're all alike; bein' a woman myself, I ought ter know; but that ain't nothin' when ye git used to it.'

"'Marm,' sez he, an', Miss Alden, he wor actoolly cryin', an' he tuk out his new red an' white hankerchief to wipe his eyes, an' sez he:

"'Marm, I'd pray from now till kingdom come ef t'would do any good. She's the peartest critter in these hyer parts; an' ef I don't git her, I don't keer a dog-gon for anythin'.'

"Sez I, 'Sile, don't yer be a fool. I'm sot on that gal myself, so ye jist go in ter win, an' I'll back yer. I never come out of the little end of the horn yit, an' I won't this time, you bet!' An' then we made it up that he was to bring you over here to-day, an' when he got a chance he were to up an' at her, an' not take no for an answer."

Amy started up, and turned toward the parlor, but the widow put her hand out to delay her:

"Don't go fer to interrupt him now. He sot thar lookin' at her till he couldn't hold out any longer, an' I'll be bound he's poppin'."

"But I must go! Grace might be alarmed if he is persistent, and she cannot marry him—she is already engaged."

"Engaged! Can't marry him!" she shrieked, all her earnestness of feeling turned in a moment into wrath, which no sense of propriety had ever taught her to restrain; "an' yer hev bin incouragin' my son to go kadovelin round yer place, keepin' company with her all summer, an' me a visitin' o' yer, an' givin' yer a present of a pure-blooded pony. I'll have my revenge, I will! Ef she won't hev my Sile, she can't hev any feller, there!" and she went foaming and raging after Mrs. Alden through the hall and into the parlor, where, as the latter threw open the door, Sile stood alone, with flashing eyes.

"Grace!" called she. "Oh, Mr. Hardiker! where is my daughter?"

"D-d-damn your daughter!" stuttered Sile, striding off, and she heard his footsteps as they fell heavily on the uncarpeted floor of the hall, and the back door slammed behind him.

"YER MIGHTY PURTY MISS GRACE."

When the widow and Mrs. Alden left the parlor, Grace was seated on the lounge, and Sile, with his chair tilted backward, was on the opposite side of the room. When they had fairly disappeared, and the door was closed behind them, his chair came down to a level, his hands came out of his pockets and, clasping his fingers, he began to twirl his thumbs and cast sidelong glances at his companion, in such a comical, sheepish-looking way that she could scarcely conceal her amusement, but sat silently enjoying his evident embarrassment for some moments, until he broke the silence, with:

"You're m-m-mighty purty, Miss Grace."

"Do you think so? Well, I'm not a bit good."

"Lord knows, you're too g-g-good for me!" with a sigh, and a vigorous thrusting of his hands in his pockets.

"I r-r-reckon now you think I'm n-n-nothin' but an ongainly oneddicated feller—wh-wh-white trash—not good enough f-f-for you to wipe yer feet on—an I h-h-hain't, nuther."

Touched by this self-depreciation, and his sorrowful tone of voice and accompanying sigh, Grace answered, with an earnest shake of the head:

"Indeed, no, Mr. Hardiker; I think you are a very good-hearted sort of a man, and I know you can improve in every respect, if you try."

He had turned his large black eyes full upon her as she began to speak, and the kind tone and encouraging words flashed a ray of hope to mingle with his overpowering desire.

"Then you'll hev me—you'll be my wife?" he cried, springing from his seat and coming toward her, just as she had risen with the intention of leaving the room.

Misunderstanding her action, as well as her speech, he threw his long arms around her and drew her toward him, the fire of consuming passion flashing from his eyes, sending a thrill of terror and indignation to her heart, terror which blanched her cheek, and anger which gave her voice, and manner to exclaim imperatively, looking him full in the face:

"Let me go, sir! You misunderstand me entirely," at which he partially released her, but falling upon his knees, the excitement of the moment partially overcoming the impediment in his speech, cried out:

"I l-love you! I love you? I know yer m-m-mighty fur above me. I n-n-never ought to a dreamt on it, but I hev, an' I can't an' won't giv yer up. I'll s-sarve ye all yer days, like a b-born slave, ef ye'll be my wife. You shan't want f-f-fer nothin' s'long's there's a dollar or a nigger b'longin' to me."

"Oh, I cannot! Indeed, Mr. Hardiker, I cannot," said Grace, drawing her hands from him and turning toward the hall door; but he was too quick for her; springing up and placing his back against it, his voice losing the pleading tone in that of harsh demand:

"Why can't yer? Am I sich a p-p-pore, sneakin', d—d drotted fool that you can't ab-b-bide me."

"No, oh no! but I am engaged to another," she gasped.

"The d-devil you air! Some darned white-livered Abolitionist, I'll be bound," stamping his feet in a rage. "I-I-I'll take care of him! who is he?" but Grace in her despair had turned to the door of the bedroom, and before he could stop her had passed out and from thence to the dining room beyond, then out of doors and around to the front of the house, from whence, hearing her mother's frightened call, she stepped up to the piazza, and replied:

"Here mamma, come out here."

No castaway on barren isle, no weary traveler on sandy desert ever more warmly welcomed friendly sail, or hailed with more joy the sight of a blooming oasis, than did Grace and her mother the coming of her father, whose welcome visage appearing in the distance, and coming swiftly, relieved them from their painful situation. The widow had followed them to the piazza with her revilings, which they endured in silence, after vain attempts to explain their position, and make clear to her, that their kindly acts had been only tokens of friendship in good faith, which efforts were received as retorts, and only added fuel to the flames of her anger, which poured forth in a torrent of burning and scathing epithets and accusations, destroying in their flow all vestiges of the respect and kindly feeling which they had so carefully cultivated for the good-natured, well-meaning woman, they had supposed her to be.

When Mr. Alden had reached the piazza, under the shadow of his protecting arm Amy went into the bedroom for their wraps, without which they were shivering in the frosty evening air. They hastily put them on, and when they had been assisted into the rough lumber wagon, whose broad bed and springless seats seemed a secure place of refuge, Grace poured forth her story into sympathizing ears.

She was full of self-reproach for the familiarity which had rendered this presumption possible, and yet said she, smiling:

"How should I know?"

"How, indeed," said her father. "Characters are like chemicals, new mixtures sometimes produce unexpected and startling effects."

CHAPTER XXVII.

DEPREDATIONS ON ARTHUR'S CLAIM—BURNING OF HIS HOUSE.

The wrath of the Hardikers, when the ebullition of words ceased, became a smoldering fire, impossible to quench, and bursting forth with renewed vigor and energy at unlooked for times and places.

That very night the beautiful pony which Grace so loved was turned loose from the stable, maimed beyond help, this cruel act making it impossible for Alden to return it on demand, and grieving the heart of its young mistress. Then began depredations on Arthur's claim, for of course they soon learned who it was that had been preferred, and were incapable of comprehending the patent fact, that constitutional and educational differences would in any event have proved an impassable barrier to the accomplishment of their desires. They bent all their energies toward driving him from the Territory, setting the very spirit of mischief to work those small ills which goad the flesh like pins, wearying and wearing upon the proudest spirit.

Carr Withers, it must be remembered, had an old grudge against Arthur and the Walnut Grove Association, and it was an easy matter to persuade him that he had a right to cut the valuable timber on Arthur's claim, and that to him belonged the fresh lime in Arthur's kiln. Remembering former experience, he chose the darkness of the night-time for the prosecution of his labors and the wreaking of the secret vengeance, a desire for which he had long and patiently nursed.

It was not until Arthur's return from Topeka that these trespasses were discovered, and accustomed as he was to the Northern method of settling all such clashing of claims, he at once sent a notice to Carr Withers of his willingness to meet him before arbiters selected from both sides, and to them submit evidence of his right to hold the land in dispute under the unwritten law of squatters' rights. No notice was taken of this, but the depredations still continued, bidding fair to denude the claim of timber, in which its value chiefly consisted. Then Arthur went before the justice of the peace for the neighborhood, with, however, small hope of obtaining relief, as the justice who had been appointed by the Legislature belonged to the opposing party, and the writ, if issued, must be served by Zeke Fagin, who was sheriff of the county. But it was his only recourse, and he made affidavit as to the damage done, charging it upon Carr Withers and others, and then endeavored to await the result with patience. The first, in fact, the only fruits of this attempt to obtain redress, was a characteristic warning tacked to the door of the cabin and signed by the secretary of Blue Lodge No. 10, "S. of S.," suggesting in words more forcible than elegant, that the climate of Nebraska would be healthier for said Arthur Fairchild, against whom was enumerated a long list of offences against the slave institution. Ten days were given him in which to remove himself and his effects beyond the jurisdiction of said lodge, after which time should he be found in Kansas, his life was declared forfeit.

A similar notice was found on the door of Alden's cabin, but both he and Arthur pocketed the papers quietly, and pursued the even tenor of their way. John was engaged in gathering the fully-ripened corn, and carrying what he could spare to market, storing away a winter stock of vegetables, selling the surplus, for which there was great demand, building shelter for the stock, and otherwise preparing for the approaching winter, of which, however, he had small dread, expecting, as he did, that it would resemble the one he had already spent in the Territory.

Arthur's time was given to superintending, and assisting in the erection of the house for his bride, into which he had put most of his patrimony, relying upon his own industry to win from the prolific soil a support and competence afterward; and with all the pride of a young and ardent lover for whom waits the dearest object of his desire, he looked upon the walls now completed and roofed in.

It was the first stone house, and by far the most comfortable and roomy in the settlement, and within the Alden household there was an air of preparation for the event which was to follow its completion.

Arthur's demeanor was singularly calm and cheerful, and notwithstanding the threats, the intrusions, and the annoyances, otherwise sufficient to have disheartened him, he seemed supremely happy.

The gentle concern manifested by Grace at his necessary absences, the glad smile with which she greeted his coming, the sweet sense of being cared for, which, under other and happier circumstances, might have been less plainly manifest, was a rich draught for the hungry heart which had waited long for the first blossoming of reciprocation.

But there came a night when he waked from rosy dreams of love to find his cabin in flames, with but time to gather up the most necessary articles of clothing, and make his escape.

Crushed to the earth, he cried out with white lips and voice of anguish: "Now, indeed, am I undone!" as, standing upon the door-steps of Alden's cabin, from whence the new building was more plainly visible than from his own, he saw the yellow flames curling in and out of its windows and doors, and bursting from the roof, beneath which had clustered all his anticipations of domestic bliss.

Higher and higher, against the midnight sky, the flames arose, remorselessly eating out every vestige of woodwork, sparkling and crackling as if in fiendish joy at the ruin they had wrought, then, as the walls fell, a smoke-stained, broken heap, leaping over the masses of sand and stone and earth, they reached the tall spires of dry grass, and, still chuckling, swept on far and wide over the prairies, and up the sides of the bluffs in the distance, a moving wall of fire, sparing naught in its progress, and leaving a blackened, desolate stretch of country for miles around. The houses and barns of settlers were only saved by the hasty burning of fire guards around their premises.

The necessity for immediate exertion to save Alden's home was a godsend to Arthur, tiding him over the first sickening feelings of despair, as it required all the men's strength and activity, with the assistance of Amy and Grace, to guide the fire they were obliged to set out, and prevent the dangerous ally called to their assistance from escaping control, and turning its destructive powers upon themselves. But, when all danger was over, and, weary and covered with smoke and cinders, they sat down within the house in the cool calm of a frosty October morning, a sense of the magnitude of his loss returned with overwhelming force.

Amy alone seemed to have retained the power of motion, for after a little time she stirred up the fire which was smoldering upon the hearth, and began preparations for breakfast; but Alden, Grace and Arthur sat motionless, and in silence. John would have comforted the young man, but he knew not how—all words at his command seemed so inadequate; but at length Arthur himself broke the silence. Lifting his eyes, which had been fixed on the coals, he said:

"Grace."

She looked at him with sympathy in her honest brown eyes.

"I am a sorry bridegroom, Grace, with naught to offer you but empty hands."

Summoning a roguish smile, and the playful manner which so well became her, she replied:

"Not quite so bad as that, Arthur. They've left us timber enough for a log cabin, I think."

The words, the tone, the manner, and, above all, the use of the pronoun *us*, which implied so much, had the effect upon him of a powerful stimulus.

It was another draught, with a deeper flavor from the enchanted cup. Tears came to his eyes, but they were tears of joy, as he arose, and crossing the room to where she sat, looked down lovingly upon the dear girl, who put forth her hand to grasp his own.

"I am indeed rich, thank Heaven! while so true, so brave a heart is all my own."

And now, with a sense of renewed hopefulness, they made ready for breakfast. Grace went upstairs to arrange her toilet, while Arthur and John washed their grimy hands and faces, laughingly piecing out the former's limited wardrobe with a coat of Alden's that fitted his trim figure as neatly, perhaps, as the clothing of the average plainsman. Arthur was obliged also to borrow John's hat and overcoat, when, during the day, he went down to Warsaw to replenish his wardrobe, and carry to the postoffice a letter written to his parents, detailing his grievances, and modestly requesting a loan for the relief of his present necessities.

Then again he went before the justice of the peace, this time adding the name of Silas Hardiker to that of Withers, in his complaint, and urging that officer, if he had a shadow of respect for justice, or for the station he filled, to issue the warrants for their arrest, and have them served immediately. Then he endeavored for many days to find these men and remonstrate with them; but they were not yet ready for the encounter, and kept out of his way.

In the meantime, a letter came to him from home, a sympathizing letter, containing a liberal remittance, but begging him to leave the Territory, where he seemed to be in the midst of so much peril, and come home, if only for a short time, until this storm had blown over. His mother wrote:

"Come home, my dear boy; bring Grace with you and come home. We love her for your sake as well as her own, and will give you both a warm welcome. If you do not feel like beating a retreat from the presence of your enemies, look upon it but as a temporary arrangement,—a visit, a wedding tour. You cannot do much on a farm in winter, and perhaps by spring the Federal government will have put forth its strong arm to quell these disturbances. At any rate, if you value your mother's peace of mind, come home. Hasten your marriage day, and come home *immediately*. Let Grace procure her wedding trousseau here and afterward."

That matter of trousseau had troubled Grace very little. The stores at Warsaw contained nothing tempting, or at all suitable for the purpose, so she resolved to dispense with anything new. A blue silk, which had always pleased Arthur, had been selected for her to wear during the ceremony, and if the proposed change in the arrangements was made, her traveling dress of the previous year would answer for the journey. So Amy told him:

"The trousseau need not stand in the way."

There was really no obstacle in the way of their immediate departure, but the boy's own strong will, and his patriotism.

"I will go," said he; "Grace's eyes tell me that she will enjoy a visit to her old home,—but we will adhere to the time we have already set. The people of this district have elected me a member of the convention for the formation of the Free State Constitution,—the future institutions of the home which I have chosen depend on the action of that assembly. It is my privilege, it is my right, it is my duty and my desire, to have a voice in determining what those institutions shall be. When I have done my work, I can play with a clear conscience," and turning to Amy, " we will go for a visit to our old home for the holidays, returning early in the spring to this new home of ours."

And thus it was all arranged as he willed.

The Constitutional Convention met at Topeka, on the 23d of October, 1855.

Their business progressed with expedition, the majority of the members extending the labors of the day far into the night, working by day in the hall, and by night in the committee-room.

" It was noticeable," said Arthur, smilingly, as he and Langtry, who were both members, were giving Alden an account of the meeting, " that each man who had, or could obtain a copy of the statutes of his native State brought it with him to the Convention, and when anything differing from that standard was offered, rose to explain that such a feature was not found in the Constitution of 'Indiany' or 'Pennsylvany,' and by dint of this repeated friction many objectionable features were removed, and a very fair Constitution produced."

" And when will it be submitted to the people?" asked Alden.

"On the 15th of December, and I should like to be here to cast my vote for it," said Arthur earnestly.

" Oh, don't you trouble yourself about that," was Langtry's reply. " We shall carry it by an overwhelming majority."

"They will have to send a much larger force than before, if they take possession of the polls again," said Alden.

CHAPTER XXVIII.

A DEMAND FOR JUSTICE — THE ASSASSIN'S AIM — THE LONE TREE ON THE PRAIRIE.

And now Arthur bent all his energies toward preparations for the wedding and his departure, endeavoring to put things in the best possible shape for his prospective long absence. He procured a land-warrant, and laid it upon his claim, that he might have a more direct title of ownership than that which a squatter's right could give. Then he visited the tardy specimen who held the seals of justice, urging him again to issue a writ of arrest, and failing in that, finally secured an injunction forbidding the cutting of timber on his premises; but, alas! as well give it to the winds, as to Zeke Fagin for service.

With Hardiker or Withers he had not yet been able to obtain an interview, yet time, inexorable and swift-footed time, moved forward with rapid strides, bringing him within two days of the wedding and departure.

He had obtained lodgings in the house of a neighbor, some two miles distant, and went over to breakfast with the Aldens on the morning of the 21st, intending to go immediately afterward to Warsaw, to make some final and necessary arrangements, among others, to engage the minister who was to perform the marriage ceremony.

For some reason, unaccountable even to herself, perhaps a mere fancy to try her power, Grace set to work to prevent his going; detaining him by the sweet, pretty wiles that fair women best know how to use. A game of chess, a song, a new magazine story, something, every time he proposed going, until the morning waned, and the sun told the hour of noon.

"I must go," said he at dinner.

"Arthur," said she solemnly, "never do to-day what you can put off till to-morrow;" then, pleadingly, "Stay with us all the afternoon, do!"

"Fie, Grace!" said her father, "let Arthur attend to his business; you have detained him long enough."

"Yes," said he rising, "I must go now, for to-morrow I will remain all day with you, and the next—" John did not hear the rest of that sentence, for as he spoke Arthur opened the door, and Langtry came bustling in with some piece of neighborhood news, and, forgetting the young folks with their joys and troubles, Alden sat down to chat with him for an hour or two, and then set out in haste to get in his last load of corn, as the clouds were gathering, and the east wind betokened coming rain.

Arthur rode one horse, and led another; his wagon needed repair, and he had left it, some days since, at the blacksmith shop in Calhoun, and to-day he intended to call for it and harnessing his team thereto, drive down to Warsaw on his errands. Intent upon his purposes, and with summer in his heart, he hurried along, not pausing to notice the changes which a few weeks had made in everything surrounding the serpentine road through the timber over which his pathway had so often led. The trees, shorn of their foliage, and no longer joyous with the songs of the birds and the whirr of the summer insects, stood bare, and gaunt, and desolate, their branches outlined against a leaden sky, while the winds, tossing and whirling the yellow leaves about, chanted a mournful requiem, which fell unheeded on his ear. The very road, usually so firm and smooth, was sticky and uneven, caused by the alternate congealing of the earth during the nighttime, and its thawing out under the noonday sun. But it impeded not his progress, for, as if divining his glad errand, the well-trained steed bore him onward at a rapid pace, and anon the smithy, which, although within the limits of Calhoun, stood apart from the other buildings, came in view.

As he neared the shop and dismounted, he heard voices, and as he advanced to the open door through which the glowing flames of the forge might be seen, three men came in sight. At last then, he was able to confront them, his enemies, Sile Hardiker, Carr Withers, and the little Irishman whom he scarce knew how to class—whether as friend or foe. With flashing eyes and menacing gestures, coming toward him, Sile was the first to speak:

"S—s—so yer g—g—going to take the lor on me, are ye? y—y—ye d—d abolition sneak! Ye 'aint got the grit to give me the satisfaction of a g—g—gentleman fer the wrong ye've done me!"

"Why, what do you mean?" said Arthur coolly. "What wrong have I done you? It is I who should and must receive satisfaction for your trespasses. You have taken my timber, and destroyed my house."

"D—d—damn yer house!" stuttered Sile, "if I hed my r—r—rights y—y—yer wouldn't need a house."

"You stole my land!" barked Withers fiercely, as the little dog vociferates when under the protecting shelter of a greater.

"An' d—d—damn yer, ye stole my gal! What's a h—house without the w—woman you love?" shrieked Sile, advancing toward Arthur with the gun which he held in his hand, raised menacingly.

"Come one at a time, gentlemen, and I'm willing to meet you," said Arthur, placing his back against the smithy wall, and deliberately raising his revolver, which of late he always carried.

They halted, looked at each other, and then slunk away, Sile muttering to himself prudently, "N—n—no, I'le be doggoned ef I f—f—furnish food for abolition powder."

When the coast seemed to be clear, Arthur left his position to confer with the blacksmith.

"The wagon was not yet finished, he was at work upon it, but it would take him two or three hours at least."

"Then," said Arthur, "I will leave one horse here, and with the other go to Warsaw, stopping on my return for the wagon."

"All right," said the smith.

"Don't disappoint me, now; I shall want it on my return," and with these words he mounted and set forth.

Speed swiftly, oh, young rider! for whom a maiden's heart beats warmly, for whom, far away, a mother prays, and for whom the murderer lies in wait.

The roads cross each other. To the left! to the left, and return to her whose undefined premonitions of ill would have detained thee! But no! to the right; the task set before him must be accomplished,—he was not wont to let the day pass with the day's work undone. Even now there is hope, should the easiest path though the longest, allure him. But no! direct to his purpose and straight to his mark, he speeds onward down the hill, and past the lone tree which rears itself like some giant by the roadside. A moment more; a flash! a fall! the sound of a shot rings out on the still air, and a horse goes riderless on the prairie.

Three hours later, a fair girl with brown eyes and pale, anxious face walked restlessly to and fro in a rude cabin,—the gathering clouds in the autumn sky not heavier than the weight upon her heart. The daily routine of work, the charm of preparation for the coming event, suggestions of glad greetings with old-time friends, made by her mother with kind intent,—alike insufficient to arouse the slightest manifestation of interest.

Long before the time at which she might have reasonably expected the return of him for whom her fears went out, with pale face pressed to window-pane, she gazed into the gathering gloom. How slowly move the hours when weighted by the brakes of mysterious, indefinable dread.

"Mamma," said Grace at five o'clock, resuming her restless walk, "it seems to me an age since Arthur went away. When will he come? It is growing dark, and those black clouds surely indicate rain."

"He won't mind a little rain, Grace. You must not allow your fears to overcome you," said her mother.

Half an hour later, she sees through the window, dimly, an approaching form,—she hears footsteps,—and with a glad cry she springs to the door.

What is it that blanches the roses which had come to her cheeks, and sends a cold shudder through her frame?

The white, set face of Sile Hardiker, with its black, wicked, wide open eyes and large, beastly jaws, confronts her. His passion calcined by jealousy to hate, hissed forth its venom in the cruel words:

"Y-y-yer wait for yer l-lover, do yer? H-h-he won't come until ye s-send fer 'im. I've l-l-laid 'im out by the l-lone tree on the prairie."

Is vengeance sweet to the wicked? Then surely the piercing cry of agony which rang out on the still air, must have sated his soul, as turning away, he rode off in the darkness.

That shriek reached John Alden in the barnyard, where he was unloading corn, and he hastened in to find Grace unconscious, and her mother bending over her.

But for a short time only she succumbed to the blow, then, recovering herself, she repeated the words which had stricken her, adding:

"We must go. We must go immediately to him, papa."

"Yes, yes," said John, "I will go; but calm yourself, my

dear. This is probably but another specimen of that braggadocio of which we have already had so much."

"I will try to hope," said she, with forced calmness, summoning all that brave resolution to waste not strength in tears which should be spent in action. With her own fair hands she assisted her father hurriedly to dispose of the corn in the wagon, that their speed might not be impeded by its weight.

"Put some hay in the bed of the wagon," said Amy.

He knew why, and acted upon the hint. Grace had hastily thrown her wraps about her, and now cried:

"Let me go too, papa!" with such a pleading tone that he could not say her nay, although the wind was chill, and misty drops of rain were falling. The roads were bad, and the creek upon the rise, necessitating the longer drive by the bridge. But she took her place beside him, and they speeded on the way in silence, though dark and darker grew the sky, and more heavily fell the raindrops.

Over the bridge and up the first slight ascent, and then out across the prairie, where their eyes, accustomed to the night, could see dimly defined against the sky the leafless branches of the lone tree, beyond which, after alighting and casting the rays of light from a lantern in all directions, they found him—all stiff, and stark, and cold, his blue eyes staring upward, his garments wet with the dew and the rain, and ghastly with the life blood which congealed as it issued from his wounds.

John Alden stood transfixed with horror, while his daughter, tearless, yet with lines of agony indented deeply on her white face, from which, in that hour of supreme grief, the girlish grace had fled,—with loving hands tenderly lifted the dear head from the cold, damp earth, and pillowed it upon her knees. She clasped the marble fingers within her own, she kissed the cold lips with a pressure that at morn would have

"SHE KISSED THE COLD LIPS."

sent the blood bounding through his veins, yet now he lay pale, calm, and motionless.

A low laugh startled them. John Alden turned his lantern so that its rays fell in the direction from which the sound came, and the light disclosed Carr Withers. Alden asked him if he knew aught of this foul deed, and the wretch mocked him with a chuckling jeer. He asked him to assist in lifting the poor body into the wagon, and he refused, and then, in the presence of the dead, in presence of the fair girl who loved him, and whose face was white and still as Arthur's own, John Alden swore a terrible oath of vengeance on the murderers. Terrified, Carr Withers moved away. Another voice now came to Alden in a whisper:

"Whisht, whisht. Though it cosht me neck an' the divil's to pay, yit will I lind yez a helpin' hand," and Pat Malone came forward out of the darkness and assisted in depositing the lifeless form upon the hay within the wagon where Grace quietly and resolutely took her place, and resumed her burden.

"It is the last I can do for him," said she, with mournful voice, raising her sad eyes to her father's, and he acquiesced.

CHAPTER XXIX.

BENEATH THE SOD—ARREST OF ALDEN—A MIDNIGHT TRAMP.

Two days afterward, on the morning that was to have been his wedding day, they laid him to rest beneath the sod of the prairie, and with aching hearts and flagging footsteps turned to take up the daily round of duties to which the inspiration of that young and ardent spirit had lent so much of brightness.

It was a weary task; life's sky which had beamed so brightly, was now dark, and threatening clouds hung low. The atmosphere was heavy with grief and apprehension. They moved forward slowly, and with difficulty—the hours seemed days—and the days, lengthened with a consciousness of misery, grew into years.

The murderer had gone back to his lair. The power which had sent him forth to work its purpose now received and sheltered him. The hand of justice was palsied, and no strong arm of the law was put forth to seize and bring him back for trial.

But through all this gloom, one gleam of light remained to the Aldens. The star of friendship shone with its mild luster all undimmed. As in the days of joy, so now in sorrow the indomitable Langtry and the tender hearted Agnes, were ever near them. Agnes it was, who, with that delicacy of which only such rare natures are capable, proffered her sympathy and sustained with her strength, the young heart bravely battling with its first deep grief.

And it was Edward Langtry who called together, at Alden's cabin on the morning of the 26th, the Walnut Grove Association, for the purpose of embodying in suitable form a testimonial of respect to the memory of Arthur Fairchild, whose services in behalf of the colony were held in deserved esteem, and whose character had gained him the affection of all; and also for the purpose of having a committee appointed to take active steps for bringing to justice his murderer. Both measures were adopted unanimously, and Langtry himself chosen chairman of a committee appointed to insure the prosecution of the criminal.

A proposition was made by some of the younger and more aggressive members that they go in force and burn down, during the night, the white house which reared its head mockingly from that eminence in Calhoun; but this was voted down by a large majority as being a retaliatory measure partaking too largely of the spirit of violence, which had, hitherto, reigned exclusively in the bosoms of the opposite party. Surely, there was law left for such an extreme case as this, and that they would faithfully exhaust all legal measures before taking the execution of justice into their own hands, was the determination of the Association when at nightfall, with sad hearts, they adjourned.

How desolate Alden's cabin seemed when they were gone. The clouds which had lifted from the sky without, then hung heavy within the household. No merry young company with song, and jest, and glee, made joyous the evening hours. On the journey of life, stern fate which urges us inexorably forward, had suddenly uncovered in their path, lately strewn with flowers, a dreary and seemingly interminable cavern, chill with the damps of death, and bristling with pitfalls into which she precipitately and unrelentingly urged their unwilling footsteps.

The forms of supper were gone through, and soon

after Grace retired to her chamber, and Amy soon followed her, for since the shock of that sad event the poor child longed for her mother's presence through the long watches of the night.

When they were gone, John put on a heavy back-log and sat before the fire for a long time, his head and heart bowed down with miserable thoughts, too miserable even, for the solace of a pipe.

At last he retired—to sleep, but not to rest, for in dreams he was traveling over an endless, dreary, desert waste, desolated by fearful storms.

A heavy knock, which chimed in with the rolling of thunder and flashing of lightning, partially roused him, then another, and before his benumbed senses were fully roused, there was a crash, the hinges burst, the door came in, and in a moment the room was filled with heavily-armed, rough-visaged men, whose countenances revealed the effects of the poisonous stimulant which had been used to nerve them for the deed.

What deed? Was he to share the fate of Arthur? and if so, what would become of his wife and daughter? The possible horrors of shame and torture to which they might be subjected, flashed through his mind in an instant, blotting out all concern as to his own fate.

"Git up!" said the voice of Zeke Fagin, "I want ye."

"What for?" John gasped.

"I've got a warrant for yer arrest, and no time for foolin', so git up an' git into yer old duds," and a pistol was held menacingly before him.

John made an effort to rise, but in the surprise and horror which had overcome him, fell back again.

"Git up!" ejaculated Zeke, "or I'll blow yer brains out."

He made another effort, stimulated by the light steps which his quick ear had distinguished overhead. "They must not come down, they could not help him, and the sight of them might suggest more fiendish deeds to these ruffians," he thought. Then, throwing on his clothes hastily, he managed to get near the ladder, and as Amy's face appeared, he shook his head at her authoritatively.

"What air ye doin' thar? Hurry up," grumbled Zeke.

"Looking for my hat," replied John.

"Here's one, dog-gon ye!" said Zeke, taking down from a peg an old straw hat which had seen rough service, and placing it on John's head with a jam, at which his followers lustily cheered.

"Now we're all ready; move on." As John did not obey immediately, at a signal from Zeke, two of the men took him up forcibly and put him upon a mule they had brought for the purpose. The others then mounted, and the whole party rode off.

"Where are you going to take me?" Alden asked.

"Ter Warsaw," was the reply, but the road they followed led not to Warsaw, but to Charleston, and in time they reached that city of dug-outs, where preparations seemed to have been made for a revel.

Tobacco and hot toddy awaited the party in several of these places, and they were partaken of with the usual accompaniment of vain boastings, and ribald song and story. In the midst of this carousal Zeke turned to Alden with a leer:

"Hed a big meetin' up to yer place to-day?"

"Yes," John said unhesitatingly, for he had recovered himself somewhat. "We held a meeting, and appointed a committee to discover the hiding place of Hardiker, the murderer of Fairchild."

"Hiding place! Ha—ha—ha! That's a good joke! Do ye hear that, boys? Sile hain't no chicken to run in to cover. Ha—ha—ha!" and he laughed uproariously, while his followers all joined in the chorus.

"He's not in Calhoun," said John.

"Thar yer off. He's ter hum, with his mammy; yer can bet yer eyes on that."

"But he has been away?" said John, astounded at this information, which he could scarcely believe to be true, as the committee had scrutinized, as they thought, every place in Calhoun, the previous day. "When did he get back?"

"Last night; I brung him up from Levensworth myself. Me an' him went down as delegates to the Lor an' Order Convention."

"If he remains in Calhoun he will be brought to justice. The friends of Fairchild are determined that his death shall be avenged."

"Nary time!" chuckled Zeke, villainously, putting his thumb to his nose. "Fact is, we've got you fellers on a hook an' you may wiggle an' squirm, but ye can't git off. Lor an" order! that's what's done it."

John did not think it prudent to give the Sheriff his opinion of the laws at this juncture, for obvious reasons, and, after a few moments' silence and another swing at the toddy, Zeke continued:

"How many wuz at your meetin'?"

"About a hundred."

"A hundred! Do you hear that, boys? Don't you wish we had got there afore they broke up? That would a bin fun for ye; we'd a taught 'em how to pass resolutions!"

"You bet!" was the unanimous reply, accompanied with oaths.

"I'm spilin' for a fight," said one big, burly fellow, expectorating his tobacco juice in Alden's direction, at which they all laughed; then another amused himself by treading on John's toes, and a third knocked off his hat. The victim's blood boiled, but, with pistols cocked on every side of him, to attempt resistance was certain destruction.

At last, after another potation, Zeke again commanded the party to move on, and they took up the line of march; this time, to John's great relief, on the road which led to Warsaw.

The ride was silent—so far as Alden was concerned—with the exception of a question or two put to the most good-natured-looking of his guards as to what sort of a warrant the Sheriff held for him, which was graciously answered. It was a peace warrant, issued by a newly-made Squire—the ink on whose commission was not yet dry when he signed a warrant for John Alden's arrest, on the oath of Carr Withers that he feared his life was in danger from said John, as he had threatened him on the night of the murder.

Alden knew on the instant that it was a trumped-up measure which concealed some deeper scheme; though what that might be, nor how much of danger to himself it implied, he could not divine; and he was revolving it slowly in his mind, when, as they came in sight of the well-known bridge over the Ariposa, he descried in the moonlight a company of men on foot. The Sheriff had discovered them also, and he ordered his men to ride to the left, hoping to put Barton's cabin, which stood there, between them and the advancing body. But this body discovered his purpose, and John heard, with relief, the command:

"File to the right," in the clear, firm tones of Sam Ward, a friend from Warsaw.

"Halt!" cried Ward, in a commanding tone, and the late braggart horsemen meekly obeyed.

"What's up," said Zeke, "that ye git in the way of the Sheriff an' his posse?"

The answer came in the form of a question:

"Have you got John Alden there?"

"Yes; I am here, and a prisoner!" John shouted.

"Come over to our side, then," said Ward.

"I am the Sheriff of Hamilton county, and I hev a warrant for this yer man. I warn ye not ter interfere with an officer dischargin' of his duty," said Zeke, pompously.

"I do not recognize the validity of any process issued under the bogus laws," said Ward, fearlessly. "Ride out, Alden, and come over to us."

"If ye do, we'll shoot!" said Zeke, and thirty men seized their guns.

"Take good aim, boys!" called out Ward, and the click of the locks on thirty Sharpe's rifles was heard; and, thus encouraged, John Alden rode out, and passed safely over to the side of his friends, where Langtry received him with an embrace, as the boys fairly lifted him from the saddle, and thrust the mule back to the side where he belonged. The men who were "spilin'" for a fight, who would have had some fun with a hundred Abolitionists, did not fire a single gun at thirty; but their oaths were loud, and fierce, and long, led off by Zeke, who first demanded that his prisoner should be given up, and, on receiving a refusal, declared that he would have him again, and that he would arrest every one of the rescuers, if it took all the fighting men in Missouri to do it.

"I will send a messenger this yer night to Col. Delaney, an' one to the Guvnur of this Territory, an' in five days I will hev five thousand men hyer to distroy ye, root and branch," swore the Sheriff, with fearful oaths, and then they galloped off to Calhoun.

Day was breaking as the rescuers entered Warsaw. Her inhabitants were roused from their slumbers by the beating of a drum through the streets, and, before it was fairly light, Free State Hall was crowded with earnest men and women, eager to know the cause of the alarm.

Sam Ward, still with pistols in his belt, was appointed chairman of the meeting, and, in a few well-chosen words, he referred to the murder of the past week, dwelling on the atrocity of that deed, the promising character and hopeful future of the victim thus cut off in his early manhood—the cold-blooded cruelty which had left him weltering in his blood through the long hours of the afternoon, and which now persecuted the friend—the almost father—for the crime of caring for his lifeless remains.

Ward declared this but a foreshadowing of what the Free State men might expect, did they fail to avail themselves of the first principle of nature—self-protection.

He instanced several cases where, for slight offences, the aggressors being Free State men, they had been arrested and punished with the extreme vigor of the law; while they, in their turn, for the destruction of property, and even for murder, had no redress. He recounted, also, the threats of Zeke Fagin, and urged that, while they might possibly be but a specimen of that gentleman's braggadocio, yet he was inclined to think otherwise, and that he feared the Territory was really in danger of an armed invasion.

Ward then called on Alden to make a statement of his case; but, overcome by his feelings, worn with grief and anxiety, weary with his long walk, John was able to say but a few words. Besides, his mind had become so impressed while Ward was speaking, with all the possible consequences of an indorsement of his rescue, by the people of Warsaw, that he shrank in dismay from the responsibility of bringing so much misfortune upon them, and he said, in conclusion:

"I can not have it so. Let me go to my own home, and meet my fate."

But as he sat down, cries arose from every side.

"No! no! Stay, we will protect you!" and so many expressions of sympathy were showered upon him, that he could not restrain his tears.

A committee of ten persons was elected, to take measures for the defence of the town, should an attack be made.

Dr. Francis Rulison was elected commander-in-chief, and

with the consent and advice of the committee, authorized Col. James H. Hale, an active, intrepid Indianian, who had distinguished himself in the Mexican War, to organize, and take charge of the field forces.

Other officers of experience were there to assist in defence if necessary, and it was plain, from the manner in which these men set to work, that the enemy would meet with a warm reception.

CHAPTER XXX.

LAW AND ORDER CONVENTION—SECRET PLANS.

The Convention epidemic was not confined to the interior. There was a gathering in Lauderdale, no longer a village, but assuming already city airs. A gathering of the chivalry of the South, the Federal office-holders, and the border men. Her streets were thronged; excitement ran high, and the crowd surged to and fro as the eloquent words of the speakers stirred up all their prejudices against those whom they styled the invaders.

Harlan, the newly-appointed Governor of the Territory, presided. He was a tall, dignified man, with an eagle's eye and iron-grey hair. He had an imposing presence, and a stentorian voice. He opened the meeting with a speech, in which he declared to the party there assembled:

"Your laws shall be enforced. I regard the Legislative body so lately convened at Shawnee Mission a legal assembly, and their laws binding on every citizen of the Territory, and it is my purpose, while the gubernatorial power is in my hands, to exercise it to carry these laws into effect. I regard the efforts of the Free State men to form a Constitution, as a revolutionary movement, which should be put down by force of arms. If the State power is not sufficient, I shall invoke the strong power of the Federal arm."

There was loud cheering at these words, voicing as they did the desire of the assembly, and the Governor sat down, assured of popularity with the "Law and Order party."

Hon. David Watkins said:

"We, the Union-loving and States' rights party have kept still too long, and allowed these Abolitionists to proclaim millions of lies. This is a great question for Abolitionists to make capital out of, but we must not allow it to go on. For the safety of our property, and the preservation of our lives against these 'higher law' invaders, we must enforce the laws."

Hon. David was a great favorite with the boys, and the hurrahs were loud and long.

Gen. Stringman said:

"I indorse the sentiments of the speaker who has just preceded me, and had I the tongue to be heard to every limit of this Union, I would proclaim it, so that the old men now standing on the brink of the grave, and the young men just rising into the duties and responsibilities of life, might hear it. I would rather my tongue should cleave to the roof of my mouth, or my right arm be severed from my body, than silently give over my country to ruthless Abolitionists. We must enforce the laws, though we resort to the use of arms. Better by far, trust to our rifles, and make blood run as freely as do the turbid waters of the Missouri that flow along our banks, than allow these laws to be disregarded. Unless we prepare to defend ourselves, no man is safe who does not indorse their sentiments. They will destroy our property and our institutions must yield to these meddling Yankees, who assert that a nigger is as good as a white man. Are you prepared to submit to be ruled by niggers? Do you want to marry niggers?"

"No!" shrieked the excited mob.

"Then do as I bid you: Out-vote them. Out-fight them, if needs be. Force them to carry their household goods and families to Nebraska, where they belong. The fair fields of Kansas are yours and mine, and no Abolitionist should be allowed to occupy one foot of her soil."

Stringman sat down amid thunders of applause, and then a tall, dark-haired young man arose:

"My friends," said he, "I am a Southerner, a South Carolinian. I have spent much time, and energy, as well as the greater portion of the fortune left me by my uncle, in planting the colony of Charleston, in this Territory. (Cheers.) I am by birth and education an advocate of the institution of slavery, but I am also a believer in States' rights, and that doctrine, in my opinion, forbids the foisting of slavery upon this Territory in violation of the will of the majority."

"Hear! hear!" shouted the crowd.

"The organic act provides for a free expression of the popular will of the actual residents of the Territory."

There was a hiss, but the speaker went on, unruffled.

"I do not consider the election of March 30 such an expression of the popular will, as the elections were carried by fraud and violence."

"Traitor!" "Renegade!" "Abolitionist!" resounded amid groans and hisses, and cries of "Put him out!"

The Governor endeavored to call the meeting to order. He rapped on the table in front of him. He shouted "Order!" but the surging, seething crowd grew more and more vehement in their demonstrations of disapprobation, and in despair he turned to the young man.

"They evidently do not wish to hear you, Mr. Delaney."

"But I have a right to speak," said Roderick, impatiently. "I am a regularly elected delegate to this Convention, and I will be heard."

"Speak the sentiments of your constituency, then," gruffly ejaculated the Colonel, his father, with no pleased expression on his face.

The young man raised his voice to its utmost compass, and exclaimed:

"The fundamental principle of the Constitution of the

United States is—" But the excited crowd did not care to hear anything concerning principles opposed to their inclinations, nor did the leaders attempt to protect the audacious young speaker from the fury of the crowd, when they finally carried him off by force.

Poor Roderick! his apprehension of the difficulties in store for him who would endeavor to promote peace by overcoming prejudice with reasoning, had not been unfounded.

Zeke Fagin sat on the platform at this meeting, and Sile Hardiker was also thus honored.

The latter had gone to Col. Delaney with his murder-stained hand. The Colonel breathed upon it the breath of smiling condescension, and relief came. A pro-slavery judge was induced to admit Sile to bail, without examination, allowing his friend, Zeke Fagin, who was not responsible for a penny, to go on his bond. And then and there was concocted among the pro-slavery leaders the plan for Alden's arrest.

"The very thing," said Stringman.

"Be sure to manage to have him rescued," said the Colonel.

"And let it happen in that cursed town, Warsaw," said Watkins. "I am suffering for a *casus belli* against the place."

"They will be in a mighty tight place," said the Colonel, chuckling; "if they give up the prisoner, they acknowledge the validity of the Territorial laws, and the authority of the officers appointed by the Legislature, and if they refuse, why, that is resistance to the laws, rebellion, and the Governor may rightfully call out the militia to suppress it."

"I may call, gentlemen, but suppose the militia won't come," interposed the Governor.

"Never you mind," replied Watkins, with a wink and a chuckle, in which Stringman and Delaney joined, and which sent Zeke and Sile into a long guffaw, "our friends here, Fagin and Hardiker, will take care of that."

Zeke Fagin therefore, knew whereof he spoke, when he threatened to bring five thousand militia-men to retake his prisoner. Unfortunately for this wily scheme, Zeke had tarried too long at his potations, and it had now one weak point. The rescue had not taken place in Warsaw.

On reaching Calhoun after the rescue, the sheriff immediately dispatched a message to Col. Delaney, by the hand of his trusted coadjutor, Silas Hardiker, the latter being thus enabled to do good service, and at the same time remain out of the reach of the committee.

On the receipt of the message, Delaney issued a circular which was distributed in all the border counties, and discussed in the meetings of the Blue Lodge.

This circular asserted that the Free State men of Kansas had not only rescued a prisoner from the hands of the sheriff, but were committing unheard-of atrocities, such as burning houses, killing people, and driving pro-slavery men away from their claims, threatening to take from the sheriff a prisoner and hang him without process of law, and called upon Missourians to come, and come immediately to the assistance of their friends, who were in imminent danger.

To the Governor, the sheriff also dispatched, soon after, a message—evidently drafted by some more scholarly mind than "Zeke's"—and reading as follows:

HAMILTON Co., K. T., Nov. 27, 1855.

Gov. HARLAN,

Sir:—Last night I, with a posse of ten men, by virtue of a peace warrant, regularly issued, arrested one John Alden, who, on our return, was rescued by a party of forty armed men, who rushed on us suddenly from behind a house upon the roadside, all armed to the teeth with Sharpe's rifles.

You may consider an open rebellion as having actually commenced, and I call upon you for three thousand men to execute the laws. The bearer of this letter will give you more particulars as to the circumstances. Most resp't'lly, ZEKE FAGIN,
Sheriff of Hamilton Co.

To His Excellency,
WARNER HARLAN,
Governor of Kansas Territory.

Of course a Governor who had unhesitatingly asserted that the laws must be enforced, could not resist this appeal, and he in turn sent forth dispatches, dated from " Headquarters," in true military style, and addressed to the generals of the militia, appointed by the Legislature, commanding those officers to assemble as large a force as possible, and at as early a day as practicable, and report to Zeke Fagin, Sheriff of Hamilton Co., to whom they were directed to render every assistance in their power toward the execution of the legal processes in his hands, adding, " It is expected that every good citizen will aid and assist the lawful authorities in the execution of the laws of the Territory, and the preservation of good order."

CHAPTER XXXI.

FORCED TO FLEE—IN THE BORDER RUFFIAN CAMP.

To Amy and to Grace, left alone in the cabin at midnight, it seemed as if the seven vials of wrath had been poured out on their defenceless heads. They clung to each other in an agony of grief and apprehension, as the husband and father was borne away. What fate awaited him? Their experience warranted a fear for the worst.

Grace was the first to awaken to the possibility that all was not lost,—that there might still be hope if their friends could but be aroused to pursuit, and tremblingly they set forth in the darkness and cold, to seek the cabin of Langtry. Here they remained with Agnes, until Langtry returned with the glad news of the rescue.

Satisfied that the loved one was safe in Warsaw, they returned to their home, cheerfully adding his duties to their own, and with no thought of deserting their post. But on the morning of the fourth day after the abduction, Roderick Delaney came to them.

"My dear Mrs. Alden," said he, "you must not remain here. Where is your husband?"

"In Warsaw," Amy replied.

"That is hardly a safe place for him, and yet it is better than this. Here you are in the line of march which the troops from Missouri will take in coming in. Their camp will probably be on this creek, and I urge, nay, I command you," said he, smiling, "to stow your valuables and necessaries into your wagon, and have them taken to Warsaw, whither I will convey you in my carriage, to remain until Mr. Alden has decided upon some safer place for you all."

This was a warning not to be disregarded, and after thanking Mr. Delaney for his thoughtfulness, Mrs. Alden and Grace proceeded vigorously with the packing.

Mr. Delaney drove, meanwhile, over to Langtry's, saying:

"I must warn our Abolition friend, as there seems to be a special feeling of enmity against him."

He found Langtry, however, immovable.

"I have broken no law," said he. "They have no reason to molest me. I will go to the defence of Warsaw if a call is made; otherwise I remain at my home, and attend to my business."

Delaney did not stop to parley with him, but went back to assist Mrs. Alden.

Langtry, with his usual kindness, sent his brother George with a team to assist them in moving, which enabled Mrs. Alden to convey at once all that they desired, and with sad hearts they bade adieu to the home where privations and toils, where sorrows and sacrifices, had come to them; but whose rough walls were still sacred with the joy of a hallowed reunion.

John Alden considered himself fortunate in being able to secure a single room for his family, in the house of a friend, into which, with their belongings, they were soon compressed. It required some labor to accomplish this, but they bore it good-naturedly.

"The philosophers say the world might be contained in a tea-cup, if force enough could be applied," said Grace.

"But it needs more skill than force to plan the disposition and adjustment of this heterogeneous mass into conditions suggestive of comfort," rejoined Roderick; "and this scientific problem I fear we shall have to leave to you, ladies, as the political question we have on hand compels our entire attention."

To the committee of safety, then, at Delancy's request, Alden went, and having introduced Roderick, left him with them for a council of several hours, returning himself to assist Amy and Grace to carry out their plans, and their united efforts soon gave the place the appearance of a human habitation.

When Roderick Delancy returned, he was in a very thoughtful mood, and did not linger long.

"I have found your leader," said he, "a man of great sagacity and good judgment. He sees, with me, that the present safety and future justification of your town consists in absolutely refraining from every act which can give to the invaders the slightest show of reason for attacking you. Under the avowed purpose of assisting the sheriff to arrest yourself and those concerned in the rescue, their real intention is to demolish Warsaw, and lynch or drive from the Territory the Free State leaders. It is the avowed purpose which makes it possible for the Governor to throw over their acts the shield of the law, and when your leaders shall have disclaimed all responsibility for the acts of these rescuers, and expressed their willingness to yield them, as well as yourself for trial, they will have deprived the ruffians of that authority, without which they are a lawless mob, and must either disband or make a cold-blooded raid upon the town, for which the whole country will condemn them."

"I see," said Alden, "and I have had some such feeling from the first, that it was unnecessary for the town to assume a responsibility for the action of a few unauthorized individuals, when it involves such grave results, even though they might approve and rejoice in the acts themselves."

"But that course will drive you away from us," said Grace, bursting into tears.

"It seems very hard, indeed," protested Amy, "that they annot be allowed to defend innocent men from oppression."

"It does, indeed," said Mr. Delaney, "and I have no doubt you think me cruel to suggest it, but it is frequently necessary for us to consult expediency rather than absolute right in our dealings with this very imperfect world, and in this case I am convinced, that if your authorities can make your people see the wisdom of this measure, and have power enough to hold them strictly on the defensive, no matter how great the provocation, the small faction of our party who deprecate this violence may be able to delay them and disarrange their plans, until finally they will be forced to retire, without even making an attack."

"Our people will control themselves, if they can be made to see that it is the right thing to do," said John, a little proudly.

"Yes; I know they possess that power of self-control, which has so little place in the uneducated Southerner's calendar of virtues, that he scarcely recognizes its existence, and mistakes its manifestations for those of fear or cowardice," and then rising, and waving his hand, as John essayed to reply, with just that little assumption of superiority which the latter could never quite like, he continued:

"It is the result of the differences in our systems of civilization you would say, no doubt; but we must not linger philosophizing—this is the time for action."

And as he would go, with many warm thanks for his kindness, and thoughtful care for their welfare, they bade him adieu.

The reliable information given by Roderick, and which was confirmed by others, that intense excitement prevailed along the border, that inflammatory handbills were being circulated through Western Missouri, and the loose elements of her population hastening to enroll themselves as

"Kansas Militia," in response to the call made by Generals Eaton and Richards, and that they were being armed with United States muskets, and that the first division was already under way, caused redoubled efforts in the preparations for defence.

Three large, circular earthworks, a hundred feet in diameter, were thrown up, to defend Warsaw from attack on the northwest, south, and southeast, the men working in the trenches day and night. In the afternoon of each day there was a drill parade, Brigadier-Gen. Hale walking beside the companies with a military air and gait, and giving his orders with a sharp, shrill voice. Then the band played stirring martial music, and many buildings were made gay with flags. After parade and drill were over, Gen. Hale would sometimes make a speech, resolute and fiery, calculated to rouse the men to the fighting point. Gen. Rulison, on the other hand, restrained them, counseling them ever "to suffer and be strong, to carefully avoid making an attack, and when they might be sent with patrol or scouting party, not to be intimidated, or aggravated into a skirmish."

An appeal for help was dispatched to several of the surrounding settlements, and in two days there were five hundred men, besides her own inhabitants, in Warsaw.

The Free State Hotel, still unfinished, but sufficiently comfortable, was made the headquarters. Two large, finished chambers, in the southeast corner of the second story, were set aside for the council-room and General's headquarters. The remainder was used by the soldiers; the large unfinished dining-room serving as a place of reception, two sentinels guarding the outer door, giving the place quite a martial air. The soldiers were not confined to the hotel alone, but were quartered in the town wherever vacant rooms could be obtained.

At night the town was closely guarded by pickets, who

were placed about its entire circumference, and once or twice during its darkest hours, a horse patrol would make the entire circuit, frequently coming in contact with the patrol of the "Sheriff's posse." Many fears were expressed that on some one of these occasions a collision would ensue, but the General's commands were, in no case to fire, except in the last extremity. Not a few oaths were sworn at these non-resistant orders, and the General freely anathematized, for the enemy soon began to send out small bodies of well-mounted men, who would gallop up rapidly to within one or two hundred yards of the Warsaw sentries, and fire at them.

Fortunately, a bullet aimed in the dark is not a reliable missile, and no serious damage was done; still, it was a trying thing, the men said, to stand guard, and even hear random shots fired, without having the satisfaction of returning them, especially when to the shots were added taunts of cowardice.

CHAPTER XXXII.

LANGTRY SHAKES THE DUST OF WARSAW FROM HIS FEET— AN EXCURSION TO THE CAMP OF THE INVADERS.

Langtry had come into Warsaw with the Walnut Grove company, leaving Agnes with the family of Harley, whose claim was a long distance from the place where the Missourians had encamped. John Alden was exceedingly glad to see his friend once more before his own departure, which must now soon take place, as himself and the Warsaw men, who had been engaged in the rescue, had been requested to absent themselves, until after the expected demand for them had been made. Sam Ward had at first refused to go, but on Alden's suggesting an excursion to the camp of the enemy, he had consented, the idea striking him as one likely to be productive of some amusement, at least.

After exchanging greetings with Langtry, Alden communicated to him this order, and no words can express the scorn with which he listened to it.

"Poltroons!" he cried; "no wonder they taunt us with cowardice. We have allowed them to violate the sanctity of our ballot boxes, to impose upon us a most tyrannical code of laws, to imprison and punish our men for most trifling offenses, while the incendiary and murderer, if but a pro-slavery minion, stalks abroad, vaunting his crimes in the broad light of day."

In vain John suggested that something must be yielded to expediency.

"Expediency!" cried he, in whose pure mind all actions

crystallized as right or wrong, and marshaled themselves accordingly. "Expediency! I detest the word! No great cause was ever gained by such humiliating concessions as we are required to make. Here we have been asserting, over and over again, that we would not submit to the execution of those laws; and, on the very first case of resistance, when, too, the right is all on our side, we allow them to browbeat us into a subterfuge."

Alden quoted to him the words of Macaulay: "A public man is often under the necessity of consenting to measures he dislikes, to save others he thinks more important"; but he would not hear, and hastened off to make known his indignation at headquarters, and endeavor to induce a change of policy. The majority of the Free State people agreed with him in feelings; but, as they had consented to be governed by the judgment of the committee, it was hardly possible at this late day to change their course of action.

John Alden remained standing where his friend left him, for a few moments, lost in thought; but a hearty slap on the back aroused him, and he turned to meet the gaze of a ruffianly-looking fellow wearing the regulation stoga boots, with pants stuffed in, and a bowie knife peering from each, an overcoat made of a red blanket, and a slouch hat, from beneath which hung long black hair. He had a black patch over one eye, which did not add to his beauty, and spoke in a coarse, gruff tone of voice:

"Come along o' me, ole feller; I've got a call for yer."

"You have! From the Sheriff?"

"You bet! Git ready, an' come along now; no foolin'."

"Well, if I must, I must," said John; "but I should like to see your warrant first."

"And so should I," said the well-known voice of Ward; a hearty ha-ha-ha! convulsing his form, which was concealed beneath that border ruffian outfit.

"I guess I'll do, when you fail to recognize me; but come, now, let's make you up in something the same style!"

Ward knew pretty much everybody, and by dint of inquiry, and inducing a search in chests and closets, succeeded in completing John's disguise. He wore a wig of long white hair underneath his slouch hat, a blue blanket over his old flannel shirt, and buckskin pants of California memory, with a pair of stoga boots containing the requisite number of bowie knives. Lastly, Ward brought two old revolutionary firelocks, which completed the costume.

"Sharpe's rifles," said he, "would betray us immediately, but we can depend on our pistols for use, and these and the bowies will serve us for ornament."

In spite of their fears for John's safety, Amy could not resist a smile, and Grace actually laughed once more when they saw the two thus accoutred, and, with two days' rations in their knapsacks, mounting to depart.

"Now, do take good care of yourself," pleaded Amy, as John kissed her good-bye.

"I assure you, Madam," said Ward, "that the camp on the Areposa is the very safest place in all this Territory."

"Not for you, I fear, though you do look as if you were 'to the manner born.'"

"We shall come back all right!" said John, "never fear."

"Yes, and heap coals of fire on the heads of the Committee of Safety by furnishing much valuable information," added Ward, who had not yet arrived at a becoming appreciation of the policy which made him a wanderer.

Knowing the country well, they struck off to the south, and crossing the little creek, after making their way through a thicket of underbrush, with a wide detour, came up to the camp as if from below.

They found the country full of travelers, men on horseback, and men in wagons and carriages, all with faces turned to the west. The camp was near the ford, and on both sides of the creek; though by far the greater number were encamped beyond, on the low plain below Calhoun. They were halted by the guard as they appeared, and asked for the countersign, but Ward was equal to the emergency; putting his thumb to his nose and wriggling his fingers, he said, scornfully:

"Thar, dog-gon ye, that's all the sign as I knows on!" and then squaring himself up, as if to be ready for the onset: "If yer want any more signs, jist pitch in; I've come up fer a fight, an' I dunno's I keer how soon I begin!"

But this was enough for the sentry.

"Pass on!" he said, and they did so. Crossing the creek, they found the camp beyond, a busy scene. Wagons and carriages were scattered in all directions, and horses and oxen were feeding on hay which had been appropriated from surrounding claims. There were several dirty-looking tents, over which were flying banners with different devices; but the large white flag with the lone red star, the symbol of the great secret "Blue Lodge," floated over the large tent which stood in the center of the camp. There were, perhaps, fifteen hundred assembled; and the smoke of many camp-fires, by which detailed cooks were preparing dinner, curled upward through the timber.

The weather was mild again, and the breezes, which blew from the south, were as gentle as those of a summer's day. Little groups were seated here and there, discussing the situation, and the adventurers moved around among them, carefully avoiding the vicinity of Sile Hardiker, who was engaged, with several others, in a game of cards.

"Hillo thar!" shouted one observing fellow; "whar did ye git that thar old firelock?"

John hesitated a moment, but Ward whispered:

"Act well your part—there all our safety lies," so he turned upon them, with an air of pride:

"Gentlemen," said he, "this hyer old firelock wor carried by my father through the dark days of the revolution—the days that tried men's souls—as I heerd a chap say down thar in Arkansaw, when he war makin' a stump speech; but I'll be derned, gentlemen, yes!" bringing down the butt of the gun with emphasis; "yes, I'll be derned ef she war ever carried in a better cause nor this!"

This called forth a general "hooray." "You're some punkins," cried one;" "A whole tater patch," cried another, and then there was a general invitation to "licker."

The universal sentiment here was in favor of an immediate attack, and there was much chafing at the delay.

"Thar are only thirty-five hundred Free State men in the Territory, and if we can't clean them cl'ar out now, we never kin."

"Slavery must and shall go into Kansas, though we have to wade through blood to accomplish it."

"We kin chaw up a whole nation of them white-livered Yankees."

These were some of the sentiments which fell upon the ears of Alden and Ward, and proved almost too much for their discretion.

"I dunno," said Ward, shaking his head, "ef a thousan' of 'em war to come down here now, with them infernal guns o' theirn, they'd make it mighty hot, I kin tell ye."

"What do you know about them guns?" said a middle-aged man, with a forbidding look, and a face like a bottle brush, so stiff and short were his hair and beard.

"Oh, I've seen 'em," said Ward, looking wise.

"What sort o' fixin's air they?"

"Terrible gun. Say they kin load 'em ten times every minute."

"Why, how'n thunder kin they do it?"

"It's done by machinery,—a sort o' revolvin' fixin'."

"Wall, how fur kin they carry?"

"I dunno. They do tell amazin' big stories, them Yanks. Can't say I b'lieve the half on 'em. I should think as how they mought kerry nigh on to a mile,—that is, and make a sure shot."

"Lookee here," said one, drawing his companions on one side. "Ef them infernal Yankees *should* take it into their heads to come down here with them blasted guns, we'd be in a derned nice scrape."

"Got to fight, that's all," said the other, "an' I don't see what in thunder we're waitin' here, for."

"Got to wait," said another. "I've just seen Fagin, an' he's in a d—l of a temper. Got an order now, from the Guv'nur, not to move until he kin git word from Washington."

"What's Washington got to do with this fuss, anyhow?" said Ward.

"That's jist what I say," said the man with the bottle-brush face. "This air our own private individooal fight, an' we don't want no United States troops snoopin' round."

"'Twar all along o' you fellows laggin' behind," said another. "Seven hundred o' us war here waitin' a week for ye, an' hearin' o' fifteen hundred in Warsaw, drillin' and fortifyin' and gittin' ready to pounce on us. In course our Gineral he got skeert, an' asked the Govnur to call out the troops."

"Fer my part, I came hyer for a fight, and I jist 'low to stay hyer till I get one, ef it's a month o' Sundays," said another.

Which combative sentiment was not unanimously concurred in.

The situation was just this. Gov. Harlan had learned too late that it was easier to raise a storm than to control it afterward, and began to be alarmed at the probable consequences of his own hasty action; and, on receiving a request from General Eaton, that he call upon the military at Ft. Leavenworth, in order to overawe the Free State people, and prevent bloodshed, at once addressed dispatches to Col. Somers, asking him to interpose the United States troops between the opposing parties, and thus prevent a collision.

To all of which the Colonel replied that he did not feel justified to act in this matter until orders were received from the government, adding:

"I would respectfully suggest that you make extensively known at once, your application to the government for aid—and I would countermand at once any orders that may have been given as to the movements of the militia, until you receive an answer."

And it was the compliance of the governor with this request of Col. Somers, which called forth such an ebullition of wrath from Zeke and his followers, whose cry was still for war,—"War to the death,"—and who threatened now to raise the black flag, and proceed at once, to the destruction of Warsaw, unless the governor should call upon the Free State men to give up their arms.

The doughty sheriff had the impudence to address a note to the governor, stating that he had writs for the arrest of fourteen of the rescuers, and that it was impossible for him to restrain his men longer than until the next morning, which caused the governor to hasten down from Lecompton, where another similar force was encamped, to hold a convention of leaders, and suggest a compromise.

Some words of non-approval from Washington, and the reception of a protest from the people of Warsaw, disclaiming responsibility for the acts of the rescuers of Alden, and declaring themselves willing to assist in serving any legal process, suggested the idea that it was not yet quite time for the precipitation of a conflict, and tended to bring the gubernatorial mind to the conclusion that a patched-up peace would be the best thing all around.

There was a stormy time at that meeting of pro-slavery leaders. The captains stood somewhat in fear of their men, who were drinking and carousing without, and clamoring to be led on to clean out the Abolitionists without delay, and hesitated to agree to anything which might bring upon themselves the fierce ire that a disappointment of the rank and file would arouse.

At midnight, the meeting adjourned, without coming to a conclusion, and Ward and Alden, crossing the creek, endeavored to enter the cabin of the latter. They found it already occupied by a dozen or more " militia," who were sleeping sonorously upon the floor.

With a little grumbling at being disturbed, they made room for the new-comers to pass, and climbing into the loft, our scouts were soon asleep, not waking until a late hour of the morning, when, after breakfasting on the contents of their knapsacks, they hastened back to camp.

They found it still more the scene of excitement than on the day before. The whiskey still flowed freely, and threats ran high. The Governor, with Col. Delaney, Gen. Watkins and Dr. Cornello, had already departed for Warsaw, and speculation ran rife as to the object of their errand, some said to compromise, and others declared they had gone to demand the surrender of the arms and ammunition of the Free State men.

Lingering about until afternoon, Alden and Ward, seeing a party ride up from the west, sauntered slowly toward them, in time to hear one of them say:

" I thought I had shot him, when I saw the fur fly off his old coat!"

And the reply:

"Well, dang it, it's only another Abolitionist out of the way!"

This party, beside a number of lesser lights, consisted of Major-General Richards, of the Kansas Militia; Judge Carr, the same who had admitted Hardiker to bail; Maj. Jenkins, one of the largest slaveholders in the Territory, and Col. Dunn, a merchant of Westport.

The Free State men could hear no names mentioned, nor yet the circumstances, only that somebody had been killed, and that somebody, an abolitionist of the deepest dye. At last, when it was nearly night, uncertainty becoming unsupportable, Alden proposed that they should go back, at least far enough to interrogate the sentries about Warsaw.

"Relying on the General's non-belligerent orders for our safety in approaching them," said Ward, jocosely; then, after riding in silence for some time: "What an insatiable Moloch is this on which so much must be sacrificed!"

"It is ever thus," replied John; "each forward step in the world's progress is over the brave and loyal hearts who cast themselves upon the spears of rampant hosts of evil, that they may make a pathway for those who follow after."

CHAPTER XXXIII.

> " One more look of that dead face,
> Of his murderer's ghastly trace!
> One more kiss. Oh, widowed one!
> Lay your left hand on his brow,
> Lift your right hand up, and vow
> That his work shall yet be done."

That night John Alden sat by the lifeless remains of his dear friend in Warsaw, and none said him nay. The pall, enshrined by the flag, whose glories the dead had rejoiced in, and whose one dark stain he had so bitterly deplored, was stretched in the long dining-room of the Free State Hotel, whose rough, unfinished walls, dimly lighted by the uncertain glimmer of tallow candles, were made sacred by that dead presence.

Never fell on battle-field a braver man, and never went martyr of old to the stake with truer heart or firmer convictions of right.

John stood there, while the brave fellows who had come to the defence of Warsaw, and who, with himself, had seen unfolded day by day, trait after trait of earnest, thoughtful, and conscientious character, passed in to look upon the still, white face, which never again would kindle with holy wrath at the wrongs of a down-trodden and oppressed race. Strong men wept bitter tears at this untimely ending of an aspiring and vigorous life, whose philanthropic aims proclaimed with eloquent zeal, had surrounded the petty trials and privations of pioneer life with the glamour of heroic sacrifices in a noble cause. And, as they gazed in silence upon the calm, pale, face, many a hand, brown with toil, was laid upon that still heart, and dewy eyes were raised to Heaven, while firm lips vowed solemnly to take up the work which the dead had been forced to leave undone—consecrating themselves there anew to the task of making Kansas a free State, and counting that but as one step forward, resolved to rest not until the whole nation stood crowned with the garland of universal freedom. And as each vow was registered above, a heavenly smile descending played about the calm, white lips, and settled upon the marble brow, which some fair hand had wreathed with evergreen—fit emblem of a noble character, and of the enduring influence for good, which, emanating from it, sweeps on in ever-widening circles, whose force and potency no human thought can measure.

And as, with bowed head, John Alden sat, he heard recounted o'er and o'er in muffled tones to groups of wide-eyed listeners, as they came and went, the sad, sad story,—

The characteristic words with which his friend shook the dust of Warsaw from his feet when urged to indorse the compromise proposed:

"I will never, no never, walk a crooked path to such a goal." He listened to the tale of the homeward ride—brother and friend on either side—the meeting of foes where two roads crossed, the exchange of words, the insolent demand, "Turn your horses' heads and ride with us to our camp;" the assumption of power, "We have orders to see the laws obeyed;" the indignant refusal to become prisoners without warrant or process of law; the firm, honest eyes of Langtry fixed upon his accuser, as he asked:

"What laws have we disobeyed?"

The evasive reply as positions were changed, and Major Jenkins reined his horse directly in front of his victim—the firing of pistols—the retreat of the ruffians to some distance for a parley, while the Free State men rode forward, hoping haply to escape. And now the narrator's voice grew husky, and the listeners' eyes filled with tears, as it was told how a little further on, Edward Langtry placed his hand upon his heart, exclaiming: "George, I'm faint! I'm shot!" and the brother, with tender care, placed his arm around the stricken man to support him in the saddle, still galloping swiftly onward. A few rods further on, and the victim feebly gasped: "My blood be upon the cause they represent! Agnes! oh, Agnes!" The strong limbs relaxed—the head bent upon the bosom—the body swayed to and fro, and both brothers came to the ground at once. Then friend and brother chafed his hands—they were cold. They felt his heart—it was still. The enemy, taking fresh courage, were coming on in pursuit. To save their own lives they must mount and hasten forward.

And the narrator's voice grew indignant, and the listeners' eyes flashed, as t'was told how, with heartlessness unparalleled, that band of murderous kindred spirits gazed upon their work, and then rode off to camp; and his friend, John Alden, oh, God! he knew the sequel. He had listened to the words: "One more Abolitionist out of the way. I thought I had killed him when I saw the fur fly off his old coat."

But the tale went on through the lonely vigil kept by the brother at the side of the dead body, while the friend returned with the sad story to Warsaw. The excitement, the indignation of the soldiers when they heard it, was intense, and great was the eagerness to be detailed as guard for the carriage which was sent out to bring in the remains, each comrade counting it a service of honor as well as of love. Kind hands had prepared him for burial, and covered the pall with the Stars and Stripes.

As John Alden sat there through the solemn watches of the long night, when gradually all movement ceased, when the whispered tones of his companions were hushed in sleep, the silence broken only by the voice of the sentry as

"MY BLOOD BE UPON THE CAUSE THEY REPRESENT. AGNES, OH! AGNES."

he called the hours, his thoughts went back through all the events of the past sixteen months, the brief time during which he had been blest with the friendship of this noble man, and he felt indeed that the hand of the assassin might deprive him of the inspiration of his friend's warm bodily presence, but of the example of patience and hopefulness under petty trials, of a constant subjection of actions and motives to the scrutiny of conscience, of loving, generous care for others, he could not be deprived.

Nor could the consequent elevation of character unconsciously imbibed from intimate association with one who breathed and walked only in the elevated atmosphere of purity, and unselfish devotion to lofty principles, be taken from him.

"Alas!" he cried out, "of such stuff are the martyrs made who lead the van of all the world's great reforms."

Langtry's last words, too, came up before him again and again—"My blood be upon the cause they represent." To the cry of the oppressed was now added the blood of the innocent.

"Ah, well!" John reasoned, "to parties and institutions, as to individuals, the consequences of evil actions come back to rest as a blight upon their lives."

Morning at last dawned, and the world of Warsaw slowly awakened to its duties, and its fears. The smoke of many kitchen fires went curling upward on the morning air, children played about in the sunshine, following the soldiers as they moved in squads to relieve the guards. The sentries came in, and friends again thronged the room to complete arrangements for the funeral on the morrow.

Then came the carriage, which had been dispatched at daylight for the loving wife, who had awaited a husband's return to the distant home on the prairie. The fears which had long haunted her were now too terribly realized.

20

Leaning upon Mrs. Alden's arm, she slowly ascended the stairs, entered the room, and with one wild shriek cast herself upon the body of her beloved, her blanched face rivaling the whiteness of his own placid brow.

There were no tears to relieve the agony of that hour; the lightning stroke, which fells the strong oak, withers the tendrils of the vine which clings lovingly to its branches; the sad, sick silence of despair, which uttereth no sound— was upon her, and sympathizing friends strove in vain to break the spell.

She took her place by his side, and, together with John and Amy Alden, watched through the afternoon and night, jealously treasuring up the few remaining hours of his bodily presence; and when all was silent, she listened while John told her of his own deep love, and reverence for her husband, and unveiled a kindred sense of loss, the depths of whose misery was exceeded only by her own. He spoke, too, of the triple chastening which had fallen upon him and his, in the loss of one whom he had loved as a son, the breaking up of their household, to be followed by the death of the dearest friend he had ever known.

And then, at last, for another's woes the fountains of Agnes' grief were unsealed, and blessed tears came to the relief of the gentle heart so near to breaking.

During the day, a deputation from the camp of the enemy, consisting of the Governor, Col. Delaney, Watkins, and others, in passing upward to the council-room, looked in by chance, and shuddered as their eyes fell upon the still form of the dead.

"Our losses of yesterday," said Gen. Hale.

"I did not think it had come to this," was the reply of the Governor, as they moved away.

And what mattered it to the dead, that in that room above was signed the compromise against which his life had been given as a protest? What mattered it, that the Governor now rode off to disperse the force which his own command had called into existence, or that the fierce spirits which he had evoked now refused to be exorcised, that they threatened and bullied him, until in very fear he was forced to take refuge for the night, within the town threatened with destruction, in consequence of his own misguided actions, or that he gave on his return, to the Free State leaders, a written permission to defend the town and himself from his friends —the militia.

But neither the concession on the part of the people of Warsaw, that they would assist in the execution of any legal warrant (the words "legal warrant" being construed in different ways by the different parties), nor the command of the Governor issued to the generals of militia, to disband their forces, as he had now no need of them, would have availed to prevent an attack, had not the elements come to the aid of the peace commissioners.

The wind, which had blown gently from the warm south all day, at evening whirled about suddenly, and came down with fury from the north, wailing and howling, and penetrating the crevices of the poorly-built cabins of the settlers, who, wholly unprepared for such an onset, shivered about their fires unable to maintain even the minimum of comfort. It was dark as Erebus, and the snow and sleet dashed wildly in the faces of the guard, who, wrapped in furs and blankets, painfully tramped their weary rounds, returning at short intervals to the fires in the forts, to maintain their vitality.

And what of the men in the open camp on the Areposa? Shrinking, and shivering, and helpless, as the wind whistled through the trees, and about their wagons, piercing their clothing, and bearing off from the body every particle of animal heat, they gathered about their fires, piling on the logs until the yellow flames darted and leaped among the branches of the gnarled oaks, and elms, and walnuts. Colder and more bitter grew the night, and as the hours wore on, the winds took on a whirling motion, sending flaming pieces of wood and coals in every direction, endangering the wagons and even the lives of men and shivering horses, till at length they were obliged to extinguish the fires, and creep for shelter under wagon tops and covers, which their relentless persecutor remorselessly tore away and sent flying off in the distance.

It was a fearful night—not even incessant motion was sufficient to preserve the warmth of their bodies, nor continual firing of guns to keep up their courage. Had their councils been undivided—had the Governor's authority not been withdrawn, or had the night been a calm and pleasant one, they might have made the attack; and, perhaps, then and there, would have been reached that decision which only came after two more years of wasted time and deplorable destruction of life and property.

But, as it was, the morning found them dispirited and disheartened. The intense cold had congealed the feeling of hostility, and the announcement that the supply of whiskey was exhausted caused a general breaking up and a homeward movement, enlivened only by threats of coming again with the return of spring, and fiercely muttered imprecations on the head of the Governor for having, as they expressed it, "gone back on them."

CHAPTER XXXIV.

LANGTRY'S FUNERAL.

> "Bear him comrades, to his grave;
> Never over one more brave
> Shall the prairie grasses weep,
> In the ages yet to come,
> When the millions in our room,
> What we sow in tears shall reap."

Somewhat of the wind's fury had ceased, but the white flakes of snow were still falling when the hour came for the last sad rites of the funeral service for the martyred dead. Notwithstanding the severe cold which still prevailed, the streets were thronged with wagons and carriages, and people hurrying on foot to the hotel, which had now become the place for holding all public gatherings. Boards had been brought into the dining-room and arranged for seats, and soon every place was filled; while in the hall, on the stairs, and in the rooms beyond, scarce standing room was to be found. There were gathered representatives from almost every State in the Union. There were men and women from Eastern homes of luxury and refinement, seated side by side with the sons and daughters of toil. There was the infant, borne in its mother's arms, and the gray-haired grandsire, mingled with the far greater number in the prime and vigor of life; and over all the numerous assembly, composed of such varied and dissimilar elements, was spread the chastening influence of a common sorrow.

A deep silence pervaded the house, and many a heart

whose tendrils still clung unbroken to its loved ones, who had come unscathed through the past week of perils, found relief in a deep sob, half grief, half thanks.

There was a hushed sound as Agnes Langtry, leaning on the arm of her brother, and followed by John Alden, with wife and daughter, still suffering from that first sad blow, passed in, and took the seats reserved for the mourners. John had tried to dissuade Grace from going; but the remembrance of the healing balm of sympathy poured upon her own wounds by gentle Agnes, constrained her to make the effort, and they sat with hands clasped, while the choir sang a sweet, sad hymn.

And then the white-haired minister, who had known and loved the noble dead in his far off, early home, spoke of the reward prepared for one taken in the performance of duty—a duty cheerfully performed in obedience to conscience and for the good of his country—from whose service he had been taken to a higher sphere, and broader field of action—of the evanescence of human life, and of that fairer country beyond the dark river of death.

He discoursed of that infinite, omniscient power which treasures up every fragment of sacrifice, of effort, of devotion to a holy cause, until the whole combined, moves with resistless power the veriest stronghold of wrong.

"Ah!" said he, in conclusion, "though we commit his body to the dust, and his spirit returns to God who gave it, yet does he still live, and move and work among us. The scintillations from the holy fire which burned in his bosom have passed into other lives, awakening and inspiring them to nobler deeds and aspirations;" and then, with a commendation of the grief-stricken widow to Him who has promised to be more than husband or child, the services were over, and preparations were made to bear the lamented dead to burial.

The military companies, with arms reversed, walked first—the Generals, upon horseback, leading the way.

There was the Warsaw company and the Walnut Grove company, deputations from each acting as pall-bearers; then the body of the dead and the sad mourners; then all of his immediate neighbors, and, lastly, the whole community. All kinds of vehicles, wagons, and carriages fell into the rear, and in solemn procession wound their way—a long, sad line—over the prairie, up the lone, steep heights of Mount Olympus, and still yet a mile further on over the elevated plain, then halted; the soldiers formed in two lines, with bared, bowed heads, and the mourners and friends passed through and stood around the open grave. The coffin was gently lowered; the ominous sound of falling earth, mingled with the bitter wailing of the desolate, childless widow, rose above the sad moaning of the wind, and broke in upon the solemn words: "Earth to earth, and dust to dust. I am the Resurrection and the Life."

The mourners then fell back, giving place to the soldiers, who, advancing by divisions, fired their rifles above the last resting-place of their loved and honored comrade.

> "Frozen earth to frozen breast,
> Lay our slain one down to rest.
> Lay him down in hope and faith,
> And above the broken sod,
> Once again to Freedom's God
> Pledge ourselves for life or death."
> —*Whittier*.

CHAPTER XXXV.

GRACE GOES TO OHIO—ELECTION OF OFFICERS UNDER TOPEKA CONSTITUTION—THREATS OF ANOTHER INVASION.

As the cortege drove homeward swiftly, silently, sadly, at the foot of Mount Olympus the attention of the Aldens was attracted by a horseman galloping toward their wagon, and gesticulating frantically, in a manner which John interpreted to mean "Stop!" or "Go back!"

In obedience, he reined in his horses, and soon distinguished beneath the mufflings of a heavy woolen scarf, fur cap, and overcoat, the good-natured person of the proprietor of the Pioneer House. As he came within hearing, Jake, who was ill-adapted to such feats of rapid equestrianism, cried out, breathlessly:

"Meesther Alden! Meesther Alden! You not want to speak mit der Sheriff Fagin, hey?"

John shook his head: "No, not I."

"Vel den! You petter not gone mit ter town site alongside. He vash dere already, for somepotty."

"Already?" exclaimed Grace. "I think he might have given you one day."

"Shust vat I dinks, but he is dere, an' he haf got two of ze shentlemens already, but I tought I come an' pring you my pony, an' you make off some blace vare he not find you dish time; I vill trive mit der ladies home. You go, hey?"

The snow was falling faster than before, and the lowering skies indicated a coming storm.

John Alden had not slept for two nights, not indeed for three, and he longed for a comfortable rest in his own bed, but there was no help for it; he must either surrender himself to the tender mercies of Zeke and his associates, or he must accept Jake's suggestion and his pony, to ride off, he knew not where. True, the cabin of any Free State settler would be open to shelter him, but few had accommodations for more than their own families, and he dreaded to incommode them. And then it was exasperating to be driven forth thus, to be hunted like a wild animal, and obliged to fly at a moment's notice.

"If there was the least hope of justice, I should give myself up," said John.

"But there is not, you know there is not, papa."

"It would be simply suicidal," exclaimed Grace and Amy in concert.

"Well, I'm sure I've no great fancy for being tarred and feathered and rode on a rail for Zeke's amusement, nor yet for being set adrift on a raft to float down the Missouri River, which are the least of ills to be expected, should I yield myself up to them for trial."

"Trial, indeed!" said Amy. "Even should a legal trial be granted, it must be but a mockery of justice with judge and jury pledged against you in advance."

"No, better to be an Ishmaelite, forever wandering, than allow myself to be taken now," replied John. So he thanked Jake heartily for his kindness, and accepted his offer.

"Where will you go?" asked Amy, as Jake and her husband changed places.

"To the South; I think the roads are better in that direction. The sheriff will probably be off to-morrow, and then I can return," said he, in answer to two pairs of eyes filled with tears.

"Dot is shust vat I dinks, and you yust coom up some-dimes, in der night already, alongside of te room numper six, you finds dat vindow open, an' a bed vat nopotty vash shleepin' in."

"You are very kind. I hardly think it will be safe for me to return in less than two days," and with a sad good-bye, John set out to seek a place of refuge.

And this was the beginning of a series of escapes; he could never sit down, even to enjoy his dinner, with the certainty that he should be able to finish it; he never went to bed without the dread feeling which was a number of times made a reality, that ere morning he might be obliged to turn out in the cold and the snow. Sile Hardiker was still at Calhoun, and to his unappeasable vindictiveness, Alden attributed much of the sheriff's perseverance in his case, as he was certainly not what might have been called a political offender, and yet his views were sufficiently pronounced to bring him under the pro-slavery ban, in case any of the clique desired to make it unpleasant for him.

Before Christmas Mrs. Alden received a letter from Arthur's mother, Mrs. Fairchild. It was a heartrending wail of anguish for her first-born, the center of many fond hopes and bright anticipations, and she begged so hard that Grace would come to her for awhile, "for Arthur's sake," that her parents could not but think well of it, providing an escort could be found for her. Grace herself said: "If Agnes Langtry will stay with you this winter, mamma, in my stead, I think we may lighten the burden of two sad hearts, and I will go; but I cannot leave you alone, with papa so often away."

Agnes was pleased, or rather she consented to this arrangement—nothing seeming as yet to raise her depressed feelings to a state approaching pleasure.

Like the plant which, deprived of the sunshine, still vegetates, though in a limp, colorless manner, she lived on from day to day, with tear-dimmed eyes and pale, sad face, the old enthusiasm, the old joyous, impulsive manner, all gone. Time and work might recall something of its brightness, and the best might be hoped, from constant and close association with such a radiating center of happiness as Amy Alden, whose face was ever turned to the bright spots in the sky, and who in turn dispensed contentment and peace to all about her.

S. R. Ward, Alden found, was going East for the winter, on business for the Association, and his wife was to accompany him on a visit to her friends in Ohio, and they very kindly consented to take charge of his daughter, and see her safely to the residence of the Fairchilds.

Rapid preparations were made for the departure, and they were soon on the way, traveling by stage to St. Louis, as the river was by this time a mass of floating ice, and navigation closed for the winter. It was a hard, uncomfortable journey, but they made it in safety; letters from Grace were received, in a few weeks announcing this fact, and also giving an account of her kind reception by the parents of Arthur. "They treat me as a daughter, mamma," wrote she, "and I think I can be a great comfort to them."

During this winter, whose heavy fall of snow, unparalleled in the memory of the traders and Indian agents who had been in the Territory for years, direct hostilities were for the most part suspended, thus giving the settlers a brief season of rest. In the meantime, however, the opposing parties were not wholly dormant.

On the part of the Free State men, the Topeka Constitution was adopted by a heavy vote, elections being interfered with only in the border tier of counties, and resulting there in serious disturbances, and the loss of some lives. Then came the election of officers under this Constitution, and they assembled and took the oath of office in March, notwithstanding the threats made by the Judges of the Supreme Court, of indictment for treason.

They reasoned, however, that their constitution was of no avail without this taking of oath and assumption of office, that they were but following the precedent of other States, and furthermore, that they could see no other way of so effectually protesting against the acts of the bogus Legislature, as by thus knocking at the door of the Union with a Free State Constitution.

Accordingly, this Legislature having convened, presented a memorial to Congress asking admission to the Union as a sovereign State, and then adjourned, to await the action of that body.

The pro-slavery party had, during the winter, made urgent and stirring appeals to the South for men and money, and the early spring brought them large accessions of both. They had also discussed and matured a policy whose first move was to prevent Northern immigration to the Territory by arresting and turning back the Free State immigrants, frequently with entire loss of baggage and freight. Supplies of food and lumber for the interior were also stopped, and even the mails delayed, and in some instances, tampered with. The long, tedious route through Nebraska was, for some months, the only safe means of access to Kansas.

The continued and oft-repeated threats of another invasion were a great clog upon the energies of the settlers, though the spring opened fair. Who could sow with diligence that an enemy might reap? Besides, the loss of horses through the severity of the winter and the scarcity of hay, in consequence of the burning of haystacks, and also the destruction of farming implements by the invaders, were serious impediments.

Well for the Alden family was it, that Amy's small patrimony was securely invested in her own name, and that her modest income was sufficient for their simple wants, for, save the rude cabin which still stood upon that piece of land from which he was at present outlawed, the results of

John Alden's labors in Kansas might now be set down as naught; verily, it seemed as if an evil star pursued him, and had he not been sustained by his wife's still unquenched hopefulness, he might have yielded to despair.

CHAPTER XXXVI.

A CHAPTER OF HISTORY.

Hostilities were begun early in the spring, by the President's proclamation, that the whole force of the United States Army was at the command of the Governor of Kansas, for the execution of the laws of the Territory. Then followed the indictment of the newly-elected officers, under the Topeka Constitution, by the grand jury, for treason against the United States, and also the indictment of the two Free State newspapers at Warsaw, and the Free State hotel, of the same place, as nuisances which must be suppressed or destroyed.

The return of Ward, about this time, was also turned to good account, Zeke Fagin who, as before, still led the van, making an unsuccessful attempt to arrest him. Ward declining to submit, without first seeing a warrant, and Zeke, on that occasion, having failed to furnish himself with that indispensable document, he refused absolutely to go. This occurrence the sheriff reported to the governor, as an act of direct resistance to his authority, and the governor, in accordance with instructions from Washington, and in the spirit of the President's proclamation, called upon Col. Somers, of the regular army, for a posse of soldiers to assist the sheriff in the discharge of his duty. They were immediately furnished, and, with the air of a Napoleon at the head of the immortal "Old Guard," Zeke Fagin galloped about the country. What would he not do for a cause which gave to him such laurels?

Unfortunately for Alden, they entered Warsaw from a side street, and came upon him suddenly from around a corner, just as he had descended the stone steps of Free State Hotel, one morning in April, and stood alone upon the sidewalk, and with an " Aha! I've got yer at last!" and a fierce grip, which tore his coat, though he offered no resistance, the sheriff pounced upon him. A tent was soon erected on a vacant lot, at some distance up the street, and John was placed within, and strictly guarded by four soldiers, while the remainder of the posse assisted the sheriff in making other arrests. This proved an unusually successful sally, and five companions were given Alden during the afternoon.

Their captors did not move, however. They were waiting for the night to cover up some deed of violence, hints of which the sheriff could not forbear to convey in taunts directed to John Alden, intimating that he was to be given over to somebody in Calhoun.

" Somebody who hez a heap o' 'fection fer yerself and fam'ly," said he, bowing with an air of mock politeness. As he did this, the sharp, explosive sound of a pistol rang on the air, and Zeke Fagin fell at John's feet. What unseen hand had thus avenged his wrongs, at the very moment when, completely in the power of the tyrant, he was forced to listen to his revilings, John knew not—nor was it ever known— though the wicked eyes of Carr Withers, which leered on Fagin for an instant through the opening in the tent, while he lay convulsed, with the blood issuing from his wounds— suggested to Alden a possible intention on the part of Withers to avenge his own private wrongs,—for Bets, his wife, received and openly returned the admiration of Fagin,— and at the same time to cast a stigma upon the Free State people, and give the border ruffians cause for an attack.

At any rate, it had the effect of rousing the loose element in Missouri to the fighting point, being heralded there as a base assault by the people of Warsaw, upon the sheriff, while in the discharge of his duty.

ZEKE AND BETS.

It was made the most of, for, before he had been carried to the hotel, examined by the physicians, and pronounced "only slightly wounded," a messenger had set forth, bearing news of his *death*, and arousing his friends and neighbors to avenge his assassination.

The next day, Fagin was carried to his *confreres* at Calhoun, and the prisoners whom he had arrested were taken to Lecompton, where they were kept confined in a log cabin.

At various times, large additions were made to their numbers, so many, indeed, that the cabin became too small to hold them, and they were placed in tents, which, with those occupied by the soldiers who were stationed there as a guard, gave the place quite the air of a military encampment.

Gov. Rulison, who, while on his way East, had been arrested without a warrant, was, with other officers under the Topeka Constitution, in a few days brought here for safe keeping.

Their arrest was preceded with a proclamation by the United States Marshal, stating that certain persons indicted for treason, were supposed to be in the town of Warsaw, and that he had *reason to believe* that their arrest would be resisted by armed men. He, therefore, called upon all good citizens to assemble for the purpose of assisting him to serve the warrants for their arrest, now in his possession. Whether in response to this call, or owing to pre-arrangement, the marshal's posse grew with fearful rapidity, and the whole country was soon a scene of warlike confusion. Travelers on the highway were arrested and confined as prisoners. Cattle and horses belonging to Free State men were pressed into service, even the settler's only cow, in many cases, being driven to their camps, and killed for beef.

An armed force was rapidly concentrated around Warsaw, whose people, entirely unprepared for attack, looked on with dismay. Their leaders were absent, many of them confined as prisoners in the camp at Lecompton, the rank and file were in the field endeavoring to plant their crops, or hewing out lumber, or quarrying stone for their houses, and the people of Warsaw hesitated to ask them to come again to their defence, without pay, when, perhaps, a non-resistant policy would serve them, as before. Besides, there was now a glimmer of hope that justice would be received from Congress, as a committee had, at last, been sent to the Territory, to take testimony concerning the election frauds of March 30, 1855. But, as the armed forces closed round the town on every side, more numerous, more rampant, more threatening than before, it was determined to make one more appeal to the governor, asking him to interpose the United States troops—which were, as yet, kept on the border—between the advancing army and the beleaguered town.

The reply was:

"There are no armed forces approaching Warsaw, except such as are legally authorized to act as a posse for the execution of the laws, and when your people submit themselves to the laws, and abandon all opposition to their execution, this force will be withdrawn."

The reply was interpreted to mean, that if the officers elect submitted quietly to arrest, others should not be molested, and they resolved to do so, trusting to the sense of right inherent in the great body of their countrymen, to see that justice was done them, when the excitement had subsided.

In the meantime, preparations were going forward, and were vigorously prosecuted by the enemy, for the sacking of Warsaw.

They proclaimed, "*This time* they were to wipe out the Abolition stronghold, and no mistake."

Of the Sheriff, nothing had been heard. He who was wont to be the life of that chivalric host, was he indeed dead, or dying from the wounds received in Warsaw by the hands of an assassin? Opinions differed—and the people of Warsaw persistently denied all knowledge of, or connection with the deed, whose perpetrator they had endeavored to search out, but without avail.

The morning of the 21st of May dawned clear and cloudless, and the inhabitants of this little Western hamlet, shaking off the drowsy slumbers of the night, began to busy themselves about their usual avocations. Suddenly it was discovered that a large armed force had taken possession of Mount Olympus, and another was encamped to the southeast of the town.

A scouting party—sent out in haste—brought back the news that they were the Marshal's posse, and composed of companies from Carolina, Alabama, Georgia, and Florida, combined with the Missourians, and numbering perhaps eight hundred or a thousand men; that they were armed with the United States rifles belonging to the Territory, and which had been intrusted to the charge of the Federal officers; that they had four pieces of cannon, and were entrenching themselves upon the hill, preparatory to making a move upon the town.

This intelligence was in no wise calculated to revive the drooping spirits of the inhabitants; but, trusting in the policy of submission, they awaited attack in silence.

About ten o'clock Marshal Kane entered the town, accompanied by a posse of thirty armed men.

He summoned several of the citizens to assist him in making arrests. Their cheerful compliance, as well as the non-resistant air of the inhabitants, seemed to puzzle him, and he lingered about until noon, notwithstanding the parties for whom he held warrants surrendered themselves immediately on his demand. Constituting himself and his posse the guests of the city, he ordered dinner at the Free State Hotel, which was promptly furnished him, after which he quietly retired with his posse and prisoners.

And now another actor came upon the scene—Sheriff Zeke Fagin issued forth from his retirement, and was received with loud cheers of joy by his confederates, many of whom had mourned him as dead.

As he rode up in front of the men, he exclaimed:

"Boys! this yer's the happiest day 'n my life! We've got orders fer to destroy the printin' offices and the tavern belongin' ter that ar d—d Yankee Emigrant Aidin' Soci'ty; and by G—d, we'll hev some fun, ef we can't git a fight out o' these hyer sneakin,' white-livered fellers! Plant yer cannon, boys! an' then hist up the flag o' the South!" and with these words he led the way into the town. While his men were executing these commands, Zeke endeavored to serve his writs. Name after name was called, but no one answered—they were not to be found—and the Sheriff's wrath rose accordingly.

Then he issued an order that the women and children should leave the town. Some of them had fled in the morning—and the men of a belligerent turn of mind had likewise absented themselves when the submission policy was agreed upon. But the remainder—now gathering up their little ones and what few things they could carry—hastened out on the prairie.

Agnes and Amy assisted a friend, with three little children, to escape to a cabin near the timber, and then returned, with others, to take up a station, where they had a partial view of the enemy's movements.

A motley-looking crew they were in their red shirts, which had the effect of a scarlet uniform.

At the command of their leader to "Pitch in," they rushed with a yell into the printing offices, demolishing the presses, type, furniture, everything belonging to a newspaper outfit; bearing the larger fragments to the river, and throwing the smaller pieces about the street.

Then they began to discharge their cannon, two pieces of which had been placed directly in front of the hotel, but the stout walls resisted the attack, and round after round was fired without making the least impression. At last they brought several kegs of powder, and, placing them within the building, applied the match, but there was only a slight explosion, sufficient, however, to set fire to the building; and as the flames arose, hissing and crackling, the Sheriff was unable to conceal his delight.

"Boys!" he exclaimed again, "this yer's the happiest day 'n my life," and his fierce black eyes sparkled with joy.

Then commenced a scene of wildest pillage. Bolts and bars were no obstruction to their entrance; trunks were broken open, and all money and jewelry taken; pictures and books destroyed—even the daguerreotypes of cherished friends were ruthlessly marred and thrown into the streets. Scarfs and dressing-gowns were donned, and the marauders paraded the town in fantastic garbs selected from the wardrobes of their victims.

Everything that could be carried away was taken, and many things destroyed which were of value only to their owners. The wines and liquors in the cellars of the Free State Hotel were freely passed about, and served not a little to inflame the passions of the marauders.

At last, near midnight, with a crowning act of maliciousness, they retired, the flames bursting forth from the dwelling of Gen. Rulison lighting up their retreat.

They carried with them their dead and wounded—two in number—one injured by the accidental discharge of a pistol in the hands of a comrade, and the other instantly killed—struck on the head by a stone swept from the walls of the highest printing office by the South Carolina flag, as its heavy folds swung to the breeze. And it was whispered as he was borne away that Arthur Fairchild was avenged—that it was Silas Hardiker who was carried lifeless to his home in Calhoun.

And now occurred a revulsion of feeling. Forbearance had ceased to be a virtue. What was Federal authority to men whom Federal power was used to pillage and destroy? "We will endure it no longer!" were the words heard from every side; and gallant Old John Brown, in the south, and Gen. Hale, in Central and Northern Kansas, took the field, and attack and repulse, advance and retreat, successively ensued; until the Governor was constrained by the success of the Free State men to conclude a second treaty of peace, which was no sooner made than broken, and the Territory was again the scene of anarchy and confusion.

The little village of Osawatomie was twice sacked and burned. Lauderdale became the scene of daily outrage; her Free State inhabitants—many of them merchants of the place, having valuable stocks of goods, and possessed of property besides—were actually driven out of the place, a hundred at a time, at the point of the bayonet; some escaping by the boats, others seeking refuge in the woods, and, ultimately, at Fort Leavenworth.

Their property fell for the most part into the hands of the "law and order" administrators. But the end was drawing near. Gen. Hale's army received large accessions through Nebraska, and became stronger and better armed every day. They made incredible marches, and gained surprising victories, and at last, in September, turned their attention toward liberating the prisoners who were confined at Lecompton.

It can hardly be imagined with what feelings of joy the prisoners hailed the rumors of his approach. The summer had been one long season of suffering to them, confined in small space surrounded with filth, and guarded by drunken demons, who frequently amused themselves by cursing and throwing stones at them. With two large cannon loaded with shot and slugs, planted but a few yards away, and the match in the hands of the gunner, with orders to discharge both in case friends should come to their rescue, they needed but starvation to complete a list of horrors equal to any known in history. But from this they were happily saved by the one indulgence granted—that their friends might provide food for them; and Mrs. Rulison, Mrs. Alden, and other ladies were untiring in efforts in their behalf.

At last, however, when Gov. Harlan had been replaced by Gov. Gage, who was inclined to administer justice without fear or favor, and who won his subsequent removal by his endeavors in that direction; and when Gen. Hale, with a large force, was within a few hours' march of the camp, Gov. Gage admitted the prisoners to bail, and they were dispatched to Warsaw by another route, so that the General, on demanding their release, could be informed that they were already at liberty, and had departed.

Then this new Governor turned his attention to the dispersion of the militia, who were again encamped on the Areposa, and threatening that of Warsaw there should not be left one vestige nor one soul to tell the tale.

It required great firmness and decision on his part to compel them to disperse. Disband they did not immediately, but scattered far and wide in little bands, devastating the Territory, and defying the power of the United States troops. But at length, meeting with retaliation from armed bands of Free State men, now roused to fury, and being routed, they were forced to retire, never again to come in a large, well-organized body; though frequent skirmishes continued at intervals on the southern borders, for at least two years more.

During the winter following, the report of the committee for the investigation of election frauds was received by Congress, and the Committee on Territories advised a repudiation of the acts of the Kansas Legislature as a spurious body, and the repeal of the whole Kansas code that had sanctioned the bloodshed and crime inflicted on the Territory.

This measure, though not adopted, attracted the attention of the people of the Northern States to the condition of the Territory, and the spring of '57 brought such an overpowering army of Northern settlers, with their "Bibles and Sharpe's rifles," that when the next election for members of the Legislature was held, the Free State men were able to hold the polls and out-vote the slave party by an overwhelming majority.

The Topeka Constitution, for which so much had been endured, was rejected by Congress, and a united effort made to fasten upon the Territory, without ratification by a popular vote, a Constitution formed by the pro-slavery faction at Lecompton, which attempt proved to be the rock upon which split the great Democratic party, North and South, Senator Douglas himself repudiating such an interpretation of the Squatter Sovereignty Bill.

This Constitution was overthrown, however, in a peculiar manner, worthy of narration. When the time came for the election of officers under it, the Free State party nominated a ticket, and turned out in such force at the polls as to elect their men by a large majority, and then these newly-elected officers, from Governor down, united in a memorial to Congress, protesting against the admission of the State under that fraudulent instrument, perhaps the only case on record of Americans petitioning themselves out of office.

Then the Free State party, gaining possession of the Territorial Legislature in 1858, abrogated by a single act, the multitudinous and barbarous laws passed by the bogus Legislature in 1855, and till *then*, in nominal force, though any attempt to actually enforce them had long since ceased, " and amid great rejoicing, the bulky volume of bogus statutes was committed to the devouring flames of a public bonfire."

CHAPTER XXXVII.

"What, we have many goodly days to see,
The liquid drops of tears that we have shed,
Shall come again, transformed to orient pearl,
Advantaging their loan with interest,
Ofttimes with double gain of happiness."
—*Shakespeare.*

John Alden's release from the prison camp at Lecompton was the first faint glimmering of the light which heralded the dawning of a brighter day.

He joined Gen. Hale's army of defence and retaliation, but the long marches, the sanguinary skirmishes, the starvation rations, the weary nights with the bare earth for a resting place, which, with his brave comrades, he endured through the autumn and early winter, were but as the mists of the morning, soon dissipated by the glorious sun of conquered peace. Many a time, when faint with hunger, suffering with cold, fatigued in body and depressed in mind with the consciousness that their families were lacking care, they were almost constrained to give up the contest, and, folding their tents, depart northward; but a few eloquent words from Hale always brought them to their feet, and with the cry of, "Free Kansas forever!" they rose with renewed zeal to the conflict. Hale was the motive power, and Gov. Rulison the balance-wheel, and under their guidance and direction the bark of State was safely guided o'er the rapids, and went floating out on the broad sea of prosperity. By a wise alternation of self-control and determined resistance, the fires of contention were smoldered, a sudden and violent explosion prevented, and the fierce under-current of opposing elements turned backward to find, at a later day, a more legitimate outlet.

As the winter came on, and hostile incursions became less frequent, the Free State men retired to their homes, retaining an organization, however, and ready to spring at a moment's warning again to arms.

"O that long and bitter winter!
O that cold and cruel winter!"

the remembrance of which might make the stoutest heart quail. Disease and famine stalked like gaunt, grim specters, through the Territory. Men, worn out by the toils of defence, prevented thereby from making a proper provision for their families; and women, whose brave souls had endured the heats of summer and the frosts of autumn, perhaps on a diet of green corn ground by hand, were unable to withstand the cold blasts of winter, which penetrated every crevice of their unplastered cabins, and now lay on beds of sickness without strength to prepare and make available, the supplies sent by generous friends in the North.

Ah, it was an easy thing, from beds of down in homes of luxury, to echo back the cry "No more slave States!" but the early pioneers of Kansas with the true spirit of devotion, cast themselves before the iron wheels of the great Juggernaut of oppression, and with their own stout arms stayed his onward march.

The cry of Agnes Langtry in her bereavement had been for work.

"Give me work! that I may have no time to look back upon the joys of the past, or forward over the long dreary path which stretches out bleak and lonely into the future."

This winter encompassed her with opportunities. In forgetfulness of self, and in alleviation of the woes of others, she found a most salutary narcotic for her own grief. Many a mother had cause to bless the sweet, sad face, whose presence at her bedside brought back the ebbing tide of hope, and recalled the vanishing resolution so necessary to recovery. With her own hands she gently bathed the fevered brow, prepared the food to tempt the feeble appetite, and fitted the clothing to the necessities of the half-clad little ones. With rare good judgment she managed the supplies sent to her hand, that there should be no waste, and that the utmost benefit might be derived from them.

Nor were her ministrations confined to Free State people alone, but, like their gentle dew from heaven, were showered upon the sick and suffering of all parties and sections, with equal graciousness.

Occasionally, during the course of these labors, she came in contact with Roderick Delaney, engaged in a like work of Christian charity. Especially was he concerned for those whom his own persuasions had induced to emigrate, and whom he found entirely unable to adjust themselves to the requirements of their new environment. Unaccustomed as they were to the rigors of a severe climate, and prevented by the slothful habits of procrastination, as well as by the political troubles, from making a proper provision for the winter, he found them quite a burden upon his hands, a willing burden many of them, without the least sense of the unmanliness of dependence.

Then too, their habits of improvidence were such, that it was almost impossible to keep them provided for.

"With your people," said he to Agnes one day, "a little goes a great ways. Give them a certain amount of good food, and they immediately calculate how many days it may be made to last by the addition of such coarser material as they have at hand; but let me give our folks a supply, and they at once proceed to 'eat, drink and be merry,' with as much extravagance, as if they had unlimited resources at command. I cannot impress upon them the necessity of economy."

"You must have patience with them," said Agnes; "that lesson requires years of 'line upon line, and precept upon precept'."

And then, as the spring came on, with all the joyous awakening of nature from her slumbers, as the river was unlocked from icy chains, and the little creek swept by with gurgling sound, and the birds came again with merry songs to warble in the branches through which the uprising sap was coursing with new life, and bursting forth in tiny leaves and buds, the Free State men again essayed to woo sustenance and prosperity from the soil. Then Roderick Delaney came once more to Agnes with troubled brow.

"What shall I do with these people?" said he. "While the wise and active have already conquered all difficulties by daring to attempt them, they shrink at the thought of toil, and sit basking in the sunshine, as free from care as if they had never known a winter's cold. I wish they could imbibe even a small portion of the industry which is abroad in the air."

"I think," Agnes replied thoughtfully, "that example would be better than precept."

"Well, they have enough of that, I'm sure. There are examples on every side of them, but they will not see, they will not heed."

"Ah, yes!" said she. "But I mean that if you were to settle down among them yourself, and endeavor to develop the agricultural interests of the country, it might have a good effect. We are more willing to take lessons from our friends than from our enemies, and your people, to put it in its mildest form, have no affection for, and no desire to imitate us in any way. But they would with alacrity, 'do as Captain Delaney does.'"

Roderick shook his head. "You are a hard taskmaster,

Mrs. Langtry, and if I succeeded no better in carrying out this last suggestion, than I did in the work you bade me attempt nearly two years ago, would it be worth while to try the experiment?"

"If we do the work set before us with our might, Mr. Delaney, it is all that is asked of us. We may not live to see the result, we may not measure its benefits," and here her eyes filled with tears, "but the world will—humanity will."

And so it turned out that Roderick Delaney became her neighbor. He purchased an additional tract of land in the vicinity of Charleston, and began the experiment which has since proved so successful, of farming on a large scale; and as Agnes had prophesied, those South Carolinians who would not till their own claims with any degree of diligence, because the reward of the autumn's crop was so far distant from the spring's toil, that to them the connection was not sufficiently obvious, learned their first lessons of industry in working for the Captain by the day or week, for the daily or weekly stipend, becoming in time self-supporting.

At Agnes' suggestion after a time he formed a neighborhood Agricultural Society, whose weekly meetings for the discussion of farming interests proved quite a stimulus to them. He induced her to visit among the women, and in her kind way, suggest improvements in their method of cookery and housekeeping, and also later, in their attire and manners. No other woman could have done this, but Agnes Langtry possessed rare tact, and besides, so unusual had been her deeds of kindness, so untiring her efforts in their behalf in sickness and in want, that she represented to them rather the spirit of charity than a true flesh and blood Yankee woman.

And now it became apparent, so near is a mutual purpose and a sympathy of aims to the boundaries of that mysterious region—love, that if Agnes desired she might have the hand and fortune of Roderick Delaney laid at her feet.

But no, the fountain of love whose inmost depths had stirred to meet the ennobling affection of Edward Langtry, was forever sealed to the advances of another. For the alleviation of the woes of others, for the welfare of humanity, and the development of a higher life in those around her, her sympathies went out to him. But there was that in her manner which said plainly, in reply to the slightest manifestation of warmth of personal feeling: "Thus far shalt thou go and no further! My dream of love is over."

As soon as it became evident that they might live in peace and safety in the cabin on the Areposa, Amy and John Alden returned thither, not perhaps in so joyous and so expectant a mood as when they had first taken possession of it, but with an enhanced appreciation, gained from deprivation, of its homely joys. Like themselves, it had seen hard usage. The doors were off their hinges, and the windows boasted not an unfractured pane of glass. The shed attached for cooking purposes was gone, and the winds had free course through the apertures in the walls from whence the greater part of the chinking had been jarred; the weight and solidity of the logs had alone prevented their being carried off. But, as we bind up the wounds of a friend, so did they with willing hands remodel and repair this humble home. They hung the doors, and glazed the windows anew; they mended the walls and replanted the vines outside, which had been ruthlessly trodden under foot. The fences, hewn out with so much time and toil, had been carried off to be used as fuel, but they were in time enabled to replace them. The fruit trees, so carefully planted and watered, and left in such a thriving condition, had been wantonly destroyed, and it was impossible to obtain others this year, as the more urgent needs must first be supplied; yet they were only too happy to be allowed to work out their plans in peace, and too busy to spend much time in useless regrets.

Again the strong oxen turn the furrow, and once more they plant the seed in field and garden, and watch the tiny shoots with eager eyes. But through all, and with all their renewed happiness, was mingled a vein of deepest sadness. Everything around and about was so imbued with remembrances of the dearly-loved son and friend for whom fate had decreed the martyr's crown, that nature's brightest tints wore, for a time, a somber hue. And in all the subsequent years of patient toil, made necessary by their conditions and surroundings, the settlers of Walnut Grove have not ceased to feel the inspiration which, during that short and troubled period, flowed from those strong and noble souls. To have communed with them in the intimate relations of close friendship, was to have breathed the pure air that nourishes the ambitions of lofty spirits.

Mrs. Hardiker had returned to Missouri on the death of her son, and the Aldens heard of her but once, and that was on the occasion of her marriage with the Hon. Dr. Benjamin Cornello, whose broken political fortunes she no doubt temporarily mended with her plantation and negroes. Zeke Fagin betook himself to the far Southwest, and afterward became noted as a raider during the War of the Rebellion.

In June—the month of roses and of balmy breezes—the restoration of happiness to the prairie home of the Aldens, was made complete by the return of their bonny, bonny Grace, lovely as ever, but with an added charm of dignity and self-poised womanliness. The years of absence, though quiet ones, had not been cheerless, and she had gained much in culture and habits of thought.

"How strangely scenes answer to our moods, mamma," said she, one day soon after her return. "Everything seemed so gloomy to me when I first went back to Cleveland. The houses, the trees, the plants, even the dear old familiar faces appeared to have been dyed in somber colors, which gradually moderated and then wore away; but never, I think, quite took on the hues which they wore when I gazed upon them with childish eyes, and basked in their brightness with the thoughtlessness of the butterfly."

Capt. Delancy she met with an easy manner, which showed her to be free from any embarrassing remembrances. On his part there was apparent somewhat of surprise at the chameleon-like character of this maiden, who two years before had awakened his passionate admiration by her artless and winning childish graces, and who now challenged his respect by her responsive sympathy with all the higher and more cultured elements of his own better nature. He sought her presence frequently, and thus there came to pass what might have been expected, the light sparkled in her eye, and the rosy blush mantled her fair cheek at his coming.

Like draws to like.

> "How can I tell the signals and the signs,
> By which one heart another heart divines;
> How can I tell the many thousand ways
> By which it keeps the secret it betrays."

Oh, mystery of love! Oh, strange romance! Again its enchanted pages were turned o'er beneath the silvery moon, adown the rustic path, and by the winding stream. Low voices in earnest tones repeated the old, old story: "I love you!" "I love you!" The wild flowers whispered it, the birds sang it, and the low winds breathed it in soft music, to which their heartstrings answered back without one discordant note.

How swiftly that summer glided by on radiant wings, bringing a rich reward to the husbandman, and full fruition to the lovers' hopes, and at its close a fair bride went with the blessing of fond parents to grace the home of a proud and happy bridegroom.

Mabel Delaney came from St. Louis to gladden the wedding party with her presence, before returning to her home in South Carolina; and during her visit, Benty, our blonde Bostonian, won from her a promise, which she was only able to redeem when the passing years had freed her from her duty to her father, who fell at the head of his troops bravely fighting for slavery and secession.

And in the years which, since then, have come and gone, John Alden's brightest anticipations of material prosperity have been more than realized. Nature with lavish hand has responded to the "open sesame" of patient toil, and graced the undulating prairies here and there with majestic trees. She has given him grain, and fruits, and herbs, an abundance for use, for storage, and for exchange. Each autumn, rosy apples peep from beneath green foliage, purple grapes cluster on the vines, and yellow pears hang gracefully from heavily-laden boughs. The golden corn waves its silken tassels, and the breeze is fragrant with the scent of the new made hay, and resonant with the click, clack of the giant mower of the prairie and the hum of the steam-thresher, as it magically separates the wheat from the chaff.

John and Amy Alden sit at evening, on the veranda of a large and commodious farm house, their faces bearing an unmistakable impress of content—content material and spiritual—beautifying and glorifying all the lines left by toil and care, by sacrifice and subordination of things selfish, to the higher motives of patriotism and humanity.

Their home is made glad by the happy voices of children—their grandchildren—dark eyed and fair-faced; the toning down of whose imperious natures, with each added year of culture and experience, bespeaks the mingling of Northern and Southern blood.

But most these children love to follow grandpa down the steps, over the velvety lawn, beyond the garden, and through the orchard, where, on a little knoll, surrounded by tall trees, and overgrown with vines, stands the old cabin, like its owner, grown grey with age. And as in youth, John Alden's thoughts dwelt much in the future, so now the past enchants him, and the young Delaneys listen with eager interest to his oft-repeated tales of the days of "Squatter Sovereignty."

"AMERICA;"
An Encyclopedia of its History & Biography

BEGINNING WITH

PRE-HISTORIC AMERICA, AND COMING DOWN TO JULY 17, 1882.

The only Comprehensive, Exhaustive, and Complete Reference Book on the HISTORY OF THE WESTERN CONTINENT. The aim of the work is to give everything in its proper setting; to show the steady, unparalleled progress of the Continent, and quicken an interest in old and young in the life and affairs of the New World.

By Prof. Stephen M. Newman, M. A.

A **Large** Imperial Octavo, of nearly Eleven Hundred Pages, Elegantly Printed and Illustrated.

Prof. Stevenson, of Ohio, says: "He who has a family of children, or to do with children, should purchase this volume at even a price equal to its weight in silver."

President Bateman, of Knox College, says: "It is a rich Thesaurus."

The Chicago Inter Ocean says: "It covers a new field, and by methods the best. It is nothing less than a treasure."

The Advance says: "The work is indispensable for the family in general, not less than for persons of literary pursuits, alongside of Webster's Unabridged, and the standard Encyclopedias."

This work is sold ONLY BY SUBSCRIPTION, and AGENTS ARE WANTED EVERYWHERE.

THE COBURN & NEWMAN PUBLISHING CO.,

PUBLISHERS,

96, 98 and 100 METROPOLITAN BLOCK,

CHICAGO, ILLINOIS.

"THE JEANNETTE;"

A Complete Narrative Encyclopedia of all Voyages and Expeditio[ns]

IN THE

NORTH POLAR REGIONS.

IT NARRATES ALL THE ATTEMPTS TO DISCOVER TH[E]
LONG SOUGHT FOR

NORTHWEST PASSAGE,

In which so many Lives have been Sacrificed, and such v[ast]
amounts of Money Expended.

The Finest Work of the kind ever Produce[d]

The Romance of History, Biography, and Science.

It gives full accounts of FRANKLIN, KANE, HAYES, HALL, a[nd]
the last ILL-FATED JEANNETTE Explorers.

*A Large, Royal Octavo, of over Eight Hundred Pages, Fine[ly]
Printed and Elegantly Illustrated.*

ONE OF THE FINEST SUBSCRIPTION BOOKS PUBLISHED.

By CAPT. RICHARD PERRY

The Coburn & Newman Publishing Co., Publishers,

96, 98 and 100 METROPOLITAN BLOCK,

CHICAGO, ILL[.]

THE HOME BEYOND;

OR,

VIEWS OF HEAVEN,

And Its Relation to Earth,

BY

MOODY, SPURGEON, TALMAGE,

AND

Over Three Hundred other Prominent Thinkers and Writers:

WITH AN INTRODUCTION AND BIOGRAPHICAL SKETCHES,

BY THE

Rt. Rev. SAMUEL FALLOWS, D. D.,

AUTHOR OF "LIBERTY AND UNION," "SYNONYMS AND ANTONYMS,"
"SYNONYMS DISCRIMINATED," "ABBREVIATIONS AND
CONTRACTIONS," ETC.

WITH ELEGANT ILLUSTRATIONS.

Agents wanted in every Township in the U. S. Prospectus will be ready January 1, 1884.

CHICAGO, ILL.
THE COBURN & NEWMAN PUBLISHING COMPANY,
PUBLISHERS,

The Cheapest and Best

BIBLES

In the World!

THE
MOST SALEABLE SUBSCRIPTION BIBLES EVER PUBLISHED.

Containing Fine Illustrations,

And a Complete Body of Helps to Bible Study, in the way of Concordance, Bible Dictionary, Proper Names, Maps, Etc., Etc.

Strongly and Handsomely Bound, and Finely Illustrated.

AGENTS WANTED EVERYWHERE.

The Coburn & Newman Publishing Company

CHICAGO, ILLINOIS.

OF THE

CIVIL WAR;

BEING THE INCIDENT, ADVENTURE AND WAYSIDE EXPLOITS OF THE

BIVOUAC AND BATTLE FIELD,

AS RELATED BY MEMBERS OF THE

GRAND ARMY OF THE REPUBLIC.

EMBRACING THE TRAGEDY, ROMANCE, COMEDY, HUMOR AND PATHOS IN THE VARIED EXPERIENCE OF ARMY LIFE.

By WASHINGTON DAVIS.

WITH A HISTORY AND OTHER VALUABLE INFORMATION FOR MEMBERS OF THE G. A. R.

AGENTS WANTED FOR EVERY POST OF THE G. A. R. AND COUNTY IN THE U. S. PROSPECTUS WILL BE READY JAN. 1, 1884.
BEAUTIFUL ILLUSTRATIONS.

THE COBURN & NEWMAN PUBLISHING CO., PUBLISHERS.
CHICAGO, ILL.

FAMOUS
Frontiersmen, Pioneers and Scouts;

THE VANGUARDS OF

AMERICAN CIVILIZATION.

Two Centuries of the Romance of American History.

A THRILLING NARRATIVE OF THE LIVES AND MARVELOUS EXPLOITS OF
THE MOST RENOWNED

Heroes, Trappers, Explorers, Adventurers, Scouts, and Indian Fighters.

INCLUDING

BOONE, CRAWFORD, GIRTY, MOLLY FINNEY, THE M'CULLOUGHS, WETZEL, KENTON, CLARK, BRADY, CROCKETT, HOUSTON, CARSON, CALIFORNIA JOE, WILD BILL, TEXAS JACK, CAPTAIN JACK, BUFFALO BILL,

GENERAL CUSTER WITH HIS LAST CAMPAIGN AGAINST SITTING BULL, AND GENERAL CROOK WITH HIS RECENT CAMPAIGN AGAINST THE APACHES.

By E. G. CATTERMOLE, A. B.

ELEGANTLY ILLUSTRATED.

AGENTS WANTED in Every Township in the United States.
Sells at Sight.

THE COBURN & NEWMAN PUBLISHING COMPANY, PUBLISHERS,
CHICAGO, ILL.

www.ingramcontent.com/pod-product-compliance
Lightning Source LLC
Chambersburg PA
CBHW020240240426
43672CB00006B/585